Accumulation by Segregation

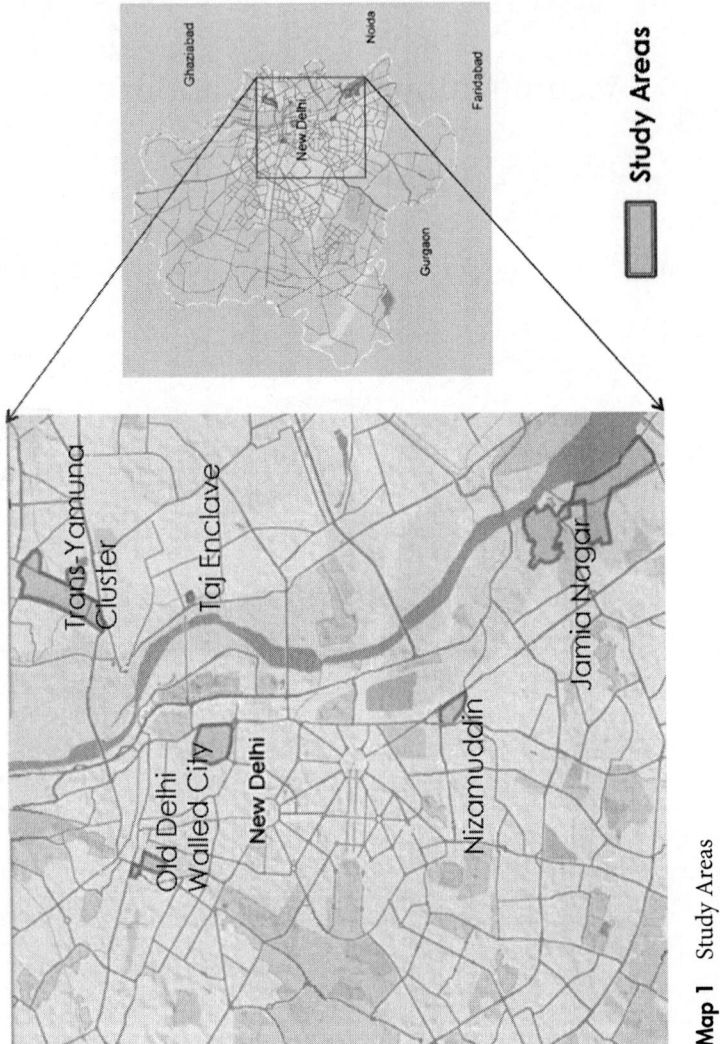

Map 1 Study Areas

Source: Author (based on google maps).

Note: This map is not to scale and does not depict authentic boundaries.

Accumulation by Segregation

Muslim Localities in Delhi

Ghazala Jamil

OXFORD
UNIVERSITY PRESS

OXFORD
UNIVERSITY PRESS

Oxford University Press is a department of the University of Oxford.
It furthers the University's objective of excellence in research, scholarship,
and education by publishing worldwide. Oxford is a registered trademark of
Oxford University Press in the UK and in certain other countries.

Published in India by
Oxford University Press
2/11 Ground Floor, Ansari Road, Daryaganj, New Delhi 110 002, India

ISBN-13: 978-0-19-947065-5
ISBN-10: 0-19-947065-0

Typeset in Minion Pro 10.5/14
by Tranistics Data Technologies, Kolkata 700 091
Printed and bound in India at Repro India Ltd., Mumbai

For
Manoj K. Jha
who cleared the space for me to speak

Stop thinking about saving your face. Think of our lives and tell us your particularized world. Make up a story. Narrative is radical, creating us at the very moment it is being created. We will not blame you if your reach exceeds your grasp; if love so ignites your words they go down in flames and nothing is left but their scald. Or if, with the reticence of a surgeon's hands, your words suture only the places where blood might flow. We know you can never do it properly—once and for all. Passion is never enough; neither is skill. But try. For our sake and yours forget your name in the street; tell us what the world has been to you in the dark places and in the light. Don't tell us what to believe, what to fear. Show us belief's wide skirt and the stitch that unravels fear's caul. You... can speak the language that tells us what only language can: how to see without pictures. Language alone protects us from the scariness of things with no names. Language alone is meditation.

Tell us what it is to be a woman so that we may know what it is to be a man. What moves at the margin. What it is to have no home in this place. To be set adrift from the one you knew. What it is to live at the edge of towns that cannot bear your company.

Toni Morrison
Nobel Lecture: 7 December 1993

CONTENTS

. . . .

ACKNOWLEDGEMENTS

· ·

Kaun jae Zauq par Dilli ki galiyan chhor kar
(Who wishes to leave, Zauq, wandering the streets of Delhi)

— Sheikh Ibrahim 'Zauq

Time spent wandering the streets of Delhi, drinking in the depths of everyday life; meeting with people, partaking in their memories and experiences; pouring over the work of the finest thinkers and maverick walkers of the world; reflecting on human existence, oppression, and emancipation has come to fruition in this work. Based on my doctoral thesis from the University of Delhi (2008–12), this book is a result of a process of great discovery and learning for me. The entire process is marked by moments of serendipity followed up with much digging, probing, and analysing. Though this process had its solitary moments, for the most part I was travelling with wonderful companions.

I was extremely fortunate in having Professor Manoj K. Jha as my doctoral supervisor. He is an inspiration for championing against ignorance, apathy, and prejudice. Every interaction with him is a lesson in *being* political and *doing* theory. I can never even begin to thank him properly because I know I will never be able to thank him enough for his generosity and brilliance, both of which know no bounds. I thank my colleagues at Delhi School of Social Work (DSSW), University of Delhi, where I taught at the time of being engaged in my doctoral work. Special thanks to Pushpanjali for being a comrade in arms and for sharing true empathy. I particularly wish to acknowledge my students in the *State, Political Economy and Governance* course. They (without knowing it, perhaps) challenged me to see familiar concepts with a critical perspective, and escape the danger of oversight and oversimplification.

I would be setting myself up for an impossible task to thank all the participants of this study, but I would certainly be amiss if I did not mention Juned Khan and Ovais Sultan Khan, Shakeel Malik and Azeem Akhtar sahab for sharing their deep insights with me; for their faith in my efforts; for their willingness to indulge me with constant conversations, walks, and phone calls; and for introducing me to numerous other people. Thanks are also due to Humera Arzu for her support in accessing newspaper archives and transcribing interviews. Grateful thanks also to the OUP team who worked on this book, for their exceptional professionalism, their openness, and for making me keep to the schedule.

It was in the work of Professor N. Sridharan that I first encountered spatiality of marginalization. I thank him for drawing me to engage with students at the School of Planning and Architecture (SPA), Delhi, as Visiting Faculty. I thank my MA Regional Planning and Urban Planning students, who not only made teaching exciting by their critical and enthusiastic response, but also helped me learn so much about their discipline. Thanks are due to Shubham Mishra for sharing his insights about mapping and getting me all excited about GIS, and to Sheema Fatima for her incisive comments on spatiality of middle-class aspirations. Thank you all for demystifying Planning for me.

The discussions and feedback received in two conferences gave my work an additional edge. I thank the Sir Dorabji Tata Trust for giving me a travel grant to present a paper titled 'Spatiality of

Differential Belonging: Variable (but Durable) Marginalities among Muslims in Delhi' based on preliminary findings of this research at the international conference organized by RC21—Research Committee for Urban and Regional Studies of the International Sociological Association at the University of Amsterdam in July 2011. I also thank Professor Manish K. Jha who invited me to present a paper at a symposium organized by him at the Tata Institute of Social Sciences in collaboration with Mahanirban Calcutta Research Group in November 2011. This paper was titled 'Muslims in Delhi: The Normative Non-Citizens of the Global Urban'. Revised versions of these were published respectively, in the *Economic and Political Weekly* (EPW) titled 'Capitalist Logic of Spatial Segregation: A Study of Muslims in Delhi', and in the Working Paper Series of the Centre for the Study of Law and Governance (CSLG), JNU, as 'Normative Non-citizens of the Global Urban: Muslims in Delhi'. Slightly reorganized, this material is included in the present book. I thank EPW and CSLG for permission to republish this material.

I cannot thank Pratiksha Baxi enough for her friendship and camaraderie. The thesis has been published as a book largely because of her support, and encouragement of other colleagues—Professor Niraja G. Jayal, Professor Amit Prakash, and Dr Chirashree Dasgupta—at Centre for the Study of Law and Governance, Jawaharlal Nehru University, New Delhi.

I am profusely grateful for the comments of the two reviewers. It is difficult for me to articulate what their feedback and endorsement means to me. Their suggestions were important in improving the manuscript. Of course, its failings are all mine.

I thank my elder brother Zafar Ullah—his intimate familiarity with the changing geography of Old Delhi and its recent history was a constant source of reference. My younger brother Faiz Ullah would go over each argument in the book with me as I wrote and revised it. Thank you for our chats (sometimes at unearthly hours). Biggest thanks are due to my sister-in-law Salma Begum, who took over the role of my mother and my daughter's mother too. This book was possible only because of her rock solid support and love.

Many thanks are due to my friend of over two decades and my partner Nasir Jamal. The games he invented ostensibly to keep our daughter Miftah busy, and the resultant interruptions, kept it real for me.

Finally, I thank my parents Anwari Begum and Azmat Ullah. Even though they are no more, the attentive memory of their dreams for me egged me on.

ABBREVIATIONS

. . . .

ABVP	Akhil Bharatiya Vidyarthi Parishad
BJP	Bharatiya Janata Party
BPO	Business Process Outsourcing
BUMS	Bachelor of Unani Medicine and Surgery
CPWD	Central Public Works Department
CSLG	Centre for the Study of Law and Governance
DCP	Deputy Commissioner of Police
DDA	Delhi Development Authority
HCC	Heritage Conservation Committee
HRW	Human Rights Watch
IAC	India Against Corruption
INTACH	Indian National Trust for Art and Cultural Heritage
IT	information technology
JNNURM	Jawaharlal Nehru National Urban Renewal Mission
JTSA	Jamia Teachers' Solidarity Association
LGBT	Lesbian, Gay, Bisexual, and Transgender
MLA	Member of the Legislative Assembly
MNS	Maharashtra Navnirman Sena
MP	Member of Parliament

NCEUS	National Commission for Enterprises in the Unorganized Sector
NCT	National Capital Territory
NGO	Non-Governmental Organization
OB	Outside Broadcasting
OBC	Other Backward Classes
PCR	Police Control Room
PR	Public Relations
RWA	Residents' Welfare Association
SC	Scheduled Caste
SHO	Station House Officer
SPA	School of Planning and Architecture
SSS	Samajik Suvidha Sangam
ST	Scheduled Tribe
TRP	Television Rating Point
US	United States
WTO	World Trade Organization

Introduction

· ·

How do we begin posing and examining anew the questions vis-à-vis the position of Muslims in contemporary India? If we are to choose the single most defining feature of India today, it will be the massive urbanization[1] that we are experiencing as a country. This development is not an isolated one but a part of the globalization project of neoliberal forces. The World Bank (2001) sees this as a part of a global phenomenon it calls 'the urban transition'. Delhi is seeing immense transformation in terms of infrastructure and facilities for those who

---

[1] According to the Census of India 2001, 98 million people migrated all over India in the 1990s, an increase of 22 per cent over the previous decade. In absolute numbers 7–8 million people get added to the urban population of India every year. Large cities are getting larger: thirty-five mega and metro cities in the country account for 37.8 per cent of the total urban population. Delhi has outgrown all other urban centres since 1951: above 50 per cent

can afford them, but the change processes have also ended up marginalizing the already poor and marginalized sections of the urban population further. The changes have, of course, also impacted urban spaces, social relationships as well as the way everyday life is lived by its inhabitants. Today, while the *urban condition* is attracting the same kind of attention that glamourized 'the rural' in sociological and development literature of the 1960s and 1970s, the Muslim populations within the urban spaces receive no mention of their position within 'the urban transition' (World Bank 2001). How do these processes impact Muslims, and what (if any) is the impact they may in turn have on them? No doubt that the urban Muslim has also been affected but not much present scholarship is invested in studying these effects. The spatial and geographical turn in social science focused on the urban in India but has bypassed the issues of segregation of Muslims in the urban landscape, except to note the fact of segregation.

In this work I turn my attention to examining urban processes that frame the creation and articulation of urban Muslim identities, and to charting the topography of discriminatory segregation. This involved an examination of the textuality of representation and concerns on how to read texts that represent, while discerning the impact of nationalistic and transnational politics on the creation of Muslim identities. Attention is paid especially to geographies of social reproduction and social control; materiality of culture and identities

---

per decade. The 2001 Census pegs Delhi's population at 13,850,507 with a population density of 9,340 persons per sq. km (300,000/sq. km in the slums) (Government of India 2001). In the Census of India 2011, 453 million people reported as being migrants, an increase of 362 per cent over the previous decade. The decadal increase in the period 1991–2001 had been 22 per cent (Census of India 2001). Large cities are getting larger: 496 class 1 cities in the country account for 59.34 per cent of the total urban population (Census of India 2011). The 2011 Census pegs Delhi's population at 16,787, 941 with a population density of 11,320 persons per sq. km. Delhi's population is projected to grow to 24 million in 2021 (Statistical Abstract of Delhi 2014).

in everyday life; residential segregation and 'community cohesion'; and the socio-political positionality of Muslims in the urban social fabric and public sphere. I also hope to have illuminated, in this bid, the heterogeneity among Muslims in Delhi, especially along class differences.

DELHI AND ITS MUSLIMS

Delhi is the largest and oldest metropolis in India (UN Habitat 2016)—arguably, the one city in India that has seen three thousand years of continuous urban settlements (Dalrymple 2003). The oldest evidence of inhabitation in Delhi are painted grey shards dating 1000–500 BC (Singh 1999). The city has been a seat of power for centuries. Historians have argued that even though the names of the various cities that saw their establishment and decline on the site were different, all have, without exception, been associated with a 'magical', 'hallowed reputation', 'intrinsically identified with imperial sway' (Frykenberg 1986: 5). Frykenberg (1986) even goes so far as to say that from the time of Alexander the Great, '... to read of the hosts which have camped on the site(s) or tramped in the vicinity of the Delhi triangle is like reading a variant version of World History itself'. Numerous travellers, such as Ibn-e-Batuta who spent eight years in Delhi between 1334 and 1342, have sung paeans to its beauty, might, and size. Some scholars contend that the architecture, city plans, and everyday life in Delhi of yore was modelled after the medieval metropolises of Isfahan and Baghdad and also, that for Muslims, urban life has historically been the embodiment of ideal life (Bayly 1986). The Urban has been called 'the flower of earthly existence', where Muslims can bring together the most basic requirements of social life required of a faithful. Even in the nineteenth century, Indian Muslims tended to live mostly in *qasbah* towns and large cities. At least in the imagination of its poets like Dagh, Hali, and Ghalib, and the perspectives of many British and Indian historians, Delhi also has the distinction of its fate being bound up in the modern age with the fate of its Muslim community (Gupta 1981;

Spear 1937). Even today, culturally, Delhi, Lucknow, Hyderabad, and Bhopal, are among the important cities contributing to the images of Islamicate[2] cultures in India.

Narayani Gupta (1981) weaves an account of the fall and re-conquest of Delhi by the British after the 1857 'mutiny'. Almost all the residents were driven out and the city ravaged and looted. The event marked a major watershed not only in the narratives of colonial misfortunes to befall India and Delhi, but also left an indelible mark on the relationship of the Muslim inhabitants of the city with the colonial state, and the subsequent fortunes of Muslims in India. In January 1858, after the British took a decision to confiscate the property of all Muslims and any 'guilty' Hindus, the rest of the Hindus were allowed to return to the city. Still, no one could enter the city without a pass, and only those Muslims were given a pass 'whose services were needed by the Public Works Department' (Gupta 1981: 23–4). In his account of the Mutiny, Ghalib (quoted from Gupta 1981: 24) said 'the Muslims' houses remained so long empty that the walls seemed to be made of grass'. The pass system was discontinued and Muslims were allowed to resettle in Delhi after August 1859 only because the British were finding that the pass system to keep the Muslims out was difficult to implement! Even then the Muslim properties were still attached to the British government and many prominent Muslims were kept under house arrest. Many Muslims chose to leave Delhi 'to seek a new life in courts of Jaipur, Hyderabad and elsewhere' (Gupta 1981: 25). In a letter written in November 1859, Ghalib lamented that Delhi was a deserted city in ruins. John Lang, an Australian writer is quoted by Gupta

---

[2] Islamicate is an adjective that may be used to refer to cultural practices and architectural traditions that are commonly accepted as containing some features of 'Muslimness'. Kesavan (1994, quoting Hodgson 1974) advocates the use of this term especially to describe those qualities that have peculiarly been historically associated with Islam and Muslims even when found among non-Muslims and even though there is no religious sanction for them in Islam.

(1981) from the June 1860 copy of the newspaper *Moffusilite* he published himself:

> [W]hen will the agitation of European nerves subside? There is no reason for it ... the people are abject because they are starved out, banished and plundered. Thousands of Muslims are wandering homeless and houseless; the Hindus, pluming themselves on their assumed ... loyalty, strut about the streets giving themselves airs ... Let not the public think that Delhi has not been punished. Wend through the empty grass-grown streets, mark the uprooted houses, and shot riddled decaying palaces. We must not over punish ....

Gupta further opines that, '[t]he British then and later were to persist in holding to the stereotype of their own creation—the treacherous Muslim and the loyal Hindu' (1981: 20). Throughout the rest of their regime, the antipathy of the colonial rulers who found Muslims a very useful pawn in the pursuance of the divide and rule policy, ensured that the status of Muslims in India only proceeded from bad to worse.

During my research I found that 1857 figures very prominently in the memories and even contemporary narratives of the *Dilliwalley* (families living for generations in the walled city—Shahjahanabad) Muslim residents. The *ghadar* (mutiny) against the British; their eviction from the *shehr* (the city), after being labelled disloyal to the colonial rule; the confiscation of their properties, including various mosques, all is remembered just as it appears in the accounts of historians of 'the Mutiny'. Residents of Bara Hindu Rao can actually trace the founding of their locality in the events that took place in the aftermath of the 'mutiny'.

The next spectre remembered is 1947 or *san sentalis*. The partition of India, creation of Pakistan, and mass migration of Muslims was the next big blow in terms of reducing the Muslims to a persistent minority status in India. It also left them in a vulnerable position open to prejudice, suspicion, discrimination, and violence. In fact, on this side of the border, the Muslims who remained or chose to remain in Delhi were actually the victims of horrific violence and killings across the newly crafted border. The memories of the partition of India are vivid as though the event is occurring while it is being narrated. Those who stayed saw the mass exodus of their friends and neighbours. Families were fragmented—siblings, parents, children left—while they remained rooted here for their inability to leave due to poverty, sentimental attachments, or simply for the lack of imagination that would have them believe that people could be divided like this.

The participants in this study pointed out that while almost all the elite and educated Muslim families left Delhi, the poor labourers and artisans left behind in the walled city and the rest of Old Delhi were largely insecure and without work. The violence and hostilities in the towns of western Uttar Pradesh also brought Muslims to Delhi. After the creation of Pakistan, the Muslims who did not leave for that country were virtually charged with criminal disloyalty to the state, and were held guilty for a historical crime in the committing of which they had no say. In 1948, when the zamindari system was abolished, most big zamindars who had not yet left the country also left for Pakistan and the small ones were pauperized. With no one left to patronize them and hostilities on the rise, those who were educated came to Delhi from Meerut, Muzaffarnagar, Amroha, Saharanpur, and Moradabad, looking for jobs. Dilli College, Hamdard, and Shama were the major institutions of Muslims that played an important role in anchoring the Muslim population in Delhi.

When the Muslims began to try picking up the threads of life and livelihoods again, the *karkhandaar*s (workshop owners) and *karigar*s (artisans or skilled workers) had to contend with a business environment that was hostile towards them. Many years after Partition, those who were discouraged by this hostility, or wished to be reunited with their family members continued to leave for Pakistan. The 1971 war resulted not only in the creation of Bangladesh but also the sealing of borders such that people could no longer cross over and reside in the other country. By this time, some families also began moving to Jamia Nagar and Seelampur because of lack of space in the old city. I found clear divisions between the businessmen and *karkhana* owners who moved to Seelampur, Jaffarabad followed/accompanied by karigars and labourers, and the educated—mostly teachers who moved to Okhla near Jamia Millia Islamia.

Emergency was imposed in 1975 in the country by the then prime minister, Indira Gandhi. Apart from other effects of an authoritarian rule, the emergency was also marked by an 'urban beautification'-inspired demolition drive run by Jag Mohan Malhotra as Vice-Chairperson of the Delhi Development Authority under the patronage of Sanjay Gandhi, in the areas around Jama Masjid–Meena Bazaar, Turkman Gate, and other areas of the city (Dupont 2008). Thousands were evicted and 'resettled' in Seelampur and Welcome. In the early 1980s, out-migration from Old Delhi continued and more Muslims shifted to Okhla or Seelampur. Hindus too shifted to Shahdara, Geeta Colony, Uttam Nagar, and Punjabi Bagh, among others. In many areas where the Muslim population was greater in number, Hindus sold their properties and moved out, and many localities became largely Muslim. By the late 1980s, segregation in Delhi on religious identity lines became almost final and complete.

When the 'structural adjustment' and neoliberal 'reforms' began in the 1990s, Muslim craftsmen found that their skills, which were losing relevance in industrializing India, were completely devalued in the 'liberalized' regime. Also during this time, Hindutva groups sponsored killings and destruction of businesses targeting Muslims in Meerut, Moradabad, Aligarh, and Bhagalpur, among others, which are called 'riots' in the mainstream and academic discourses (Harriss-White 2005; Khalidi 1995). As a parallel strategy, the *Sangh Parivar* also upped its ante regarding the alleged 'appeasement' of Muslims. Imageries of Muslims as 'anti-liberal', 'backward fanatics' were strengthened in the mainstream owing to relentless and planned tirades. Muslims fell literally under siege and violent attacks on Muslim communities become the order of the day. Bharatiya Janata Party (BJP) leader Lal Krishna Advani undertook a Rath Yatra in 1990, which left a deadly trail of violence targeting Muslims all along its route across north India. In 1992, when the Babri Masjid was demolished, there was more violence across the country. This frenzy culminated in a genocidal pogrom in Gujarat. The state was openly proclaimed in the mainstream discourses as the 'Laboratory of Hindutva'. Gujarat 2002 left Muslims in Delhi (as elsewhere in the country) stunned by the ferocity of the attacks (Engineer 2002; Sheth 2003; Spodek 2010). The stark and horrific images of the violence probably stunned the entire country too, for there were no more instances of communal violence targeting Muslims for many years after 2002. But even in the absence of overt communal violence, India too was gripped by global Islamophobia and all Muslims were conclusively branded as terrorists or potential terrorists in the public consciousness in the wake of the United States-led, so called 'war against terror'.

Meanwhile in Delhi, Jamia Millia Islamia anchored not only a residential locality but also a generation of youth trained in professions for which there is place in the 'globalized' market. Muslim students of Jamia received education and training which armed them with skills and proficiencies needed in liberalized and privatized markets. This lead to their 'rediscovery' as 'human resources' by technology-enabled firms with offshore jobs of transnational companies outsourced to India. From a small community of teachers and students, Jamia Nagar grew into a hub of service class professionals. In Seelampur, the small manufacturers (with their capital contained in segregated areas), and semi-skilled and unskilled labourers too are 'benefited' by manufacturing jobs brought to India by globalization. Paradoxically, both localities are eminently suitable for being 'integrated' into the globalized economy geared for profit maximization because they are 'segregated' localities. This renders the workers and manufacturers with a limited capacity to bargain because of their inability to move to other spaces. Around the same time, the culture of the walled city–Jama Masjid—became commodified. Tourists and visitors now visit Old Delhi for its culinary culture and historical–architectural heritage. The state (by setting up support for the 'conservation of heritage'), the civil society (by propagating 'walks' and 'talks' staged around the area), and the media (by popularizing the most 'delectable' experiences) are all participating enthusiastically in the cultural marketization of the area.

Today, the Indian Muslim languishes deeply in poverty and back-wardness (Khalidi 1995). Much is known regarding the socio-economic status of Muslim communities across India. It is confounding that this knowledge exists amidst the continued allegations and uproar over 'appeasement' of Muslims by the Indian state. Muslims and their faith Islam are experiencing an unprecedented focus and attention on vari-ous aspects, mostly not of their picking. Muslims and poverty, Muslim women and their status, Muslims and media practices, communalism and communal violence are the oft-invoked frameworks in which Muslims and their issues are mostly discussed. Meanwhile, the com-munity has fallen behind in almost all aspects of development and progress compared to even the scheduled castes (SCs)/scheduled tribes (STs), as pointed out by the Prime Minister's High Level Committee (PMHLC 2006) appointed to report on the social, economic, and educational status of Muslims. Chaired by Justice Rajinder Sachar, the committee (popularly known as the Sachar Committee) concluded in its report that Muslims fare poorly on most socio-economic indices. The statistics it presented are stark. The Sachar Committee found a clear and significant inverse association between the proportion of the Muslim population and the availability of educational infrastructure in most localities.[3] It reported that efforts of the Reserve Bank of India to extend banking and credit facilities under the Prime Minister's 15-point programme of 1983 have mainly benefited other minorities marginalizing Muslims.[4] They are grossly under-represented relative

[3] According to the estimates based on the 61st round of NSSO survey in 2004–05, 25 per cent of children of Muslim parents in the 6–14 year age group have either never attended school or have dropped out (PMHLC 2006: 58). While 65 per cent of eligible Muslim children finish middle school, only 17 per cent of 17+ years old Muslim children pass matriculation. (PMHLC 2006: 60–2).

[4] The average amount of bank loan disbursed to Muslims in Priority Sector Advances (indicated by amount outstanding per account for Muslims for all districts in the year ending March 2005) was one-third of the amount disbursed to others; and half that of other minorities (PMHLC 2006: 131).

to their populations across all government institutions[5] including the
highest levels of government service.[6] But prison is one place where
proportional representation of Muslims is higher than their population percentage.[7] Most of the variables indicate that Muslim-OBCs
(other backward classes) are more significantly deprived in comparison to Hindu-OBCs.[8] Marginalized thus, India's 13.4 per cent Muslim
population contributes only 6 per cent of the gross domestic product
(GDP). The report also provides some indications regarding urban
Muslims reflecting in its findings that a larger proportion of the
Muslim population in India is urbanized, but also that urban Muslims
are worse off than those in the rural areas.[9]

[5] Representation of Muslims does not match their population proportion
in any state (*Sachar Committee Report*: 171). In 15 states where Muslims average 17 per cent of the population, they are 8 per cent of the lower judiciary
(p. 372). The Muslim community has a representation of only 4.5 per cent
in the Indian Railways of which 98.7 per cent are positioned at lower levels
(p. 131). The representation of Muslims is very low in universities and in
banks (p. 169). Also, their share in the police constabulary is only 6 per cent
(p. 172), in health 4.4 per cent, in transport 6.5 per cent (p. 173).

[6] Only 2.2 per cent officers in the Indian Administrative Service (IAS)
are Muslim, while they comprise only 1.8 per cent of the Indian Foreign
Service (IFS), and 4 per cent of the Indian Police Service (IPS). No Muslim is
a Secretary-level official in the Central Government (PMHLC 2006: 165).

[7] At the end of December 2015, 15.8 per cent among the convicts were
Muslim, while 20.9 per cent of the incarcerated under trials were Muslims
(NCRB 2016).

[8] The work participation rate shows the presence of a sharp difference
between Hindu-OBCs (67 per cent) and the Muslims. The share of Muslim-
OBCs in government/PSU jobs is much lower than Hindu-OBCs.

[9] A substantially larger proportion of the Muslim households in urban
areas is in the less-than-INR 500 expenditure bracket. When compared to
other socio-religious communities (SRCs), urban Muslims face much higher
relative deprivation than Muslims in rural India. The fall in poverty for Muslims
has been modest during the decade 1993–4 to 2004–5 in urban areas, whereas
the decline in rural areas has been substantial. (PMHLC 2006: 159).

While for the majority of the Muslims in India it may not be shocking to be confronted by the Sachar Committee's finding that they are behind SCs and STs on almost all accounts of development, progress, and representation, it still is a piece of information that has not received the kind of academic attention it deserves. Ample information exists about Muslims lagging behind in their performance on most socio-economic indices across India. We know that it is so, but we are yet to begin to pose questions regarding what makes it so. This work is an attempt to a take a step in an exercise to frame and pose questions.

In the city, as a mechanism for capitalist accumulation, Muslims find the space that they lacked earlier because their unique positioning makes these areas ideal for a new kind of economic exploitation. No one is complaining because not everyone is discriminated against in the same way. The 'good Muslim–bad Muslim' (Mamdani 2005) binary imported from the US has been customized for India-specific conditions, and the good ones are treated differently. The specific details of the stereotypes of the 'good' and 'bad' Muslim in the official discourse notwithstanding, the bottom line was that in all probability 'good Muslims' were elite, affluent, and influential, while 'bad Muslims' lacked all these qualities. An important thing to note in this regard is that elite Indian Muslims also bought into the argument of 'good Muslims–bad Muslims'. While they may have sympathized with the poor Muslims, they also agreed with the mainstream discourses that because of poverty, lack of education, irrationality, and having been targeted by communal violence, Muslims were prone to retributive violence. They sought to distance themselves spatially and socially

---

Fazal (2013) reports that in the period 2004–05 to 2009–10, a faster rate of poverty decline (7.6 per cent per annum) was recorded among Muslims, while poverty decline among Muslims (3.1 per cent per annum) was slowest in urban areas. At the end of the year 2009–10, Muslims counted among the poorest (25.1 per cent) after SCs (30.3) and STs (32.5) while the national average remained at 21.6. Incidence of poverty among Muslims was 6 per cent higher than national averages in rural areas and 4 per cent in urban areas.

from the 'bad Muslims'. Everyone wants to be that Muslim who is less discriminated against and gets a bigger piece of the commodified life of canned comforts. It is to be noted though, that the collapse of this binary is written within it—in the implicit deduction that when the chips are down, even the 'good Muslim' was a 'bad Muslim'.

While all these changes are taking place, social science research on Indian Muslims across disciplines continues to focus on the socio-economic backwardness of Muslims, researching them only as slum dwellers (Mistry 2005; Hussain 2008; Engineer 1991; Faridi and Siddiqui 1992; Mondal 1992).

In 2008, several bomb blasts took place at many sites in the city. Two boys suspected to be terrorists who planned and executed these blasts were shot dead by the Delhi police in Batla House, Jamia Nagar in an 'encounter'. One was arrested and two allegedly 'escaped'. The one arrested and one of those killed were students of Jamia (JTSG 2009). In the entire last decade, there has been a spate of arrests of Muslim boys and men, which has only intensified notwithstanding protests (HRW 2011). Most are being found to be unsubstantiated cases that law enforcement agencies have been unable to defend in courts of law (JTSA 2012). Also, most Muslims arrested are educated professionals, giving credence to the global spectre of the techno-savvy, educated, radical, 'Islamic' terrorist. I argue that this is the disciplinary power of the state to rein in even the elite Muslims, who had begun to raise their voice against their stereotyping. Recently, the news media has begun to give some space to instances of discrimination but the reportage has been mostly limited to elite Muslims not being able to get their children admitted to elite schools (Perappadan and Zaman 2012), being discriminated against in renting houses (Ashok and Ali 2012), and mistreated at airports (Menon 2012), even when they could afford all these things. At the same time, research interest is beginning to emerge in the upcoming middle class among Muslims. Studies and articles have begun to appear now which conclude that Muslims are practicing 'self-segregation' (Gayer and Jaffrelot 2012).

Meanwhile, middle-class Muslims continue their struggle to run businesses and keep their jobs in the global recession, while also trying to educate their children. They struggle to keep the foothold they received in terms of an opportunity to find better livelihoods and lives, be it that this is only within the capitalism-inspired view of Muslims as incarcerated resources—capital, human, and cultural. Lower-class Muslims form a sizable chunk of the unorganized, daily wage workers, doing the dirtiest and worst paying jobs in the city. Muslims are overrepresented among the destitute, waste pickers, and street children in Delhi (Mander and Sehgal 2012; Sheikh 2016). The study concludes by asserting that Muslims have been silenced by various discursive practices and the disciplinary power of the state and a deeply discriminatory society, such that any meaningful speech that raises their real issues is denied to them.

Before structural adjustment altered not only the economic landscape of the city but also its spatial constitution, various Delhi neighbourhoods were not as strictly segregated along the lines of class and identity. Differences existed but boundaries overlapped and were not airtight. People had to iron out the creases of the differences that undeniably existed among them. This is not to say that there was bonhomie between all kinds of people, but even though prejudice was always palpable and often expressed in overt discrimination, occasionally erupting in violent episodes, *it was not easy to overlook or 'unsee' the other*. The class, caste, and communal divides often existed *within* a localized community, and people had to confront them and negotiate with them in their everyday lives. In Delhi today, the spatial segregation has reached a point where residents no longer have to engage with difference. This choice not to engage and the degree of its availability is a function of positions of privilege and class (which conflate with religious and caste identities) of the person. The more privileged you are, the easier it is to shut out and forget that other less-privileged people also exist. The privileged go to working class neighbourhoods, slums, or segregated Muslim enclaves probably only for research, fieldwork, or seeking exotic culinary experiences. While the people on the other side of the class divide—providing services to the affluent, working in their homes and businesses—have to traverse the boundary every day and can see the differences clearly. But in order that their wares and services are saleable, increasingly they are required to leave behind or obscure the tell-tale signs of who they are when they meet their employers such that even here the powerful are not confronted by the difference. An everyday critical engagement is neither a requirement nor a necessity anymore.

THEORIZING THE CITY

When the new science of sociology began, urban spaces were one of the first subjects of study. Marx, Weber, and Durkheim, credited as being the founders of sociology, were essentially dealing with social changes brought about by the advent of industrial capitalism and, by corollary, of urbanization (Saunders 1981). Nevertheless, the first urbanists or urban sociologists occupied themselves with what they called 'urban ecology' (Park 2005 [1936]). The ecological school of urban sociology, also known as the Chicago school, first through the work of Albion Small and his successor Robert Ezra Park (1926), developed a notion of 'human ecology', which drew from Social Darwinist ideas of the biotic and symbiotic development of plant ecology to study groups and urban processes (Roberts 2006). Park himself is reported as having said that his conception of city and community was not a geographical one, but rather resembled a social organism. The school's approach put a lot of emphasis on the 'scientific' view rather than what they criticized as the 'moralistic' view, but various commentators have noted that the Chicago school's urban ecology remained an ambiguous and theoretically deficient view (Roberts 2006) because of its 'ecological fallacy' arising from reliance on environmental determinism (Taylor 1973: 122). Social Darwinism led Park to not only proclaim that the city was a 'natural' habitat of the 'civilized man' but also that social phenomena were an outcome of unplanned, natural processes that inevitably form a chain of events akin to stages in individual life (Roberts 2006). Obviously, such a view did little more than just describe, and in any case had no interest in analysing the conflicts (such as race conflicts in contemporary cities in the US) which, for them, were but merely a stage in the natural scheme of things that were 'progressing'.

Louis Wirth's book *The Ghetto* (1928) and article 'Urbanism as a Way of Life' (1938), considered classics in urban sociology, have an essentially pessimistic view of the urban in which he regarded urban society as representing a break from its 'natural' situation. Urbanism, according to Wirth, gave rise to anomie and other negative processes, despite its claims to utility and efficiency (Smith 1988). Another classic of second generation of human ecologists, *Street Corner Society* by W. Whyte (1943), represents the Chicago school's enduring interest in deviance. The Chicago school also made something of a 'classic' model of a city formulated by E.W. Burgess (1925) in the form of concentric zones representing a core of commercial and elite residences, a middle ring of low-income neighbourhoods, and an outer periphery of manufacturing districts.

While the researchers related to the Chicago school, with their urban ecological view of the city, did look at the changes brought to everyday life by technological advancement, they mostly neglected to study the inequality of resources among classes, capital flows, and built spaces. Beyond a vague notion of benign neglect they also overlooked the role of the state in the maintenance of the inequalities. The school instead focused its energies and attention on ghetto life and essentialized it rather than looking for structural processes underlying the so called 'culture of the ghetto'. This approach was attacked by C. Wright Mills (1970) for neglecting structure and for being what he called a 'situational approach'. Castells (1976) also criticized the school scathingly for not realizing that the changes they were studying could not have been an outcome only of individual preferences and stylistic matters but were, in fact, the processes of industrial capitalism. Castells emphasized that the concentric zone model was an outcome of the specifics of urban processes in one city, and that it could not be used indiscriminately as a universal model. Further, Wirth's views on the disintegration of the community and individualism were shown to be not specific only to urban societies. In fact, Herbert Gans (1962) called urban neighbourhoods 'urban villages' because the modes of association in the neighbourhoods he studied in Chicago were similar to those in rural neighbourhoods.

In the final analysis, the contribution of the Chicago school remains its attention to peculiarities of city life *and* to its spatial pattern. Even though the Chicago school appeared deficient in theory, it did go on to be influential in later 'interactionist' works in the realm of social psychology and urban 'micro' studies. In reaction to the theoretical deficiencies of the Chicago school, by the 1960s urban studies had taken a Marxist (or a Weberian turn) (Roberts 2006). Interestingly enough, while symbolic interactionism located itself as a micro-theory in opposition to structural approaches which they alleged are macro, it is possible to see the Marxist approaches as those in which macro and micro level features of social phenomena can both be interpreted (Ritzer and Goodman 2004). In fact, these approaches can beautifully show how the structure *writes itself* in the everyday experiences of individuals.

With the engagements of Castells, Harvey, and Lefebvre, the Marxist turn in urban studies marked a new concern in the practice of Marxism itself. Merrifield (2002), in his lively book titled *Metromarxism*, elaborates on initial anti-urban tendencies in Marxist thought which envisioned revolutionary practice as flowing from countryside to city, as in Guevara's thought, and which derided cities as bourgeois in the complex anti-cosmopolitan attitude of the Soviet Bolsheviks. Debray, whose writings are said to be inspired by Castro and Guevara said, '[a]s we know, the mountain proletarianizes the bourgeois and peasant elements, and the city can bourgeoisify the proletariats' (cf. Merrifield 2002:3). Merrifield credits Antonio Gramsci for coming up with a Marxist praxis which identified *organizing* as a more central issue than the supposed dichotomy of urban and rural. According to Merrifield, Marxist urbanism embraces the urban with all its paradoxes and possibilities. The 'urban' turn in Marxism also probably facilitated its meeting with the 'cultural' and the 'spatial'. This promulgation of Marxist thought is discussed in some further detail in a section in Chapter 4 of this book which deals with textuality and the work of critical theorists.

The next major turn in urban studies, which brings us to the present situation, came with the post-Fordist and post-industrial turn in Western developed societies in the 1980s (Harvey 1987). Globalization and structural adjustment programmes driven by international monetary organizations pushed the economies of the developing world to 'liberalize'. It involved the 'reorganisation of economic activities and cultural attributes' of societies on a global scale (Banerjee-Guha 2010). This is recognized by many authors as a logical extension to the enduring story of capitalism and has been aptly termed neo-imperialism (Harvey 1985). Several trends stand out as a result of this process—namely shifting of manufacturing and other low paid services to the third world economies (often rapid shifting from one location to another), and privatization and deregulation of the economic sphere to facilitate an extreme fluidity of capital. Other effects were increased migration flows—both inter and intra-national (Sassen 1998)—and, technological changes—especially in modes of communication and transportation (Castells 1989, 1996, 1997, 1998). A very important impact of all this has been the incredible pace of urbanization (Castells 1994) and the emergence of what has been called world cities (Friedmann and Wolff 1982), or global cities (Sassen 1991) from which the capital flows are being controlled. Social, political, and cultural changes as an impact of globalization are too many and too intricate to even begin to enumerate in this space. Suffice to say that the trends here are of deeper and wider inequalities between the haves and have-nots, xenophobia of different kinds proliferating across the world (Appadurai 1996, 2006), and the citizen being reduced to a customer—served by the state proportionate to their purchasing power (Katz 2001). It has been noted that in the wake of globalization, even democratic governments have done little to reduce inequalities. All this and more obviously has spatial ramifications which have occupied the attention of the scholars of the 'urban'.

In her book *Theorizing the City*, Setha Low (1999) traces the historical development of the anthropological study of the city, and delineates a number of theoretical approaches that were developed over time and continue to be drawn upon by urban anthropologists. According to her, '[t]hese approaches include urban ecology models; community, family and network analyses; studies of the power/knowledge of planning and architecture; supralocal/local linkage analyses; and political economic, representational, and discursive models'. The present study locates itself somewhere in what Low calls the political–economic, representational, and discursive model of study. Elaborating on the 'representational cities' approach further, Jane Jacobs (1993) says that this is an approach in which messages encoded in the environment are read as text. Jacobs argues that 'ethnographic studies were commonly prescribed the role of rendering more real the exotic and marginalised, but were seen to have little value in terms of the modern project of theory-building' (Jacobs 1993: 828). Jacobs suggests that in this new radicalized ethnography of the city, the urban built environment is also a discursive realm.

Geographies of Discrimination

Despite their theoretical deficiencies and Darwinian moorings, the Chicago school researchers did look at segregation, and were among the first to engage in the systematic study of residential segregation in urban America based on racial and ethnic differentiation. Thomas and Znaniecki's (1958) epic study, *The Polish Peasant in Europe and America*, and Louis Wirth's *The Ghetto* (1928)—a study of the Jewish immigrants—reflect the school's interest in the ideas of the 'marginal man' as formulated by Park. Park posited that the mind of this 'marginal man' was where the changes were taking place, which needed to be studied for a study of the 'processes of civilisation and of progress' (Park quoted from Roberts 2006:16). In grasping the determinants of segregation, Robert Park defined it as involving a link between the social distance and physical distance between communities (Park 1915).

Examining the phenomenon of *de jure* segregation is a good place to start examining the role of the state in segregation. European Jewish ghettos are widely thought to be precursors of all such segregation having continuity into the Russian 'Pale' till the Nazi German laws of segregation and later culmination in the horrors of concentration and extermination camps (Wirth 1928). South African apartheid is another such example of residential segregation by law in recent history (Christopher 1990). Similarly, Israeli state policy relating to the segregation of Arab-Israeli citizens in Israeli towns has also been studied as an example of specific laws and policies directly pertaining to discrimination (Falah 1996). These studies show that in instances of extreme segregation of populations by law, even when the two communities have to share a space it was/is not as equals. In most cases, it leads to a very limited social interaction accompanied with an economic interaction of a coercive, debilitative nature. In a less extreme method of segregation, zoning, and public housing policies are often used by states as exclusionary devices even when these policies do not explicitly exclude (Berry 2001). Extension of financial support for housing is another such example. Jackson (1985) established in a study in the US that while housing loans were given only to white families for houses in whites-only neighbourhoods, the white families also demanded and imposed exclusion of Black families. Michael Katz (1990, 1997, 2001) has written extensively on the history and functioning of welfare in the US, framed along the debates on the 'deserving' and 'undeserving' poor. He concludes in his work that the discrimination against African-Americans is an underlying thread in the working of the welfare state.

Massey and Denton (1988) are credited with a framework for understanding residential segregation in what is widely recognized as a more nuanced and a more spatial approach. They specified five dimensions of residential segregation, namely, (i) *evenness*, which was related to the distribution of the minority community's members across the city, and was said to have an inverse relationship with segregation, (ii) *exposure*, which was the measure of the degree of the potential contact of the minority group with the rest of the population of the city, (iii) *concentration*, which was the amount of the physical area that minority groups occupied relative to their proportion in the population, (iv) *centralization*, which was the proximity of minority groups to the city centre, and (v) *clustering*, which was the extent to which minority groups live in contiguous areas. Massey and Denton (1993) also wrote a compelling book tracing the history of segregation of African-American people. Calling these 'apartheid', their main argument was that the practices of segregation were responsible for the existence of the Black ghetto, and that the poverty between Blacks and Whites is different because of racial discrimination and segregation. Citing empirical studies and reviews of literature pertaining to racial segregation in cities in the US, Galster (1988) concludes that both 'market forces' and 'illegal discriminatory acts' were responsible, *equally*, whereas others (Clark 1986) were concluding that private discrimination had waned, and with reference to poverty, it was only benign market forces that were responsible. In the late 1990s and early 2000s, the debates on segregation also turned towards what has been called Black self-segregation. These alleged that white prejudice and discrimination driving segregation had markedly alleviated, and could no longer be held responsible for the continued segregation of Blacks; instead it was the preferences of the Black people themselves that were responsible. Noting these debates, Ihlanfeldt and Scafidi (2002) point out that this implied that enforcement of fair housing and lending laws would not be required. Many statistical studies citing secondary data but also numerous studies conducting primary research reached conflicting conclusions. Ihlanfeldt and Scafidi's (2002) analysis found statistically significant self-segregation, but it could not be said to play more than a minor role in explaining the residential segregation of Blacks.

In Brazilian literature, racial discrimination as a basis of segregation is not emphasized as much as class differentiations (Oliveira 1996). Oliveira's own opinion is that, '... although residential segregation by race and class are interrelated and driven by similar socio-economic factors, the relative lack of racial segregation in the *favelas* of Rio de Janeiro has facilitated more effective political engagement around class issues without eradicating racial identities' (1996: 72). Comparing favelas in Rio de Janeiro and ghettos in New York City, he says that African slaves in the US were always a minority of not more than 20 per cent, mostly concentrated in the southern US, whereas Black people sold to slavery in Brazil were of a much higher proportion to the entire population and spread all over Brazil. White people in colonial Brazil were actually a numerical minority and later, after the promotion of European immigration in the last two centuries, whites are barely a majority in present-day Brazil. Also, the US saw much more sudden abolition of slavery and violent conflicts following the abolition compared to Brazil, where the process was much slower and long drawn out.

On the matter of nomenclature, Oliveira (1996) says, that the term 'ghetto' in the US currently alludes to economic conditions *and* race/ethnicity but also has 'physical and social dimensions of poverty represented by the decay and abandonment of neighbourhoods, crime, substandard education, unemployment, the decline of "family values" and so forth'. He says that while the stereotype of the *favelado*s refers to laziness, and social and political disorganization, it does not carry negative connotations about race or ethnicity *per se* because favelas are not exclusive race neighbourhoods. In a primary study, Perlman (2007) found that 'living in a favela' was reported by people to make them more prone to be targeted by discrimination, generally, and especially in employment, than 'race' itself. Later, Perlman (2009) says that 'favela' was considered a very pejorative term as it is no longer characterized by shanty squatter settlements on undesirable land (marshy, steep hills) in the city. As the land is developed, increasingly, favelas are no longer free places for poor people to settle, and now have fierce real-estate markets. Nor does Perlman find that they are home to acute and chronic poverty any longer. According to her, favela residents are victims of a 'myth of marginality' which is an 'ideology' that justifies inequity and blames the so-called marginals for social problems, while legitimating dominant discourses and norms. Perlman says that, '[a]lthough they are neither economically nor politically marginal, they are exploited, manipulated, and repressed; although they are neither socially nor culturally marginal, they are stigmatized and excluded from a closed class system' (2009: 150).

On similar lines, Loic Wacquant (2008) compares French working-class quarters *banlieue*s and Black ghettos in the US, and again comes up with the conclusion that it would be an error to conflate the two. Wacquant (2008) points to these places in France and the US as being products of different historical processes and arising from different criteria of classification. In banlieues, it is primarily the class position 'modulated' by ethnicity, while in a ghetto it is ethno-racial identity, irrespective of class. Also, importantly, Wacquant (2008) points out that they are products of different political construction and bureaucratic management. He elaborates further by saying that even though both are deprived zones of inequality, the Black ghettos have a task of containing undesirables and a dishonoured category of people who were needed as labour in an industrial society, but are no longer needed in post-industrial set-ups. He says that to talk of a 'French ghetto' is a 'sociological absurdity' and amounts to 'transatlantic smuggling of American concepts', an uncontrolled usage of which is 'scientifically fraudulent and politically irresponsible' (Wacquant 2008: 160–2).

THE PHILOSOPHICAL AND CONCEPTUAL FRAMEWORK

In choosing the broad direction that my work would take, I was immensely inspired by the speech that Max Horkheimer gave in 1931 at the inauguration of the *Institut fur Sozial Forschung* (the Frankfurt school). Given the advent of the Nazi Party, the approach laid out by Horkheimer in this inaugural address, was incredibly courageous. The speech titled 'The Present Situation of Social Philosophy and the Task of an Institute for Social Research' (Horkheimer 1993 [1931]) provided me a manifesto or creed on which I could base the approach of this work. Horkheimer (1993) emphasized that the study of human society necessarily required an interdisciplinary approach, which must have philosophy as its core. It was this philosophical core that would bind the multiple strands of the approach. It was useful that Horkheimer (1993) advocated the use of a new avatar of the Marxist perspective and methods that included sensitivity to social and cultural considerations. The Frankfurt school's critical theory rescues Marxism from vulgar economic reductivism, and was especially useful in providing me a position which was does not fall in the dichotomous traps of macro–micro, or little narratives and grand narratives, among others. Critical theory posits itself at a vantage position which made it possible for me to discern the structural roots of processes expressed in the everyday narratives of the participants. It is this approach that is the biggest strength of this effort. What was of utmost importance to me was that in the speech, Horkheimer (1993) also emphasized that research must have an emancipatory aim, and towards achieving this end it must bring out the role played by consciousness in social, cultural, political, and economic processes, and not just focus on the manifest condition of an oppressive milieu.

The Muslim question in India is considered one purely about identity. In my understanding, while identity is a necessary conceptual tool to study Muslims, it is extremely limited in the way it is usually employed, focused on the individual-self in relation with either the 'significant other' or selves of the other members of the same group. In this work, I have rather employed a dramaturgical view of identity as a process of role-prescription. Two things about this view are of special interest to me. First, that identity is conceptualized as a categorization based on definite 'social criteria'. What these criteria prescribe may be disconnected with the actions of the carriers of the identity. As such, conflicts reflecting the broad structure of dominance in a society are scripted into identities. Second, the self is conceptualized in a wider arena of what Giddens (1991) calls 'reflexive modernity' or 'high modernity' and globalization, and asserts that in the global situation, the self and society are 'intimately' linked.

In order to shift the frame of reference in this study of Muslims in Delhi, I employ spatiality and positionality as additional conceptual tools to reframe the questions confronting urban Muslim populations in India today.

If space is a place with social content, by a corollary, 'the social is inexorably also spatial' (Massey 1992: 80). As such 'spatiality' is the expression of the relationship between people and spaces. It operationalizes the way in which spaces and people communicate. A fundamental postulate of geography is that the relative positions of communities partly determine the form and intensity of social interactions. These in turn build back the main structures of geographical space, while increasingly distorting them. The use of a concept such as spatiality enabled me to examine the spatial relegation of a community, and understand it as the ultimate symbol of its social marginalization—which highlights but also recreates social difference and distance.

My use of the term 'positionality' in this work is influenced by feminist theory within which positionality was coined to describe the situated positions from which subjects come to know the world (Maher and Tetreault 1993). Here, the social situatedness of a researcher (in terms of her identities) is clearly understood to be shaping her analysis (Nagar and Geiger 2007).

While the feminist notion of positionality seems limited to a subjective view of people's experiences, and factors that shape or influence experiences, Eric Sheppard (2000) specifically adds geographic situatedness to render the concept more useful for analysing globalization. 'Positionality within the global economy...', Sheppard argues, is an expression of situation '... within the global economy in general and to the trajectories of particular places' (2000: 308). He suggests that within the studies of globalization, an intense focus on territories and possibility of networked spaces has meant that the very role of connection between territories in creating relational inequalities within globalized/networked spaces has gone largely overlooked. And finally, a third notion of positionality used in this work is the Foucauldian notion of individuals 'positioned' in the world they experience as a web or network of overlapping or competing discourses (Roberts 2006). It is in this broad and multiple usage of positionality that this work is engaging in its study of the Muslim population in Delhi.

We may read this along with Harvey's (1976) suggestion that the production and organization of spaces in the city take place primarily to aid the aim of capitalist accumulation. In his essay 'Revolutionary and Counter Revolutionary Theory in Geography and the Problem of Ghetto Formation', Harvey (1972) wrote an account of how Baltimore city's residential structure was produced by interacting policies of financial and government institutions, and by privately and publicly financed multiple submarkets. Through an absorbing analysis of discriminatory banking policies and speculative rent tendencies of the landowners, Harvey concludes in agreement with Lefebvre (1991) that in the process of urbanization, distinctions between land and capital, and rent and profit have blurred (Merrifield 2002). I deduce from this a need to see accumulation beyond the industrial production of goods to include investment in land and property, while keeping in mind that the key word is still 'accumulation'.

Lefebvre is noteworthy for making a potent suggestion in his book, *The Production of Space* (1991), that the production of space is not only an achievement of capital and power, but may also be potentially used as a tool that can reconstruct and liberate the social world. Lefebvre arms us with this tool of Marxist 'spatial decoding' that facilitates an understanding of how cities develop under capitalism. He insists that cities must not be viewed as a material end product but as spaces for production of social relations. Lefebvre is credited with an instrumental view of space in which he maintains that space is not just a geographical or geometrical conception, but an instrument that needs to be conquered and integrated for the maintenance of capitalism. Within the scheme of capitalist modes of production space has to be considered along with raw material, instruments, and labour, among others, even though it is unique in not being 'used-up' or 'reproduced' in the sense that others in the set of productive forces are (Zieleniec 2007: 65–6). Lefebvre accepts that the city is a market, a space that has been commodified by capitalism, but he highlights another quality of the urban as a place of play and leisure. This, he points out, is an explanation of spaces that are produced for ideological purposes beyond purely accumulative purposes. Thus, he describes space as being 'neither a "subject" nor an "object" but rather a set of social relations and forms' (Lefebvre 1991: 116).

For a critical knowledge of space, Lefebvre (1991) conjures up a spatial version of the Marxist conception of fetishism and then challenges this fetishism. Since in his understanding spaces are not material empty vessels that are filled up by other things, but rather exist because they are produced within the framework of capitalist production, he asserts that this production of space is obscured by the emphasis that spaces are physical and natural and *just exist*

(Zieleniec 2007). In order to tackle the issue of production of spaces, Lefebvre insists that we 'must account for representational spaces, representation of space, but above all for their interrelationships and their links with social practice' (1991: 116). Thus, following Lefebvre's lead I shall consider these three elements:

- 'Spatial practices refer to the physical and material flows (of groups, individuals and commodities)... ' interactions, and negotiations that occur in, across, and between sites, and the experience of such flows that shape '... the ownership, use and designation of land within the hierarchy of administrative and organizational division of space, with an intrinsic element of social control' (Zieleniec 2007: 72–3).
- 'Representation of space is space envisioned and conceived by assorted professionals and technocrats: planners, engineers, developers, architects, urbanists, geographers, and others of a scientific bent. This space reflects the arcane models, signs, and jargon used and transmitted by these specialists. Usually ideology, power and knowledge lurk somewhere within it, or radiate from it. This is the dominant space of any society, intimately tied to the relations of production and to the order which those relations impose' (Merrifield 2002: 89–90).
- 'Representational space is space as directly lived through its associations and images and symbols, and hence the space of 'inhabitants' and 'users', but also some artists and perhaps of those, such as a few writers and philosophers, who describe and aspire to do no more than describe. His is the dominated—and hence passively experienced—space which the imagination seeks to change and appropriate. It overlays the physical space, making symbolic use of its objects' (Lefebvre 1991: 39).

In this book, these are the threads—methodological, philosophical, and personal—which are scrutinized and interwoven to produce a narrative of Muslims in Delhi. The narrative, hopefully, is complex and presents life not in a fractured but rather in a holistic manner.

As mentioned earlier, the aim is not just to produce new insights into the subject of the study, but to also present an emancipatory reading of the spaces in Muslim localities in Delhi.

THE ARGUMENTS AND THEIR ORGANIZATION

The literature on Indian Muslims reifies the Muslim condition so that the meaning of communal prejudice and discrimination is either to be found within the Hindu–Muslim relationship, or worse, in some alleged internal qualities of the faith—Islam. Through an ethnographic exploration of everyday life infused with Marxist urbanism and critical theory, this work charts out the changes taking place in Muslim neighbourhoods in Delhi in the backdrop of rapid urbanization and forces of capitalist globalization. It argues that there is an implicit materialist logic in the prejudice and segregation experienced by Muslims. Further, it finds that different classes within Muslims are treated differentially in the discriminatory process. The resultant spatial 'diversity' and differentiation this gives rise to among the Muslim neighbourhoods, creates an illusion of 'choice', but in reality, the flexibility of the confining boundaries only serves to make these stronger and shatter-proof. It is asserted that while there is no attempt at integration of Muslims socially and spatially, from within the structures of urban governance, it would be a fallacy to say that the state is absent from within these segregated enclaves. The disciplinary state, neoliberal processes of globalization, and discursive practices such as the news media, cinema, and social science research, combine together to produce a hegemonic effect in which stereotyped representations are continually employed uncritically and erroneously to prevent genuine attempts at developing a specific and nuanced understanding of the situation of urban Muslims in India. The book finds that the exclusion of Muslims spatially and socially is a complex process containing contradictory elements that have reduced Indian Muslims to being 'normative' non-citizens and *homines sacri* whose legal status is not an equal claim to citizenship. The book also includes an account of the way in which residents of these segregated Muslim enclaves are finding ways to build hope in their lives. It enumerates possible ways in which a viable resistance to the systems of domination may be imagined and closes with a *problématique*—some questions and formulations that may revitalize the discussion on building a vision of the ideal Delhi.

In the following pages, I have attempted to present an image of the areas studied for this work, composed of small strokes that capture the changes in the landscape. The images have much detail in terms of narratives of quotidian life and accounts of political life of the participants of the study. Nevertheless, because of the nature of the methods and the breadth of view sought to be captured, the account is largely structural in its approach. My own observations as a participant were not limited to my role as an ethnographic researcher immersed in the culture being studied but extended to my membership of this heterogeneous group. These also form strong colours of the palette adding to the accounts of the spaces being described. The description has a keen eye for the historicity of the localities so as to contextualize contemporary changes.

The first section is titled 'Accumulation by Segregation'. It includes two chapters: 'Materiality of Culture and Identity' presents an account of the Old Delhi areas and Seelampur, while 'Variable but Durable Marginalities' describes the features of Jamia Nagar, Nizamuddin, and Taj Enclave. These chapters focus on the 'spatiality' of the Muslim population of Delhi, that is, the making of the segregated enclaves through the ways in which city residents place themselves and others socially. It is shown here that the social construction of meaning in relation to places takes place through different institutions, social relations, and discourses (Harvey 1996) and that spaces always change in importance, interpretation, and relevance in relation to the people that occupy them (Goffman 2010 [1971]).

When I began my fieldwork and writing, I gave in to the temptation to evolve a typology of segregation of Muslims based on the leading traits discernible in each area. But I recovered soon enough. As time and my work progressed, I saw the flaws in this project. In these two chapters the readers will see that even though I foreground a few major traits of an area, many of the traits were visible, however faintly, or were beginning to make an appearance in all the segregated enclaves studied. For example, during the time this work was being written and rewritten Zakir Nagar in the Jamia Nagar area evolved as a culinary hub for South Delhi. Also, I first recognized and identified segmentation of the labour market on communal lines in Seelampur; it is at the foundation of the formation of and difference between all segregated enclaves.

The second section is titled 'Discursive Bases of Segregation'. It includes Chapters 3 and 4. Taking the narrative further in Chapter 3, 'Muslims in Delhi: The Normative Non-citizens of the Global Urban', I conceive of Delhi as part of the global urban where global processes are manifested in the local. Simultaneously, the 'local' itself becomes mired in contradictory processes of urban governance and development—devaluing citizenship. I seek to discern more clearly the linkages between the processes of globalization and the peripheralization of the poor from the spaces of affecting governance. As citizenship becomes a function of power for contestation and capacity for claim-making, elites and corporate lobbying become more and more privy to governance mechanisms, and the major task of the state becomes that of a manager of inequalities. In such a situation, Muslims find themselves experiencing an acute deficit in citizenship. Because of their discursive subalternity, they are rendered incapable of expressing any concerns that relate to their other identities such as being part of the unorganized workforce in the country. I place this discussion within the realm of state power and governmentality directing a closer examination of how these manifest in a segregated locality of Muslims. Again, the issue of space and identities remains important in the chapter, but the matters related to the 'positionality' of Muslims are brought forth more prominently.

Titled 'Media Representations: Providing the Discursive Logic', Chapter 4 is an attempt to further develop the discussion on the discursive subalternity of Muslims. Although media practices generally, and Bollywood cinema specifically, have been an arena for analysis pertaining to the stereotyping of Muslims, I claim in this chapter that this analysis itself has got mired in stereotypical ways of seeing and analysing. I discuss some of the prominent stereotypical identity constructs more closely. Focusing on representation as a process of essentializing identity, I connect this to Lefebvre's 'representation of space', focusing on dominant discourses in the news media and Bollywood cinema regarding Muslim localities.

The last section of the book, comprising two chapters, is titled 'Counter-Discourses'. Chapter 5 contains a description of 'Avenues of Hope and Optimism' and attempts to capture and present an account of social spaces of counterhegemony. These are actual places and institutions inside or connected to Muslim localities in Delhi, where hope and optimism is carefully being fostered. Also included are ideational spaces that encourage hope among the struggling. These are scraps of memory—real or imaginary—that speak to the collective consciousness though they are rarely heard in the din of dominant discourses. I try hard in this chapter not to fall prey to insipid optimism and attempt to capture some of the trials and tribulations of these spaces too.

The sixth and final chapter is 'Coda: The Problématique of Envisioning the Ideal Delhi'. This brief chapter is an exercise in critical conjecture, and is meant to be an exercise in intellectual pessimism following Gramsci. I attempt to argue that inequality and segregation in the city not only frustrate the possibility of it becoming an ideal place, but also obstruct the vision for an alternative image of the city.

I make a 'Closing Gesture' with a short statement on the ideal city.

Accumulation by Segregation

. . . .

CHAPTER ONE

Materiality of Culture and Identity

Civic neglect by the state, discriminatory treatment by its agencies, and insecurity among urban Indian Muslims have long been offered as apparent reasons for their marginalization. Violence and/or threat of communal violence and everyday prejudices combine to give impetus to spatial segregation. But it would be a mistake to conclude that the discriminatory segregation of Muslims in the city does not have deeper roots. It would be a bigger mistake to imagine these neighbourhoods as static, unchanging, decadent spaces. Today, the older Muslim neighbourhoods are altered in size, composition, and scale of economic activity and have turned into contiguous clusters of several neighbourhoods with distinct features. New localities have also come up, many of which are gated enclaves of the more affluent among the Muslims. In short, during the last decade, Muslim neighbourhoods in Delhi have undergone changes that are complex in nature and merit fresh scrutiny.

Discourses on related issues have long focused on the fact that margins separate and exclude. But Muslim localities in Delhi today are not all homogenous slums or classical 'ghettos'. While some debates on segregated neighbourhoods across the world take recourse to the ease and familiarity offered by the concept 'ghetto' in their attempt to grasp the processes causing and sustaining segregation, other streams of debates have also spoken of 'hyperghettoization' (Wacquant 2008).

Historically, the term 'ghetto' has been used for localities in various European cities which were spaces of difference segregating the Jewish minority in Christian societies. Recorded references of ghettos date as far back in time as 1084 (Wirth 1928). Not all of them, though, were oppressive. Indeed, many were also Jewish settlements offered as spaces of 'protection' from violence (but not economic exploitation) by city regimes to Jews who were, nevertheless, a community reviled and loathed by the Christians (Wirth 1928). Ghettos were also easy targets of anti-Jewish pogroms for centuries culminating in the ghettos of Nazi Germany, which were merely slums in which all Jews were pushed before finally being deported into extermination camps (Arad 1980). Beginning with the settling down of European Jewish immigrants in the United States (US), the nomenclature continued to be used with the same symbolism of stigma and segregation, but underwent an expanded meaning of being applied even to those segregated enclaves where European and other ethnic (Irish, Italian, German, and Puerto-Rican, among others) minorities resided. The usage was also expanded to refer to 'racially' segregated Black neighbourhoods (Glaeser 1997). The term 'ghetto' carries with it considerable amount of baggage of the history of dehumanization of communities. I, thus, tread this ground carefully and prefer not to use this term.

The use of the term 'ghetto' for Muslim neighbourhoods in Indian cities is problematic because it 'normalizes' segregation. It makes it appear that since societies have always shunned and segregated 'the other' living within its precincts, there is nothing strange in this. There is an implicit resignation to there always being inequality in the city, and continuity of conflicting interests of various groups.

We must view this under the illuminating light of Marx's insistence regarding his predecessors being wrong in visualizing history as a repetitive series of conflicts between 'haves' and 'have-nots'. He noted that while the medieval workers were exploited by being forced into certain occupations only and barred from others, it may appear that modern workers are free to 'choose' where to sell their labour. Marx asserted that modern workers, even though 'free', are existentially constrained from making this choice. And this is the difference that makes their condition 'historically specific and functionally distinct' from that of earlier exploited classes (Coser 1977: 44). We may consider the analysis apt for explaining alleged choice in matters of segregation of the Muslim population in Delhi. Within the original ghettos, the Jews were confined through coercion, violence, and oppression, whereas in Delhi the Muslim population sometimes has been perceived to practise what has been often called self-imposed segregation by scholars (Gayer and Jaffrelot 2012) because they appear to have 'chosen' to live in segregated Muslim enclaves, but the fact of the matter is that choices on this account are existentially limited. This makes their segregation a historically specific and functionally distinct condition which may not bear any similarity to the condition of the Jews in ghettos of yore. And usage of the term 'ghetto' is, therefore, misleading.

In this work, I attempt to present an account of the creation, existence, and working of these islands and oases of a marginalized people, whose sense of belonging with each other is a complex feeling that is subject to forces such as regional, linguistic, and class identities or professions, among others, even though they have all been lumped together because of their 'Muslimness'. For them, being on the margins of the city is less about one's undeviating and subservient status in the city and more a process of experiencing a continuous progression of events and processes such as globalization, liberalization, communal violence, terrorist attacks, and the targeting/stereotyping of Muslims as 'Islamic' terrorists or their supporters. These experiences have meant that people need to continually review and evaluate afresh the opportunities and choices available to them. This research undertakes an ethnographic exploration into how individuals and families experience these changes in the spatiality of Muslim neighbourhoods; how people negotiate the intersection of these multiple, differential boundaries; and how a structural cause can be read into the narrative of their everyday experiences.

SPATIALIZATION OF DISCRIMINATION IN DELHI

Studies of the spatialization of inequality in Delhi since independence have mostly focused their enquiry on slum and resettlement colonies and urban planning perspectives (Baviskar 2004, 2006; Roy 2009). A volume on Delhi edited by Dupont et al. (2000) mainly concerned itself with Delhi as a city of migrants since independence, prominent among whom are Punjabi 'refugees', who came in at the time of the partition of the country, and later, the working class migrants from Uttar Pradesh and Bihar. The volume speaks of the resettlement colonies. The articles other than these concern themselves with the history of conservation and architecture of the post-independence city. The contributions to this volume, and much of the urban studies of contemporary Delhi continue to engage with similar concerns.

In India, the provision of public housing for members of the scheduled castes (SCs) often turns out to be a mode of segregating them from the rest of the population into Harijan, Valmiki, or Ambedkar colonies (Dupont 2004). An analysis of caste-based segregation in Indian cities (Vithayathil and Singh 2012) found that among the seven cities studied, there was a high level of caste-based segregation at the ward level, and on comparison, this was found to be more prominent than segregation by socio-economic status at the same level of disaggregation. The researchers note that the data for population based on religious identities not being available at ward level, they were not able to study segregation on those lines but indicated that in some cities 'religion is likely to be a more important axis of residential segregation...[and that] analysing residential segregation by religion would improve our understanding of socio-spatial inequalities' (Vithayathil and Singh 2012: 64–5).

Segregation of Muslims has attracted less scrutiny in this regard as far as scholarship in urbanization and urban sociology is concerned. Some of the treatment of the question of segregation in cities along the lines of religious identity has been quite perplexing. For example, in his book titled *Urbanization and Urban Systems in India*, Ramachandran (1989) presents a classification of cities based on religion and ethnicity. He remarks that, 'it may be reasonably argued that when the population of Muslims in any city equals or exceeds 20 percent of the city's population, they add a new dimension to the city's socio-cultural milieu' (1989: 173). Without qualifying what he means by 'a new dimension' or divulging how he reached that conclusion, Ramachandran proceeds to apply 'the same yardstick to other religious minorities in cities', and comes up with three types of cities, namely, Muslim cities, Sikh cities, and Christian cities 'in addition to the cities which have a predominantly Hindu population with only an insignificant proportion of religious minorities' (1989: 173–4), while making no mention whatsoever of the segregation of Muslim populations within cities.

In 2006, the Sachar Committee reported: 'Compared to the Muslim majority areas, the areas inhabiting fewer Muslims had better roads, sewage and drainage, and water supply.... For instance, a Hindu dominated urban slum in Lucknow had better quality roads, drainage system, sanitation, water supply and sewage disposal compared to another slum populated by Muslims' (PMHLC 2006: 149).

In an illustration of how built environments and real estate markets impact communal relations, Field et al. (2012) conducted a study in the city of Ahmedabad exploring the relationship of segregation and rent control with communal violence. They reported that 71 per cent of the population of the city lived in exclusive, homogenous neighbourhoods by 2002. They actually found that more incidents of violence occurred in mixed localities in the 2002 violence. Field et al. refute Ashutosh Varshney's (2002) view that communal violence is less likely to occur in mixed localities because increased interaction fosters increased tolerance, and say that in their findings, the reasons indicated lie in the holding patterns of housing units. Most mixed localities in 2002 in Ahmedabad were actually *chawls* built for mill workers where the rents were low and tenancy rights secure. While the mills were now defunct, the secure tenancies ensured that these properties could not be sold in real estate markets. Therefore, they did not shift to segregated areas even though the tolerance levels remained low. Field et al. conclude that the tenancy rights of minority tenants amidst 'mounting tensions between Hindus and Muslims in Gujarat led to a territory war rather than segregation in these locations. As tensions mounted, acts of violence and intimidation were used to push out residents belonging to the religious minority group' (2012: 509).

In the introduction of the *Urban Studies Reader*, Patel (2009) notes that many small towns and medium-sized cities have become characterized by communal conflict and communal riots. She lists Ahmedabad, Vadodara, Godhra, Hyderabad, Meerut, and Moradabad among such cities and raise the question whether 'the control of the local governance structures by a majority community aids and sometimes instigates such conflicts' (p. 18). It is important to take note of her question, 'why is it that riots have become a form to claim a space in the city rather than social movements' (p. 18). Recently, a volume containing a study of middle-class Muslims in 12 cities across India put forward in its Delhi chapters the conclusion that Muslims self-segregate (Gayer and Jaffrelot 2012).

In this chapter, I take a closer look at uncovering divisive and discriminatory processes of identity formation. This is done by treating the Muslim neighbourhoods in the framework of Lefebvre's (1991) 'representational spaces'. Thus, these spaces are treated as *texts* that are imbued with structured social meanings that are lived and perceived. In this understanding, it is easy to see that these spaces reassert the social difference. The exploration focuses on negotiations of Muslim people with the spaces they are confined in and identities that are foisted upon them. Lefebvre's analysis is especially handy for my purpose because it creates a chance for an explanation of everyday lived realities, and ideological discourses related to segregation that do not stop at economic causes. It also offers me a way of understanding segregation that does not make it seem like a problem of land-use as explained by Parks and Burgess and other sociologists of the Chicago school (Merrifield 2002). Harvey (1996) pointed this out and recognized that in American cities racism and xenophobia play, what Merrifield calls, an 'obvious role' in the formation of ghettos (2002: 140). This is where scrutinizing the issue of representation may be of great consequence, and this moment presents itself as a chance to engage with the issue of identity in simultaneity with the issue of spatiality.

MUSLIM NEIGHBOURHOODS IN DELHI: A NARRATIVE
OF DIFFERENTIATED DISCRIMINATION

For the purpose of commenting on complex issues related to space and identity, I limited my fieldwork to five small and big clusters of the Muslim population in Delhi: (i) Old Delhi, including some parts of the walled city and some localities outside Shahjahanabad; (ii) Seelampur and other Trans-Yamuna Muslim areas in the north-east of Delhi; (iii) Jamia Nagar in South Delhi; (iv) Nizamuddin, including Basti Hazrat Nizamuddin and Nizamuddin West; and (v) Taj Enclave, also in north-east Delhi. In this section, I attempt to piece together a narrative of temporality and spatiality of the Muslims in Delhi from the experiences, memories, and stories narrated by the participants of this study to me individually or in conversations in families or groups.

Old Delhi

Purani Dilli or Old Delhi is located in the Chandni Chowk, Lok Sabha, constituency, which is considered the heart of Delhi. It is considered to consist of the entire walled city of Shahjahanabad and some of the old residential and business localities outside the walled precincts—towards the west of Shahjahanabad. This part of the city is also often popularly called Delhi-6, which is a short form of the PIN code of the area—110006.

The old residents of the area have an outlook towards their lives which shows an immense amount of historicity. They are keenly aware of the continuity in their culture that other areas of Delhi lack as they assert that Muslims and Hindus both shared *Dehli ki tehzeeb* (culture of Delhi), even as they bemoan that what you see is just a shadow that remains of the grand tehzeeb.

In their account, the 1857 *ghadar* (mutiny) marks a major watershed in the narratives of misfortunes that were to befall Delhi and its Muslims. Sixty-seven-year-old Mr Qamar, who runs a shop selling saris and bridal wear in Chandni Chowk, recounted to me stories of the re-conquest by the British as if he was a witness himself to a Delhi ravaged by them.

> All the Muslim residents were either massacred or driven out. Many took refuge in areas outside the city. Most settled ... including prominent families in areas like Qutub road, Bara etc., and... what is that place near Sheila[1] ...? Nabi Kareem [pause] Yes ... Nabi Kareem. Muslims needed a permit to enter the city. They used to come in the morning ... take permits ... Hindu employers would have to tell the British government that they needed these artisans ... [pause] Hindus did not need any permits ... and then they would have to leave in the evening.

In physical surroundings that still have the remnants of the historical eras woven intricately in their present, the memories are as fresh as ever. The residents of Delhi-6 who live outside Shahjahanabad can still feel the sting of being thrown out of the walled city by the British. Shahjahanabad was the *shehr* (city) and those who could go back to living inside its precincts felt themselves fortunate, even superior.

Mr Merajuddin Qureshi lives in Ahata Kedara and shifted here from nearby Quraish Nagar in 1984. Both these localities are outside the walled city but in Delhi-6. He says,

> *Jo shehr ke ilaaqe hein, Jama Masjid, Kashmiri Gate... wahan ke log aisi batein karte hein. Bachpan mein main yeh suna karta tha ke Faisalganj ke log jo badshahi shehr mein rehte the... yeh jo Ajmeri gate, Dilli Gate, Kashmiri Gate waghaira ho gaye, yahan ke log sirf apne aap ko hi Dilliwalley samajhte the. Yahan Bare mein ham to sab mile jule hue hein.*

---

[1] Sheila is a cinema theatre in Paharganj, Delhi.

(trans. The city residents from Jama Masjid, Kashmiri Gate ... they used to talk like this. As a child I used to hear that people from Faisalganj, the royal city... the areas around Ajmeri gate, Dilli Gate, Kashmiri Gate, they considered only themselves Delhi residents. Here in Bara now, we are all mixed together).

Many participants in the study stressed that Old Delhi, especially the walled city, is not an 'only Muslim' area. Right from the beginning continuing till today, there are a large number of Hindu residents within this area. Khalid Zafar, a 24-year-old chartered accountant says,

> It is a myth that all the people in Old Delhi are Muslims. Also, many people mistakenly believe that Delhi-6 and Jama Masjid are one and the same thing. There are many other areas that are covered under Delhi-6. Chandni Chowk, for example, is one of the biggest commercial centres of the city. It is Delhi-6 too. Delhi-6 is not a predominantly Muslim area and the culture that is made fun of nowadays is not just Muslim culture. The Hindu residents of the area also share that culture.

Sumaiya, a young teacher at Rabia Girls School in Daryaganj says that Old Delhi culture is considered Muslim, strange, and inferior. She also agrees that in the popular imagination regarding the old city, people get confused in talking of religion and culture—'mix-up *ho jata hai...*'. She recounts,

> It often gets mixed-up... when I was studying in college I was in [the Delhi University] North Campus. We used to often have discussions, tutorials ... so one day it was our group's tutorial. People were arguing that Delhi is a metropolitan city and it has no culture, there was passionate discussion on this topic. I was adamant that Delhi has a culture, it has a *tehzeeb*, it has a history. The discussion continued for a long time ... it was the month of Ramzan and I got tired. I said after a while that please stop it, I'm fasting and I'm tired. So then everybody who was arguing was shocked. One guy exclaimed, 'You are a Muslim!' I said, 'Yes, I am'. Actually, Sumaiya is also a Hindu name in South India, so they had gotten confused. Then he replied, 'Okay, okay fine. Yes, Muslims do have a culture'. Then I was ready to fight again! I said, 'How could you say if

there was Muslim culture that it does not count? That if it is a culture of Old Delhi it does not count? You can say that New Delhi has no culture but if you only say Delhi, it means Old Delhi. And it is the culture of the Old Delhi Hindu and Muslim, because it is a three–hundred-year-old city, it has a distinct ambience'.

Just like the culture, a part of the Old Delhi legacy is the partition of India, the creation of Pakistan, and forced mass migration of Muslims from Delhi. This was also the next big blow to Muslims in terms of reducing them to a persistent minority status in India (Hasan 1997). *San sentalis* (literally, the year '47) figures prominently in all narratives bemoaning the departure of the 'cream' of the Muslim community.

Khalid Zafar's father, Mr Zafar Iqbal, is one of the original inhabitants of Chitli Qabar, Old Delhi.

All the government servants had already left. The only people who were left were poor labourers, artisans who worked on handicrafts. Before Partition, Chandni Chowk, Kashmiri Gate, Khari Baoli, all these areas had a lot of Muslim population. All the traders in Subzi Mandi were Muslims and all the small workshop owners in Bara Hindu Rao... Kashmiri Gate was a market, a posh area of Muslims. Karol Bagh had the cream of Muslims. Even today if you go there, you would find numerous mosques there, because people were so well-to-do. Daryaganj, Paharganj all were emptied .... After *sentalis* the refugees started settling slowly into the empty houses.

The environment was very negative. Anyone who had the means kept migrating even after 1947. People whose families had migrated would visit them in Pakistan and then out of loneliness and weariness of the hostilities here they would simply stay back. There you could stay anywhere, start any business .... Here in Delhi it was difficult to work in non-Muslim areas ... One of my friends' father had a shop in Dariba .... It had belonged to his grandfather .... It was two shops away from Hari Ram Shri Ram. He was harassed so much that he had to finally sell the shop. My wife's maternal grandfather had a shop of *surma* (kohl) under Suraj Masjid in Dariba, he also had to sell the shop because he could not work his business after *sentalis*. Now in this kind of environment what would a person do? He'd have to go to Pakistan. In the [19]60's this continued and you should note, only after the 1971 war, the borders were closed finally and the option to leave was no longer there.

Mr Haji Umar who lived in the walled city at the time of Partition, opines,

> My view on this issue is that after 1947, the Muslim who was already backward educationally and economically was hit very very hard. And with the formation of Pakistan, the cream of the Muslims in India left... good families .... There were 28 Muslim collectors in U.P., every single one of them went to Pakistan .... Those who were left behind, there was no body to take care of them ... and also after the formation of Pakistan the thought in every other person's mind was that, 'I have to go Pakistan ... I can't live here'. Thousands of families were destroyed because of this thinking... They didn't work at their trades and lived off whatever they had...selling off even the household utensils .... If you ask your father, he'll tell you brass was sold at Jama Masjid for ten *aanas* a kilo .... So the only thing they put their effort in was thinking that sooner or later they will have to leave. After the 1965 war, Muslims were jolted badly ... but many still continued to believe that they'd have to leave India. It was only after the 1971 war with Pakistan that it became clear to everyone that they would be here for good; it was only then that these people put serious effort into establishing businesses.

Mr Qamar says, in those days, the situation of Muslims was quite pathetic. It was a desolate place no one visited. But slowly, the walled city was rehabilitated by Muslims from towns like Meerut, Muzaffarnagar, Moradabad, Bijnor, Amroha, and Saharanpur. They began coming to Delhi partially in the wake of the partition and resultant hostilities, but more because of the abolition of the zamindari system in 1948. Mr Azeem Akhtar, who retired as DCP (Deputy Commissioner of Police) Delhi Police, and has also held the position of Chair of the Delhi Waqf Board, adds,

> All the Muslims who were educated and in government services were told to go to Pakistan. The elite and big landlords also left. But the smaller zamindars became paupers (*sadak par aa gaye...*) .... There was no one

left to give patronage to the artisans. The educated and the illiterate came
to Delhi to look for survival. The only jobs that were available were with
two Muslim institutions Shama and Hamdard...

Many other participants tell similar stories. Mr Haji Umar, who came
to Old Delhi in 1965 from Muzaffarnagar, and now lives in Seelampur,
agrees, '*Dobara dilli che jo abaad hui hai, woh bahar ke logon se hi hui
hai... Jab mein unnis sau pesath mein aaya tha, Jama Masjid ke log
kehte the "aao bhai yahan raho, chahe kiraya mat dena humare paas
raho", aisa tha...*' (Delhi-6 was rehabilitated by people from outside...
When I came here in 1965 till then people in Jama Masjid used to say,
'come and live here, don't pay rent if you want but live with us', that is
how it was...).

Meanwhile, Hindu and Sikh refugees from across the border
also began to settle down in Delhi. The assets and jobs given to
them had to be commensurate to what they had left behind. They
were allotted houses left vacant by Muslims in Old Delhi but there
were disproportionately too many of them to be accommodated
thus. Many were given plots of land in parts of south Delhi such
as Lajpat Nagar, Sriniwaspuri near Ashram, and north Delhi
such as Kingsway Camp, among others. The more affluent were
given houses in Karol Bagh, and shops in Kashmiri Gate, which
were erstwhile posh residential and business areas dominated by
Muslims, while the working-class and middle-class refugees were
allotted smaller housing in lower-class areas like Bara Hindu Rao,
and middle-class areas such as Beri Wala Bagh, respectively. The
old posh areas became almost exclusively Hindu because all the
original inhabitants and shop owners had left. The new colonies
were also exclusively Hindu. Only some of the middle-class and
lower-class areas in Old Delhi remained home to people belonging to both the communities. While the hostilities did not vanish
as a result of living together but the inevitable touch of everyday
life kept things smooth. The 'refugees' had to get to the business of
living. Many of the participants in this study talk of them as highly
enterprising people who according to Haji Umar, '*unki hi dukaan
se saamaan khareeda, unki hi dukaan ke aage baith kar becha, aur*

unki hi dukaan khareed li! Banyon ko khatam kardiya punjabiyon ne. Ye Partition ke baad jo dilli mein aye, tau ye hua… Bilkul khatam kardiya banyon ko.' (trans. They bought goods from them, sat and sold the same goods in front of their shops, and then bought the entire shop! Punjabis finished the baniyas. When they came to Delhi after Partition, this is what happened… they finished the baniyas absolutely.) While we may not take the word 'finished' at its face value when talking of the baniyas of Delhi, it is a fact confirmed by some other participants of this study that this kind of competition for gains did take place between them.

During Partition, Mr Zafar Iqbal's grandfather and two uncles left Delhi to go to Pakistan. His father, a young man of twenty-five, who worked with a Hindu trader and considered him his *ustad* (teacher), stayed behind and continued working in his ustad's handicrafts business. Mr Iqbal says,

> I was born in 1952 in this house. This entire house was ours at that time. My father used to say the house used to be full and alive… but his entire family—parents, sister, brothers, maternal grandparents, numerous uncles and aunts—everyone had left during Partition. After *sentalis*, there were very few people left in the neighbourhood. My father rehabilitated the house with others because of loneliness.

With a large and steady flow of in-migrants, by the late 1960s, Old Delhi was falling short of space to accommodate all their families and businesses. Many began to relocate their small manufacturing units—*karkhane* (literally, factories)—to Seelampur. Slowly, families began to shift their residences too. Around the same time, some families, especially those of teachers in various schools, few professionals, and government servants also began to shift to Jamia Nagar. The families moving to Jamia Nagar took the decision because of the area's proximity to Jamia Millia Islamia—a central university, but the small manufacturers and skilled workers wished to maintain their close proximity to Old Delhi for availability of work orders and supply of raw materials so they chose Seelampur. Mr Haji Umar, who is famous as *Lipstickwaley* (lipstick maker) because he now owns a small factory that manufactures cosmetics in Jaffarabad, Seelampur, describes how he came to decide where to move from Old Delhi,

> When Jaffarabad started getting settled, the first to arrive were those people from Old Delhi who were facing a space crunch as a result of families getting bigger... *karigars* (workers–artisans) and *karkhandaars* (small–manufacturing-unit owners). The houses were very small... daily life became difficult... I was also one of them... I've struggled a lot. I came to Jaffarabad in 1971 .... Actually, I visited this area the first time in 1964 when we heard that India had shot down a Pakistani plane and it had crashed here in Trans-Yamuna ... I came here to have a look at the plane... I used to live then at the Bara Dari ... I had a large family to look after and very little space to accommodate them in, so I decided to move. A lot of my friends were moving too... many went to Okhla. I also decided to go to Okhla ... because of Jamia... I thought the children would study there ... but when I first went there, I encountered the first difficulty.... It was a bit late in the evening and I could not get any conveyance to come back to Old Delhi. The second difficulty was that there was no labour there .... Then I came to Jaffarabad and surveyed the area.... Both the facilities existed here. Some workers stayed here those days but many came from Old Delhi every day to Jaffarabad to work. It was very convenient that if I needed to go to Old Delhi even at two o'clock at night, I could get a tonga *wallah* calling out '*Dilli chalo*' and on my way back also I could get a tonga for Seelampur at any time. Most people who came here were not original *Dilliwalley*. They were like me— people who had come from outside, like Amroha, etc., and then they had also brought their families. Most people came from Mewat, Amroha, Sambhal, Moradabad, Rampur, and Bareilly.

In their accounts, the participants are unanimous in identifying Emergency as the next blow to Old Delhi residents who had barely begun to recuperate. The career of Jagmohan (a protégé of Sanjay Gandhi) in urban governance and planning took off in the Emergency imposed by Indira Gandhi, with a beautification drive that entailed forced evictions. Numerous localities in Old Delhi, including many Muslim localities like Turkman Gate and Meena Bazaar were demolished, displacing several thousand families. Most of these were relocated to Seelampur and Welcome.

Mr Mohd Sultan was a young worker in a factory in Old Delhi when Emergency was declared in 1975. He says,

> When Emergency was declared I was in Connaught place, we didn't know what was Emergency ... the factory where I used to work was behind Moti Palace. Our *seth*, who employed me, he ... [pauses] used to write the title Oberoi... He was from Lahore... I used to work in his factory. He used to supply mixies to Bajaj .... He told us not to discuss politics outside. I and 5–7 boys who were my friends used to sometimes stand near Rivoli. Oberoi *seth* warned us ... If we said anything, police-men in plain clothes were all over the place and if they arrested us, he would not take any responsibility. We asked him what an emergency was. He said whatever it was, if the police did arrest us, nobody would ever know what became of us! [laughs]. We said okay, we only joke and laugh, but we'll stop that too. Those days I was not mature enough to understand. Now I think it was a big lesson for politicians in India ... The 19 months of Emergency were not a good way of ruling India, according to my thinking [it was] murder by order.

Commodification of Space: Community as a Living Museum

Jama Masjid always had a number of visitors because of its historical significance, but in the 1990s, tourists and visitors began flocking to neighbouring areas of Jama Masjid in unprecedented numbers. On any given day you can find Delhi's Muslim and non-Muslim intellec-tual celebrities taking groups of people on guided themed 'walks' here. Despite or rather because of the fact that of all the Muslim clusters in Delhi, Jama Masjid and other parts of the walled city get the most visitors of the general kind (while Seelampur mostly gets social work-ers, planners, and other social science researchers), the people of this Muslim neighbourhood seem to be living in an almost-time-warp. What is part of daily life for some Muslims in other localities becomes here a full-time occupation for residents. Their lives become a distinct cultural theatre for visitors to watch and be entertained. They oper-ate their businesses—their 'museum kiosks'—with cultural finesse to make a living. The businesses are old and owners are full of curious old stories of the grandiosity of the old days, and VIP visitors who frequent or used to frequent their businesses. Not only the historical monuments and spiritual/religious shrines in the areas but the less significant buildings, the history and legacy of Partition, the clothes, the restaurants, and the smells become live artefacts and installations for the visitors and tourists (many of them Muslims from other parts of Delhi and elsewhere). Muslims and 'Muslimness' which have been a taboo for long become unusual, even bizarre, spectacles for the adventurous.

Walter Benjamin (2009) rued in the streets of Paris that the modern era lacked the aura of other times. It is here in the arcades that he begins his extensive work on fetishism of commodities, and deepens it because it was in the arcades that he saw how a dreadful world of oppressive relations of production became repackaged and made ready to be sold in glittering display windows. He asserted that this fetish character seeped into all aspects of everyday life so much so that the *very image of everyday* was fetishized, when people went through the intense, pleasurable experience this image provided (Merrifield 2002). According to Merrifield, while Marxist thinkers in the political economic track *see* the capitalist modernization in the urbanization processes, Benjamin *felt* the 'experience of capitalist modernity' (2002: 65).

Reading Lefebvre (1991) and Benjamin together brings to us the understanding that modern spaces were increasingly 'produced' not as spaces of work and production, but as spaces of commodification and consumption. Marx had said that 'the strangest things are often the most trivial' to which Lefebvre quipped that 'the most extraordinary things are also the most everyday' (quoted from Merrifield 2002: 79). I am reminded of Lefebvre's influence on Guy Debord (1983), who took the concept of space as spectacle a little further and said that not only has it been commodified but also banalized. The consumer is also a 'tourist' who goes to witness this banalization at leisure.

When I asked the participants of this study regarding the tourists and outside visitors, most were nonchalant about it. 'It's good business', most seemed to say. Mr Zahid (name changed) who runs a very famous *kabab* shop in Chitli Qabar says,

We welcome them and their business. But it is of no more importance. They are just looking for a different experience .... No one is interested ... and why should they be? They've just come here to have a good time with friends .... It would not be hospitable to spoil it. They don't want to go deeper... Some of them come very regularly. I have been in Newspapers and Magazines a couple of times [pointing towards framed article cuttings on the wall]. Almost every other day, I get photographed by my customers [laughs]. If my customers saw me during the day, they won't know who I am. I don't go to the shop in a lower and t-shirt ... I dress up especially for them ... [laughs]

But some would like to distance themselves from these performative aspects of daily life and livelihoods within the walled city, especially those, whose livelihoods do not depend on the connection. Khalid, the chartered accountant, has studied in Summerfield School in Vasant Kunj and works in south Delhi. He says he has a very muddled relationship with the place and keenly feels the disparaged connotations that his identity gets because he is not only a Muslim but a *Purani Dilli* Muslim. The disparagement alludes to the antiquated and peculiar culture of the place.

(GJ) How has it been, Khalid, being the person you are and living in Purani Dilli?

(KZ) Basically, its like though I have been living in Old Delhi but my schooling, my graduation and all ... was all outside this Old Delhi thing, so basically I have never been a part of it as such, though I know the problems that are there ... but the thing is the life that I have had there, the friends that I have had there ... now it's all been very modern and most of the times they have been all non-Muslims and they reside outside Old Delhi, so basically I feel if in today's life ... if you want to be successful what you need is a good education ... good at communication, I mean convincing skills.

(GJ) Right...

(KZ) So I feel it was more like a ... super hyped .... Initially it was like... I mean when I was a kid, up to a certain age it didn't matter, I was not into these things, there was no Hindu–Muslim thing, but when I gained consciousness related to these things, basically then I started to think, get irritated, what is it? Chitli Qabar and all … it sounds weird! Then much later I thought that instead of hiding this part of my personality, it is better I showcase what actually I have, basically I do not hesitate now when people ask me where do I reside. Rather I take it positively; instead I give them an impression that though I was born and brought up in Old Delhi, I still have the same modern upbringing as you have, so now it's not an issue any more.

I ask Khalid about the tourists and visitors.

(KZ) Jama Masjid is so near to me but still I do not visit the place so often, but whenever I go, obviously I feel good, I mean there are tourists coming from different parts of the country just to see Jama Masjid.

(G) Have you seen these tourists coming into the residential areas?

(KZ) No, no …. Most do not come into the residential area, they keep themselves restricted to the Jama Masjid and the main street where Karim's and other joints are there. The general people do not even get into the inner streets …. But recently, there was a lady from Jamia who is doing her research on Jahanara. I had taken her for a walk in the area. Aaan … I don't think of it much but this place does have so much history… People come here to see the place and experience the history ….

Mr Qamar remembers that his father used to remark that for a long time after Partition, the only visitors that the Muslim areas in Shahjahanabad got came from consulates in cars to buy meat for diplomats. Beginning at the southern gate of Jama Masjid and walking towards Turkman gate, I can see the performative display all around me. A visit to Karim's restaurant, Sheerin Bhawan, and many other businesses is much recommended in articles in leisure and lifestyle magazines or newspaper supplements (http://www.livemint.com/Leisure/jCDl9CGtowdefkZgFdYD8L/Heritage--The-Old-Delhi-dictionary.html; http://timesofindia.indiatimes.com/life-style/food/food-reviews/Delhis-age-old-restaurants-we-swear-by/articleshow/14688546.cms; http://www.huffingtonpost.in/anubhav-sapra/11-musttry-iftar-eateries_1_b_7685156.html). If you read these articles, many of which are written by Muslims, you may be forgiven for thinking that they are talking about a museum. In this part of the chapter, this is the issue that draws my attention and I attempt to discern why in the 1990s, Jama Masjid and the adjoining Muslim areas have emerged in the walled city as a museum-like space for tourism and leisurely activities.

In the globalized local spaces, this process must be seen in the light of these locations competing with each other for economic growth. While the mainstream discourse rightly or mistakenly sees this as promotion of cultural heritage and even communal harmony and cultural tolerance, it is (also) a method of hiding the disparities in the process of the city's attempt to create an attractive image to promote consumption and monetization of culture (Paddison 1993). Thus, it is no coincidence that this cultural marketization of areas such as those adjoining Jama Masjid happened only in the 1990s. This is the period when India's fling with structural adjustment began. The production and management of the image of the city is an intrinsic part of this adjustment (Jessop 1998). This image production is manifested in the creation and promotion of places that use cultural heritage to ensure economic benefit.

It must also not be thought that this is a spontaneous process. It is rather a process that is governed by local authorities and the state in a bid to create and showcase cultural infrastructure for both domestic and international tourists. The area has also seen in the recent past, considerable regulation and creation of such cultural infrastructure. The government support to projects and initiatives that showcase the cultural infrastructure is important to note because the museumized culture in conventional museums or communities assist the State in its protracted efforts to define nationhood.

Shahjahanabad was one of the five controlled conservation areas identified by the Delhi Master Plan 2001. In the Delhi Master Plan 2021 (DDA 2007) the area has been re-designated as a 'special area', emphasizing 'heritage', unlike the earlier plans where the 'historical' character of Shahjahanabad was emphasized. This shift in terminology is important to note as it is in line with the neoliberal heritage tourism approach. Local bodies are given the responsibility of preparing special conservation plans. The Delhi Urban Heritage Conservation Foundation Regulations (1999), drawing power from the Delhi Development Act, 1957, aim at 'promoting and conserving civic and urban heritage' (Section 3a). The Delhi Heritage Committee formed in 2005 joins a host of existing bodies and organizations[2] to administer heritage conservation in Delhi.

Who gets to shape and 'consume' museums and what has to be on display is a function of power. Communities whose culture is on display have no power to shift the 'regimes of curiosity', that is, the discourses which shape the museum collection and display (Hetherington 2006).

The displays in contemporary museums are carefully curated not only to impress and amaze but also to communicate to visitors a narrative regarding the cultures on display. There are non-governmental organizations (NGOs) and private organizations that mainly conduct what are now called heritage walks and food walks. One such NGO's website says that they, '... take you to the most obvious destinations in Delhi as well as to places and people who you would never meet or see'. Not only organizations but even individuals (with a bit of background in history) have taken to organizing these heritage walks. Many of these are also conducted by educated elite Muslims who can slip into the roles of insider/outsider with much ease and capitalize on these for celebrity space in the social media.

From the early museums which had a humble ambition to awe visitors with spectacular disjointed things, the later museums wish to suggest that there exist an 'infinity' of things such as those kept on display in the museum. They are narrative museums that seek to represent the 'total'. Owing to its roots in the modern ideas of Enlightenment, the museum is also seen as a space for learning, and

---

[2] The Heritage Conservation Committee (HCC) has been set up under the Ministry of Urban Development. Other bodies mandated with heritage conservation are the Archaeological Survey of India, the Delhi State Archaeological Department, the Delhi Development Authority (DDA), the three Municipal Corporations of Delhi, the Central Public Works Department (CPWD), the Delhi Cantonment Board, the Indian National Trust for Art and Cultural Heritage (INTACH), and the Aga Khan Trust.

thus, for self-realization for the visitor. It is this disciplinary potential of the museum that endears it so much to those in the business of civilizing and improving public behaviour. I contend that this project of lofty intentions is marred by the fact that what is portrayed as self-realization is often only self-aggrandizement. The difference between the two in the mind of a visitor to a museum is blurred.

Modern museums are expected to not only teach but also entertain. Because of the mainstream view of the Muslim neighbourhoods as exotic, strange, and even dangerous, in the marketization of the cultural heritage and history of these spaces, it is also pertinent to note that they are likely promoted as ideal places for those visitors who seek an 'adventure', and think of themselves as those who 'dare to go where not many people go or can go', either because they actually think that they are brave or because they think they are superior in their benevolent tolerance. This is in line with museums that market their collection—display directed at 'thrill seeking visitors' (Noordegraaf 2004).

The idea of a museum is, thus, a clue into using display to infuse a displayed item with a meaning, and then getting people to buy into the logic and narrative behind this meaning. Commodity culture uses this idea generated by museums effectively. In a departmental store or mall bereft of conventional aggressive selling, the item on sale is infused with a meaning merely by the manner in which it is displayed. The sale requires people to buy into the meaning so that they buy the item. It is not only the commodity that is being bought but also an aesthetic 'value-addition' to the item which emerges only on display.

Landscapes are 'culturally loaded geography' (Sauer 1963 [1925]). They have a palimpsest-like quality. They are shaped by culture and marked by it. Spaces can thus be understood also as cultural records. Commodified culture and its banalization become apparent in the spatiality of the community occupying a space. The museumized community is a heterotopia where not only reality but even time is suspended (Bennett 1995). Take for example, the haveli where Mirza Ghalib lived for several years before his death, which had been ignored for long and was lying in a dilapidated condition. Parts of the haveli were acquired by the Government of the National Capital Territory (NCT) of Delhi and converted into a Ghalib museum in 2010, while a mostly forgotten Ghalib museum already existed in the premises of the Urdu Academy in Nizamuddin. The new museum commemorates Ghalib as a poet of love and beauty whereas the Ghalib who was a prolific letter writer and chronicled the 1857 revolt and the treatment of Delhi's Muslim population by the British, has been totally short-changed.

The spatial layout of the museum is important if it is to do its job effectively. The narrative of the museum also depends largely on how it is spatially planned and spread. In this regard, two things are of consideration known in museum science terminology as 'permeability' and 'visibility' (Hillier and Tzortzi 2006). These would define the pathways that visitors follow during their explorations and also how they 'sample' the displays (visually, or also for example, in the case under our consideration, culinarily). Built environments are necessarily a network of spaces and equipment which a visitor negotiates in order to move from one place to another. It is the ease of movement and the extent to which all of the spaces are accessed that refers to permeability. Visibility refers to the relationship of spaces to the degree to which one can be seen from the other. Even in a conventional museum, these relationships are not obvious to all visitors (Hillier and Hanson 1984).

What is visible to a person and which spaces they can permeate are both contingent on their position. In a 'museumized' neighbourhood, visibility and permeability both change depending on the visitor's vantage point. The ways in which they can experience the space, grasp the meaning of the 'display' in the everyday life of the residents, and indeed, even access different networked spaces is not an inherent property of that space, but a dynamic interplay of the positions of the displayed 'community' and discourses influencing the visitors. It is this play of power that renders some communities museumized, and others not so even though their visibility and permeability in terms of atria and equipment may be comparable. It is not a consideration whether the roads are wide or narrow and whether they are connected at right angles or winding and labyrinthine that increases or decreases the degree of visibility and permeability, it the class position of the residents and visitors that defines these relations.

Any good museum worth its name has a good layout guide that directs the visitors. The organized walks in the living museums do a job akin to this. The scale at which the information of what is present and accessible in these guides makes it possible for the visitors to reach an interpretation of the display narrative. As more information is provided regarding access and visibility, the probability of visitors reaching various alternative interpretations becomes higher. The more tightly controlled and predefined a walk's route is, the higher the possibility that the visitors are closer to the 'intended' meaning. These walks and their pathways are also largely determined by popular perceptions and also a consideration of which displays would make for a more compelling, awe-inspiring impact. The printed walk guides predict this visitor behaviour by providing the visitors information in various formats such as layout plans, pictures, and written text, among others. The various books and articles meant to tell people about Old Delhi often include such things as maps and written narratives that include facts, opinions, accounts of experiences, and pictures. The newspaper and magazine articles with their specialized maps, and the guided walks and tour organizers serve well to museumize the community, and their historical and cultural infrastructure, because their intervention makes for a more focused viewing and experience, in a way similar to that in which, say, a museum places its most popular painting in a visually isolated space, where the viewers can engage with it without any distraction (Hillier and Hanson 1984). The unpleasantness of unemployment, degrading houses, and civic amenities can be distracting to those who have come to eat at Karim's, and to the cultural voyeuristic flâneur, it helps that their position and identity renders the residential areas not as visible or penetrable as the bazaar.

According to Cosgrove (1998 [1984]), landscape has a discursive quality—it has a discourse that frames a social group historically in their relationship to the material surrounding of the place they inhabit, and also to the other groups. He further stresses that this discourse shapes the way things are seen epistemologically, as well as technically. The museumized space could then be a very strong ideological device which could shape the viewer's gaze, and thus, the meanings that the items of display represent. Even in a public museum, the term 'public' is not used to contain an open, amorphous, and inclusive meaning, as used in a term like 'public space'. Bennett (1995) actually talks of how bourgeoisie control over museums has meant that there is emphasis on museums as a space of 'polite and rational discourse'. In other words, rather than a democratic public sphere for assembly and discussion, according to Bennett (1995), the museum is a 'bourgeois public sphere'. In the museumized parts of the walled city too, the access is regulated and controlled by various discursive means. The pathways of movement for visitors are well charted out. In fact, *movement* rather than *assembly* is emphasized. The 'chaos' of the streets of museumized Jama Masjid (or any other Muslim segregated enclave) is a fetishized and commoditized random busy 'movement' because it has been reduced to a spectacular display for the consumer. It no longer has the potential to turn into an 'assembly' for political contestations. All this aids the impression that museumized communities, like museums, are merely 'places', while in reality they are spaces infused with hegemonic discursive content like all museums. The museumized community is thus a manifestation of appropriation of discourse. This is also where it becomes apparent again why the history of the museum is closely intertwined with the history of colonialism and the history of capitalism.

In the spectacle put up for the tourist in the areas around Jama Masjid is a modern *construction*, presented as if it is of old historicity and its contents are *given* and *unchanging*. Religious identities are, in a similar way, often presented as if they do not require any definition because they are so natural. The issue of connection between identities (including religious identity) and places, and the idea that identification of people with a place is a part of their awareness of themselves and each other, leads me towards the debate on construction of nationalistic identities. As such, a place that is identified with certain people is also a discursive construction and can be infused with particular and pejorative meaning. The landscape and monuments also acquire space in the collective memory invoking recollection, commemoration, and even oblivion. The spaces, thus, not only have monuments or cultural historical infrastructure but are also dotted with memory (Halbwachs 1992). It is in this light that the labelling of Muslim areas as 'mini-Pakistan' must be seen. A reductive, essentialist view of collective identities has been challenged by Hobsbawm (1983), when he identifies what he calls 'invention of tradition' which is somewhat similar to Anderson's (1991) conception of 'imagined communities'.

Spaces (with monuments and landscapes contained within them) form the material spatial axis along which the co-ordinates of life can be plotted. But time also remains an important co-ordinate. However, Lefebvre (1991) emphasized that it is not space or time itself that constitutes life content, but rather the everyday practices, history, and change around material things. This conception of production of space along with Lefebvre's call for difference, unavoidably leads into the matter of identities (Fraser 1997). Contemplating on these conceptions, I am led to think that communities are not necessarily imagined only on the nationalistic terrain. The difference between Anderson's 'imagined community' and Lefebvre's 'representation of space' may be only a matter of scale. In fact, whether the two are different at all may be the right question to ask.

Trans-Yamuna Cluster

On the eastern side of river Yamuna, popularly called Trans-Yamuna in Delhi, is a belt of exclusive or predominantly Muslim settlements beginning from Seelampur and extending towards Loni Border to include New Seelampur, Gautampuri, Jaffarabad, New Jaffarabad, and Welcome, among others. Seelampur and Welcome are the first two localities in this belt. These areas are part of the North-east parliamentary constituency.

While Seelampur's foundation was laid by the first Prime Minister of the country it was, even at that time, a resettlement colony. Welcome is a resettlement colony of people evicted during Emergency from Yamuna Bazar, Dilli Gate, Turkman Gate, Daryaganj, and Ballimaran areas of the old city and various other parts of the city. A sizeable portion of these evictees were Muslims.

Haji Umar says,

> Seelampur's foundation was laid by Pandit Nehru. He made provision in this area for people who were displaced from Jamna Bazaar—most were tonga drivers and washermen. It used to be called Bela Road... and Pandit Nehru gave them 80 sq yards each, people who came later received 40 sq yard plots, and then it was reduced to 25 sq yards... Seelampur did not get settled in one go... it happened in parts...

In later years, a large number of people from western UP also migrated to Seelampur. A portion of this belt is that of *jhuggi*s (shanty), squatters, and slum resettlement colonies, and has lower-caste poor Hindu population too in varying proportions, but in the largely Muslim population, Hindus remain concentrated separately on Hindu-only streets. Jaffarabad and Chauhan Bangar primarily house Muslim small manufacturers, and the skilled and unskilled labourers employed by them. Most manufacturing units function from the ground floors of the buildings, doubling as living and sleeping areas for the workers at night. The upper floors contain residences of the owners and/or their tenants who also work in different businesses in different capacities.

New Jaffarabad is a contiguous locality but is very different from the rest. It has upper-middle-class residents who are for the most part the manufacturers who have managed to afford to separate their residences from their place of business. Many of the residents are also professionals, being the children of the older residents, who acquired education and professional training or relatives who have shifted here to be near their families. The houses are comparatively large and there is a mosque that is air conditioned. Increasingly now, many buildings are built like flats—different floors occupied and owned by different families. The roads are wide and well-paved. The locality is gated though not very stringently guarded so it is possible for anyone to walk into the locality during the day.

Prior to conducting fieldwork for this research, I had never been to Seelampur. My first contact was a community worker—Sarvar. He had earlier been employed in an NGO connected to a church organization, but when I first made his acquaintance he was associated with an organization working with Muslim women. I spoke to him about my research and Sarvar readily offered to take me to Seelampur, help me understand the area, and put me in touch with prospective participants. My visits to Seelampur with Sarvar (and I realized this only later), were confined to a small part of this Muslim locality—only slum blocks. As my circle of contact in the area expanded due to coming to know of relatives of my participants in Old Delhi or Okhla, I realized that the Trans-Yamuna Muslim areas were much more than just a block of slums. Armed with experience of home interviews and walks in a much larger area, and localities like Chauhan Bangar and New Jaffarabad contiguous to the New Seelampur jhuggis, I asked Sarvar whether he was aware of the existence of these areas. He said, of course, he was! When I asked him why he had not told me about these areas for so many visits over a period of several months, he said, 'I have been bringing many visitors from numerous NGOs and researchers to show the area for many years now. They always ask me if I could show them the slums where Muslims live. So I show them the slums. Research happens only in slums, doesn't it?'

The part of Seelampur that Sarvar always put up for display was the very picture of dereliction. The lanes criss-cross the small shanties and one-room dwellings of low corrugated roofs. People literally live half their everyday lives on the street—sitting and working in front of their houses, some even bathing or cooking. There is not enough space and there are no public services to speak of. In the name of educational institutions, there are a few government schools, where most people allege that they teach nothing. Some children go to the madrasas after school only to learn to read the scriptures. There are also many madrasas running in the neighbourhood in shacks or bare structures where children live, and learn to read and memorize the scriptures.

The residents of these Madarsas are predominantly children from those areas of Bihar which are often ravaged by floods.

Almost everyone I spoke to in this part of Seelampur owned or was employed in small manufacturing workshops in other parts of this cluster—New Seelampur, Jaffarabad, and Chauhan Bangar. Some, mostly women, were home-based workers. Stripping wire or sorting out metal from scrap; making bangles, artificial jewellery, and scissors; stitching sequins to cloth; and tailoring in denim units were the main occupations. Most said they came from the walled city or were from various towns of Uttar Pradesh and Bihar. Everyone tried to sound as if they came from 'home' to go somewhere and just happened to 'stop-by' at these localities in Trans-Yamuna—'*hum to yahan ke nahin hein...*' (we are not from here). They feel that they belong elsewhere—because belonging is also association and identification. In her work on forced displacements during Emergency, Emma Tarlo says that:

> A map indicating the key sites of demolition may look more like a bombardment plan than a development plan (the similarity is not incidental), but it testifies to the varied spatial trajectories of the displaced. This means that although today the inhabitants of Welcome are based within the confines of a single colony they carry with them memories and experiences of elsewhere. (2003: 15)

Limits to the choices available to the Trans-Yamuna Muslims also circumscribe this sense of belonging. In my conversations with Huma, a home-based worker, who strips insulation off wires to extract copper all day long in her one-room house in J Block Seelampur, says, '*bohot gandagi hai yahan .... Koi suvidha bhi nahin hai. Log itne kharab hein koi kisi ki madad nahin karta. Par ham bachpan se yahin hein, yahan ka to sara system humko pata hai. Kaam hai ... aur kahan jayen ... wahan kya karenge?*' (trans. This place is so dirty... We get no services ... People are so bad that no one helps anyone. But we have been living here from childhood, we know the system here. We have work ... if we moved from here, where will we go? What will we do there?).

Javed is a young MBA from IGNOU who has just joined his father's business—a small workshop for stitching denim clothes in

New Seelampur J Block. For many years now, he has been giving free tuitions to children around his street. He says,

> Even though education quality in schools is bad, people are making attempts to keep their children in schools ... because they realise that not giving them an education will put their children behind in the world .... They would also like to build a decent life .... So enrolment is not a problem but there are many drop-outs. I used to teach this boy—he had polio in one of his legs but he was very good at Maths. He finished well in his tenth and twelfth board exams but couldn't afford to study further .... Now he is a vegetable hawker in the locality. I felt bad when he started this work. I know that not everyone who studies gets a good job or becomes a big businessman or an officer but education has its own value. My father is illiterate. He can only do some basic calculations for his business and can sign his name. Now, I have an MBA degree. What am I doing with it? I have begun working with him. We employ 10–12 workers. I have found out about the machines that can do special kinds of stitching on jeans. We can get better orders ...

People are keenly aware of the stigma that their identity and their address carry. In their life experiences and shared memories of evictions or communal violence, people know that their 'Muslimness' warrants violence. In a group discussion with boys from J and K block, they share with me experiences that are but mere examples of awareness of carrying this stigma and being confronted by it in everyday life. One of the participants had gone to buy a TV, wishing to pay in monthly instalments. Another had wanted to sell an old mobile phone. They said the shopkeepers or salespeople become uncomfortable the moment they tell them their name and, sometimes would bluntly refuse to do business with them when they mention their residential address. One participant said that a mobile phone shopkeeper in Sadar Bazaar actually told him after seeing his election identity card that he would not buy the old phone because the seller was a Muslim and from Seelampur. Another boy said that when he went for his first year exam in BA at a Delhi University college, the invigilator saw his address on his identity card and asked him sarcastically if people in Seelampur also study.

The boys say that these things happen also because Seelampur is unduly linked to criminality. I ask them if there is any truth in the description. The boys argue that J Block and K Block New Seelampur actually do have some illegal activities but that it all happens under the patronage of the police. One of the participants, Javed takes me for a walk around the two blocks. Once we reach the other end of the block, there is an open and bare stretch of land strewn with a lot of garbage. Right across this is the police station. We continue our walk on the slabs covering a big drain which doubles as a road for the lane of jhuggis facing the drain. Javed tells me, 'look ahead on your right-hand side … you'll see a boy sitting on a chair. I'll tell you about him after we have passed him'. I try to notice as much as I can in a very casual glance. He is a young man in his early twenties sitting on a dirty plastic chair in a pair of trousers and torn vest. He looks quite unwell and listless. As we pass him I also notice that he has a wad of currency notes in his hands. Later, Javed tells me the man sits here every day— the entire evening and night selling drugs. Javed says all his customers are for the most part well-dressed college students coming from other parts of the city. They come on bikes and buy their merchandise. I am amazed at the smoothness of the entire set-up. The drug peddler is bang in front of the Seelampur police station. It would be impossible for the police personnel to not know of him and his activities, even if they tried hard. When I mention this to Javed, he says from the point of view of the police, it is the best place for them to keep an eye on him and make sure that he is honest about their 'cut' when he closes his sale for the day. I know the answer but I still ask Javed why no one does anything about it. Javed looks at me incredulously and asks, '*usse kya hoga?*' Translated loosely, the question means, 'what will happen if they do?' His look and tone shows a complete lack of trust in the system and the fear of possible retributive reaction.

I ask everyone in the group about how often they go out of the area. Most say rarely, because they live and work there. For days on end they do not venture outside Seelampur. The young men do their shopping at Gandhi Nagar and Krishna Market, among others. They say their mothers and sisters shop mostly at the local Seelampur market. For leisure, they sometimes go to watch a film at the Delite theatre but they are careful not to venture out too late at night and go too far.

Mohsin's family is originally from Raipur, Chhattisgarh, but he was born in Seelampur. He has finished his bachelor's degree from Zakir Husain Delhi College in political science and is pursuing a master's degree now from Jamia Millia Islamia. He is interested in higher studies and keen to build a career in academics, but is already deeply involved in his father's wire-stripping business. All his close friends are also involved in various ways in the same trade. Mohsin says that he was once returning home after a late night leisure trip to India Gate. It got very late and no auto driver would agree to go to Seelampur. His two friends and he were joking with each other a little loudly while walking in central Delhi, still looking for an auto, when they were stopped by a PCR (police control room) patrol van. The constables very casually asked them what they were doing out so late and where they were coming from. When the conversation turned to where they lived, the tone of the conversation changed and the atmosphere was immediately charged with tension. Many more questions followed in a more hostile tone. Mohsin says that it must have been 20–5 minutes before the police let them go, but not before threatening to arrest them if they created any more ruckus on the roads saying, '*chup chap jao ... sadak pe danga machaya to andar kar denge*'. They used the Hindi word '*danga*' which is a rare synonym, mostly used to refer to communal riots, instead of '*shor*' for noise. Mohsin says he got so scared, that since that incident, he stopped staying out late at night.

A 'Mini-Japan'

Mr Sultan who in his youth used to live in Old Delhi and was employed in a factory making mixer-grinders for Bajaj, now owns a small manufacturing unit for making food processors in Chauhan Bangar, Seelampur. He says, 'I have often heard people call Seelampur "mini-Pakistan". This is propaganda. The truth is that this place is "mini-Japan". From a needle to parts of aircrafts everything is made here.' Mr Sultan takes me to meet his friend and neighbour, who owns a factory manufacturing metal sheet cases for various specialized electronic machines. Mr Monis Siddiqui is trained as a mechanical engineer.

> Muslims are not just some nobodies, they are the heart of India. They are what make any institution in India complete. Still Muslims are treated as if they are not Indians. See I'll tell you of my own experience. I tried meeting and working with some [Hindu] people. They treated me as if I was their adversary. Once a person took me outside and asked me, you are a Muslim? I said, yes, my name is Muhammad Monis Siddiqui. He said sorry, sorry. I cannot deal with you...because I later found out he was member of the RSS. He openly refused! So this is the environment in which I have to function ... I have to face difficulty. How will I survive in such an area? If today I were to go to some other area... See, I am registered in Bawana industrial area but could not function there. So I decided to dispose-of the plot ... I was told that if a Muslim tries to dispose-off a plot in the area they are to be given only 50 per cent of the price of the land .... This is how the environment is turned against us. Which category citizens are we? We have not been able to understand this till date... What would we be able to do .... How will we survive... How would we ever be able to expand our businesses .... People live here in Trans-Yamuna because there is business here. As far as the discussion on mini Pakistan and mini Japan is concerned ... my opinion is ... you go anywhere in the world, people live within communities. If not, then you feel alone. I am not complaining that we cannot live in other areas but can we work in peace?

> (GJ) You do business with other people from outside the area?

> (MS) Yes, we have to supply our goods outside. All kinds of goods are produced here and supplied all over the world. In the export line, all goods are produced in and supplied from backward areas. The exporters order and procure from here and he supplies [further]. Whether he procures from Moradabad, or from Chauhan Bangar, Mustafabad, Saharanpur, or Okhla, the man who is sitting in Okhla industrial area... the exporter ... stores goods from all the places and then exports it. Ultimately, the labour in these areas are here only. If someone shifted, let us say to Nand Nagri, they will not find many labourers to work in their factories. Goods have to be supplied where the buyers are, but we have to build contacts with the intermediate buyers. They are here. Whoever

works in one line they build their contacts in that line only. Suppose I work in sheet-making fabrication, all types of metal cabinets, if there is anyone who wants to order some kind of cabinets … In my factory I make almost all kinds of cabinets, from stabilisers to electronic instruments. So I'm famous for this specialty. People would say let's take it from SM Engineer or Lucky Star or Deluxe metal, they come to these areas only and they will buy from here even though their supply may be in Dubai. We have to be here.

(Mr Sultan): I got to know this today only, what you said about getting only 50 per cent back if you sell your property.

(MS): No, no! Not get back. It is the brokers sitting there who do not let you sell at the prevailing prices of your land in the area. They do this only to Muslims.

(GJ): What if you do not want to sell out?

(MS): Suppose if you operate your factory in these areas… they will have this attitude towards you …. They will never co-operate with you. They'll make you feel like oh this guy is a Muslim, a *mulla*. What is a *mulla*? Does he have green-coloured blood?

(GJ): So does the everyday operation of the manufacturing unit become difficult?

(SM): No, that can be managed… but the behaviour…. You would spend time with the other person… that is not good. Suppose you helped someone injured and took him to hospital but the police register a case against you only…. So we don't have that respect in society as a Muslim that we should have. [pauses] I mean we are Muslims but we are also Indians. My grandfather, great grandfather, great-great grandfather—all the old generations were Indians. Then this discriminatory treatment forces us to be segregated. Why don't we want to live in New Delhi? I can buy a house there, I can live there, I can go to a good place, I can buy a house in Greater Kailash. I own land in Greater Noida but I don't want to go there. I know that if violence happens, I will be killed there. And what is the thought behind it, that this is a Muslim. Kill him. This man has arisen in life. Cut his life short. What is happening today? What is happening in Nainital? If 50 or 100 Muslims live there, they are doing well there, working. And they are powerful. Their aim would be not to fight with anyone. Their motive would be to keep standing strong, work, bring up their children, take care of their workers … but the way they are being treated today is that people think they are Muslims, they must be forced to run away from here. If he knows this, why would he work there? So our minds are pressured, they are Muslims torture them. Why can't we rise? We never get any support from the environment. Take the banks, why can't we be given finance on the surety of our land? They say that this area is negative. I do not understand it. Are there no defaulters in Greater Kailash? But that area would never become negative. If any of the small businessmen here get a loan of 10,000 rupees from a bank, they would repay because they would wish to take another, larger loan. So if you never get this support you will never rise? The government never actually talks of segregating us but we have been scared. We would go and live in areas where four of our own people live. You know this ... we live in such a society... this is what forces us, scares us so much so that a man cannot rise the way he wants.

(GJ) The global recession of the last 4–5 years, has that influenced Muslim manufacturers in Seelampur? Or would you say that this area is not so well connected to the global markets?

(MS) We could have actually taken benefit of this situation if somehow credit was available to us. We could have gotten much more work. We are connected but the connection is difficult to maintain. Take the issue of electricity. It is privatized in Delhi. Everyone is getting enough of it. In our area in Seelampur, we still face scheduled load-shedding twice a week but in reality there is load-shedding four to six hours every day. So whatever work we have to do ... how will we expand? We will become a negative area, then the police comes and harasses us for no reason. So these types of difficulties do not allow us to take advantage of the larger environment. The other thing is that with the slowdown, there is less investment from the other end. The small manufacturer doesn't have savings or capital to ride it out. If we were trading also, then the scenario would be different. Some items always sell but other trends change. The manufacturer is someone else, trader is someone else. Gandhi Nagar is a market of traders in jeans and hosiery .... It never sees slowdown because everyone will always wear pants ... but manufacturers in Seelampur also see shifts in items that they get orders to manufacture. Sometimes it is this, sometimes that ... we manage but if we were in trading it would be different ...

(GJ) What is the presence of Seelampur people in trading?

(SM) Almost none. All traders are non-Muslims. Muslims are all small manufacturers.

(GJ) If someone were to start engaging in trading?

(SM) If at all they succeed they leave. It cannot happen while living here. There are no traders here. If you want, you will have to buy a shop in Gandhi Nagar .... Not many would be able to afford that. Gandhi Nagar does have a few rare Muslim traders. Trading is also bound to locality. For example, all the foreigners come to Laxmi Nagar, they purchase from there. How can anyone operate from here? Manufacturers have to stay here because they also co-operate with each other. If a small manufacturer goes to some other area and they require 10,000 rupees, who would give them that kind of support? Here we help each other in whatever way we can.

They are not only constrained by religious-identity-based segregation in bargaining for a better deal, but they are also unable to get beyond operating in the lower echelons of the supply chain in any item of industry. The *mandis* in Delhi, the garments business, spare-parts and machine-parts manufacturing, scrap dealing—in all these arenas, Muslims are kept in the lowest rung of the businesses by a mix of spatial segregation, lack of credit facilities, and discriminatory business practices. If these skilled and unskilled workers of Seelampur could sell their labour and set up their manufacturing units outside the Muslim neighbourhood freely, without discrimination and fear for property and life, their material conditions could be different, but as Wacquant (2009) points out, these neighbourhoods become prisons for their inhabitants, incarcerating their members as a dishonoured category, while severely curtailing their life chances in support of the 'monopolisation of ideal and material goods or opportunities' (Weber 1918[2009]) by the dominant group living outside the limits of these neighbourhoods. Communal spatial segregation, by way of restricting labour mobility, is one of the ways in which labour market segmentation is maintained. Muslim workers constitute one segment of the labour market, whose ability to compete with others is limited by their identity and positionality.

The conditions in Chauhan Bangar, Jaffarabad, and New Jaffarabad within Seelampur district are diverse and very different from the slum shanties of Seelampur colony. But the element of incarceration impacts not just the geographical mobility of persons (or workers), but also the geographical mobility of capital. It is conventional economic wisdom that immobility of factors of production causes market inefficiencies, and is, therefore, bad for free markets. But capitalism is not exactly famous for its propensity to just and equitable distribution, and its rewards to different segments of the market differ. Communal prejudice and threat of violence add risk, weighing against the mobility of capital owned by Muslims. Communal segregation ensures capital accumulation in other parts of city, at the cost of the Muslim areas.

CHAPTER TWO

Variable but Durable Marginalities

. . . .

In the previous chapter, I have discussed how the 'city' or the 'urban' is itself a product of capitalism. I have also shown how capitalism through liberalization and globalization is manifested in the segregated Muslim areas in Delhi. Further, I have established that the capitalist project of accumulation actually finds segregation of Muslims in Delhi useful. In the final analysis we can conclude, following Harvey, that capitalism reproduces itself spatially, creating a 'landscape in its own image' (1985: 43). Maximizing profits is the avowed aim of capitalism. In this bid, activities aimed at accumulation move quickly to areas where this can happen most easily. Manufacturing activity from Old Delhi shifted to Trans-Yamuna, which offered cheaper rent and lower wage rates. Lack of and/or minimal enforcement of any regulations is an added bonus. The usual explanation of this sort of process is that this increases the value of these spaces and displaces economic activity in older urban areas. The people who can afford to migrate to these areas are portrayed as reaping 'benefits' of the higher level of economic activities in these areas (Fainstein and Fainstein 1978). In areas of newer growth marked by communal segregation, such as the Trans-Yamuna Muslim neighbourhoods, the population within is only being fleeced of the true value of its labour and other fixed capital it owns. While their position may seem better than what it could have been, given the constraints of communal prejudice and threat of communal violence, their gains remain, at best, only marginal. In the overall logic of a city as a vehicle of capital accumulation, the segregation of the Muslim population in specific neighbourhoods with their contained labour or fixed assets therein serves a specific purpose. The old city, meanwhile, after having been looked upon as an area of degrading living conditions and even destitution, is being rediscovered by the neoliberal consumer of art and culture for its historical, culinary, and architectural heritage. While the tourism industry provides many their livelihood, a people are caught in the cesspool of stereotypical representation, that 'museumifies' them by being obliged to put on display what people wish to and pay to see.

For a long time in independent India, Muslims have been languishing in poverty because in the prejudiced social structure, their labour was of marginal and of no special economic virtue. Moreover, most of the crafts that they engaged in were actually slowly loosing relevance in the increasingly industrial India (Khalidi 2006). In the neoliberal environment, Muslims are being discovered as a 'human resource' that is (fortunately/unfortunately) positioned at a specific use in the accumulation project which has little use for prejudice per se except to the extent that it aids capital accumulation. Muslims are grateful for jobs and businesses that take advantage of their skills, time, labour, and assets and other integrative advantages that this relationship brings with it. For example, those restaurants in New Friends Colony community centre that would not undertake home delivery to Jamia Nagar neighbourhoods, now distribute pamphlets with menus offering discounts and home deliveries. Banks that continue to red-line

Muslim neighbourhoods as far as credit is concerned and limit their business with Muslims mostly to savings accounts, wish to facilitate Muslims spending (evidenced by the unprecedented increase in the number of ATMs installed in Jamia Nagar and Seelampur in the last 1–2 years). The point is that these neighbourhoods are integrated in the city economy, but only so far as the balance of accumulation of capital is tipped in favour of spaces elsewhere.

JAMIA NAGAR

Jamia Nagar is at present a cluster of several contiguous small and big localities. In the early 1980s, it consisted mainly of small settlements separated from each other by small tracts of forest-like growth. Mr Shakeel, whose moderately wealthy family came from a village in Aligarh in western Uttar Pradesh to invest in the soon-to-be booming real estate business in the area, opines that most of these people were scared to live in the vast open areas adjoining the river Yamuna. There were still some wild animals in the woods and nights were especially difficult with swarms of mosquitoes and fear aroused by howling hyenas, among others. Jogabai and Okhla were old villages of Hindu Gujjars, Gaddis, and Yadavs. Ghafoor Nagar and Batla House were small clusters of double-storied houses and narrow lanes similar to Old Delhi where mostly teachers and clerical staff, among others, working in Jamia, lived. Some residents held jobs in other Muslim educational institutions or government jobs. There were also some residents who had been evicted from Turkman gate in the walled city during Emergency.

Some Old Delhi residents bought land here recognizing the opportunity for investment but confess today that they never seriously entertained the thought of shifting to Jamia Nagar. At best, for *Dilliwallah* Muslims, the proximity to the river Yamuna and open spaces posited the area as a picnic spot. Culturally, and in terms of infrastructure, and access to markets and other amenities, among others, the two places were poles apart. Also, the claim of Jamia Nagar to being the locality of the 'educated' tended to make the

Dilliwallahs, who were mostly artisans, feel out of place. But even in the early 1980s, the residents of Okhla 'village' were conscious of their 'rurality'. Taking a ride in the DTC route 402 and 403 buses connecting the area to rest of the city, they would say they were going to *Dilli*, or to the *shehr* (literally, city). Slowly, the openness of the area began attracting some Old Delhi residents, whose joint–extended families had grown too large to be accommodated in the small dwellings in the walled city. High premium was placed on education and people saw their shift to the area as a progressive move. Any sacrifices and hardships in daily life were mentioned with pride and borne with a brave face. It was their chance to an almost-escape. With the promise of education and possibly jobs, Jamia Millia Islamia (henceforth, Jamia) slowly but steadily attracted people from U.P. It remained a focal point of community cohesion, even for those who had neither studied at Jamia nor worked there. Mr Rizwan (name changed) came to Delhi as a young journalist from Aurangabad in Maharashtra. He initially landed up in the Hauz Rani area, which is an old village in South Delhi inhabited by a large number of Mewati Muslims. Mr Rizwan says,

> ... that the place was steeped in the orthodox and feudal culture and values of Mewati people. I felt like the odd one out who was always uncomfortably different from everyone else in the locality. When I came to Jamia Nagar the first time I felt like I belonged there because Zakir Nagar's openness and diversity allowed me to blend right in. I was about to get married and felt that even among strangers here, my family would be safe.

In 1990, as part of the Ram Janmabhoomi[1] movement, widespread Hindu right-wing mobilization by the *Rath Yatra* (literally, chariot

---

[1] Literally, the birth place of Ram. A long-standing controversy exists over a mosque in the holy town of Ayodhya in UP which is alleged to be the birthplace of the Hindu god Ram. The controversy is mired in numerous legal disputes, but more importantly, is at the epicentre of anti-Muslim mobilization in the country by the Hindu right.

journey) led by L.K. Advani, leader of the Hindu nationalist party, the Bharatiya Janata Party (BJP), left a trail of anti-Muslim violence and massacres in many parts of North India. Beginning with this event and culminating in the 2002 Gujarat pogrom, in the entire period that includes the decade of the 1990s, Jamia Nagar saw a surge of in-migrants from various parts of north India, especially Bihar and U.P. The area saw unprecedented expansion. All the green forest tracts were gone and many new colonies came up.

Faizan, a young media professional says,

> After exhausting all the possibilities of expanding horizontally, this locality has now begun growing vertically—building multi-storied flats to pack in as many people as possible in a bid not to spill over the boundary. It is a comforting thought to know that there are hundreds of thousands of individuals like you and families like yours, who have similar fears and desires. Muslims arrived here at various points in history … points when history wasn't too kind to them. [19]75, [19]92 … and 2002. Willingly or otherwise—they were forced to take some decisions.

In the meantime, Jamia also grew from a laidback educational institution with moderate academic ambitions to a hub of professional courses. Teachers, social workers, engineers, lawyers, and media professionals were being trained there and finding jobs in the new liberalized regime. Upcoming firms in the information technology (IT) and media business sectors in India—business process outsourcing (BPO) organizations, software firms, and TV channels, among others—needed a large number of skilled people to perform jobs and were willing to hire even Muslims. These industries seized the opportunity of hiring this highly skilled labour being trained and turned out by Jamia. The creation of space for this segment of workers marked by their identity was a deviation, however slight, in the long-standing trend of very low representation of Muslims in public services as well as in corporate jobs. But by and large here too, Muslims got recruited mostly in the worst and most precarious jobs.

Ghayur Mansuri works as a hardware and networking engineer with a leading IT company. He says,

> I am acutely aware of the competition and ... since our childhood, I've heard stories of discrimination, so I was very anxious about being unemployed. I was so happy to get a well-paid job. I am well-trained and work really hard to keep up with the technology. My team leader says I am an asset in the team. I always reach office on time and leave the last but the anxiety is always there ...

Many young undergraduate girls and boys who work in BPOs report getting paid more than their parents. Their families are proud of their achievements and lead materially comfortable lives. They also articulate a feeling of relief and gratitude on the one hand, and on the other, a nagging fear of losing the job. Their readiness to work in inconvenient shifts and for excruciatingly long hours complements their high-quality training. This combined with an awareness of their identity, makes them docile employees, who rarely complain.

A middle-class locality to begin with, Jamia Nagar became more diverse in terms of economic classes. The affluent among the residents clustered together in parts of the locality—Zakir Nagar Extension, Jogabai Extension, and Johari Farm came up as affluent enclaves. Even though affluent, the residents could not leave the neighbourhood either because of their perception of threat or experience of violence or, in numerous actual instances, when house and plot owners in other parts of the city where Hindus lived, would not sell/rent their property to Muslims. The residents of these oases of affluence sought to put up gates to enclose themselves and preserve their exclusivity. They were in Jamia Nagar but they felt they did not entirely belong with the other residents of the area.

Sometimes willingly and sometimes grudgingly, people also 'self-categorize' themselves, exaggerating the similarities of those in the same group and exaggerating the differences between those in different groups, thus 'stereotyping' them (Oakes et al. 1994). One's self-concept is influenced by the gaze of the 'other'. In simpler terms, the awareness that I am being looked at and judged as a stereotyped individual belonging to an already formed category influences even the way I think about my 'self'. This exchange of gaze between 'self' and 'other' is a dynamic process that depends only a little on actual experiences or information but draws a lot from the historical context and emotional content of inter-group relations. Accordingly, stereotypes cannot be seen as irrational and invalid cognitive prejudices, and exaggerated stereotypes are only a result of a rational selective perception (Turner 1999). The 'rationality' in this selectivity is to do with the decision that the perceiving person finds it more useful to see the other not as individuals with unique identities, but as one belonging to a social category identity.

At this point, it would be useful to draw in a discussion of power acquired by the individual through association or through belonging to certain social groups. The members of the groups that have more power see their own image in a more positive light, and position themselves at a relatively higher status. The more powerful group seeks to distance itself from the less powerful. While the powerful group employs increased ethnocentric and discriminatory practices and attitudes, in the context of Hindu–Muslim relations this results in involuntary segregation of Muslims because they find it extremely difficult to rent or buy accommodation in Hindu areas. An offshoot of this process is the institution of gated enclaves of affluent Muslims within and outside these large pockets of Muslim population. Still shunned from the affluent Hindu areas, they resort to using a new group membership as a source of positive self-esteem. This is true for such areas as New Jaffarabad in Seelampur, the above mentioned localities in Jamia Nagar, or housing societies like Taj Enclave, also included in this work.

In Jamia Nagar, the experience of relative affluence is to be seen also in the light of the fact that many professionals and their families come to Delhi looking for a life denied them in small towns. Students, computer engineers, media persons, call-centre executives, teachers, public relations (PR) professionals, lawyers, property dealers, marketing and sales people, and business people here lead culturally very different lives vis-à-vis the values/lifestyles/aspirations from those back home. In this regard, I also explore the area from the perspective of the present first generation migrants to Jamia Nagar. Belonging to the middle-class, a majority of these migrants to Jamia Nagar are from Bihar. (The lower-class Bihari migrants who lack skills or education mostly migrate to Seelampur.)

Mr Qamar says, '*Yeh jo aap yahan Jamia mein padhne–likhne wale ladke dekhti hein, yeh zyadatar Bihar ke bachche hein.*' (trans. These Jamia students that you see here, most of them are young people from Bihar.)

Moin Ahmed, who is a software engineer, and is himself a first-generation migrant from an educated but lower-middle-class family in Ranchi (erstwhile Bihar, now in newly created state of Jharkhand), says,[2]

> (GJ) … and would you say that most of the Bihari people who have come to Delhi to make their career are actually in [the] service sector?
>
> (MA) Most. There are two different kinds, one is [those] who have studied somewhere and they got job opportunities and they migrated to Delhi, there are other guys … because of the other problems, there is no work there and they are in Delhi like labourers, rickshaw pullers and all, [a] lot of them are from Bengal and Bihar. In the last 4–5 years, you see many Bengali people, otherwise this field was only dominated by Biharis, and you will find they are lessening because the situation there in Bihar is getting better, so they are having labour there as well…
>
> (GJ) … educated Biharis who are coming to Delhi are doing better than other Muslims in their fields … I spoke to a young person in Zakir Nagar who is from Munger and she has studied planning in the Netherlands; many of her relatives are living in Zakir Nagar working in technical sort of jobs as you said, and she said they had nice houses in Munger, huge houses, and here they are living in these hovel-like small flats … She is a planner so she was saying that these flats are an architectural nightmare, but they are happy here because there are some dreams they are perusing here… especially the women, because they can go to Batla House whenever they want to for shopping, they don't want to go back to Munger ever. What is your opinion on this observation?

---

[2] Interview conducted in English.

(MA) Two things ... see if they are living in Munger, the men... they won't be having a job which can bring home every month, a lakh rupees or something, so that money which they are bringing, again the problem of numbers is very much[sic], people are thinking whatever you are earning in Delhi is a lot ... because that money is a lot compared to where he belongs, so why somebody is earning 50,000 or more is not that much happy, because you have your ...

(GJ) Expenses...?

(MA)Yes, exactly, in schools, in transportation, your living, just eating, everything is expensive, but opportunities are there, because of this school mafia you see big-big schools and all, people say my son is going in this school. Secondly, it's like Muslims used to earlier go to the Gulf; he is a plumber in the Gulf earning [a] few thousand rupees, just a bit more than double that he could have earned here, and when he comes, he is coming from foreign, so all his earning he can spend in 2 months and he shows I am something, so that thing is also to show people that they are not able to come and see [the] Lal Qila in Delhi, *ke hum Lal Qila gae the*, we did this and we did that, so that type of boasting which is actually not very natural ... He feels better ... that I am good, I am better than my relatives. I am living in Delhi.

(GJ) Even though my living conditions may have actually worsened ...?

(MA) They don't think that about living condition[s], they are happy, we are not living in big houses but here we are living better... We are in a big city, so what, nobody asks the question what we are in a big city? Our children have more exposure than that small city ....They go to malls and they do this... They know what is an escalator and elevator ... Others... they are thinking that since his brother or his uncle came to Delhi and got a good job, so he is earning very much and sometimes he goes for foreign travel on work as well, if they will study in Delhi they will also do this.

So they think that now they are growing and they will grow, so this is one thing, and some of them have actually grown, and some of them, what happens ... parents are there .... All the children have come here ... Now they don't have any option, either be alone or come here in a small home to be with their children, so this is also a big fact ... now what happens, they are living in [a] rented house and they realize, what we will do with property there, now nobody is going back to live there, so they sold a big house there and bought a 100-yard house here, so this is also a story...

(GJ) And would you say that this story is happening a lot here?

(MA) Very much, very much! If you do a survey, you will get a lot of ... number of people are coming, and those who have not yet come are thinking of coming, because two children or three children ... [the] daughter is married and she and the guy is working in Delhi or nearby and [the] son has got [a] job in Delhi, now the best option is to come to Delhi; now their parents, they look after the grandchildren also. And those who don't come ... like my wife Ranam's mother ... the big house in Patna is a problem for her ....Nobody is there to take care of the house. All the three sisters are married—one in Panipat, one in Faridabad, and one in Delhi. The son is in Canada. She is a teacher but if she gets even five days off, she comes to Delhi. So whatever there may be... she feels better to be with her children. I think when she retires, the first thing she will do is sell her house and shift to Delhi.

(GJ) From among the people that are known to you, is this observation that my friend made true, that a good number of women are working but most are not working women, their husbands are earning. Essentially, that they have money to spend and markets are full of stuff...

(MA) Yes, where can they spend that money and what can one do if you have a lot of money, but you don't have [a] good mall there, if you have money but you haven't got multiplexes there?

(GJ) Where to spend it and on what?

(MA)Yes, where to manifest that I have money, that manifestation really gives you satisfaction and that is a big problem...

In conversations with women, it does come across repeatedly that have *more freedom* to order their time and space even though both may be in short supply. Many women are professionals and work in regular jobs, many more offer support services—running crèches, playschools, tuition centres. Many of them also run small businesses—Zakir Nagar and Batla House markets have many shops being run by women—boutiques/tailoring, cosmetics and toiletries, undergarments. Both young and old women who do not have paid work also report liking their lives here better. It does not matter if the houses are small, lanes decrepit, and sewage lines overflowing. In fact, they like it that small houses necessitate that they cannot live in joint families, even though almost the entire extended family lives in the neighbourhood. There are repeated references to combining the best of the benefits of joint and nuclear families. Most women do not wear any usually recognized form of purdah/burqa. Those who do, wear scarves and stoles worn stylistically over the head, *abaya*s and *chadar*s in unusual colours and slim-fit styles, a far cry from the tent like garment worn by purdah observing middle-class women in most small towns. They socialize, go shopping often and hunt for bargains—Batla House market is a thriving, bustling witness to small joys of finding cheap and not-so-cheap delights of urban consumerist aspirations. My neighbour Naghma is a young housewife and mother of two. Her husband owns a thriving milk and milk-products shop in Abul Fazal Enclave. Naghma has most of the day to herself and her daily chores. In her stylish beige burqa and stole wrapped over her head and face, she is a regular sight in the building as she goes to drop and pick up her children, who study in Jamia Nursery and primary schools. Visiting Batla house with a few other women in the building is a regular engagement. She says,

> I feel something is amiss if I'm not able to go to Batla House for an entire week. I buy everything I need from Batla house. When my sister comes from Bulandshahr she says *baaji,* you have such a nice life here. We shop a lot together. I do all the work on my own. I take the children to the doctor. Samir [her son] had some problem in [his] teeth; I took him to Jamia Dental College. I was a bit nervous, but I did it. When I came here after marriage, I felt so frightened I could not talk to anybody. Now I do everything on my own... I'm not frightened so much anymore.

Shaheena Begum is from Moradabad. All four of her children studied in Jamia. The eldest—her son—married his classmate from Deoband, who was also a hosteller in Jamia. Shaheena did not like it at first, when both of them settled in Delhi for good. Now her daughter is also married and lives in Delhi. Slowly, when all the children came to Delhi, they insisted that she too leaves Moradabad. They have sold the house because there was no one to take care of it. When I ask Mrs Shaheena if she misses her Moradabad life, she laughs and says there is hardly any time. At 62, she looks young for her age and is quite active. She is the centre of life for all her children who live at a walking distance from each other. She says, she is engaged all the time in helping them run their lives smoothly—looking after the grandchildren, shopping for them when they are too busy, and cooking everyone's favourite dishes.

> *Zamana kitna badal gaya hai, yaqeen nahin hota. Moradabad mein, apne muhalle mein, main kabhi burqe ke baghair nahin nikli. Yahan bachchon ne kaha, Ammi burqa pehennna chhor do. Bachchhon ko mein ne bohot dil mazboot kar ke dilli bhej diya. Mere sasural waley kehte the, kitni sakht dil hai chhote-chhote bachchhon ko khud se juda kar diya. Aaj jab bachhe kehte hein, Ammi aapne haemin ilm diya. Unke ilm ne meri zindagi bhi badal di.* (trans. Times have changed so much, it is difficult even to believe. In my locality in Moradabad, I never left home without a burqa. Here the children said, Ammi stop wearing a burqa... I had sent the children to Delhi after hardening my heart. My in-laws used to say, how stone hearted she is to separate her young children from herself... Today when the children say, Ammi you gave us knowledge. Their knowledge has changed my life too).

People ascribe various meanings to their migratory experience and the motivations therein. This, in turn, gives rise to altered realities. The descriptions of everyday lives of people in the locality may be weaved together not only in order to unravel the discourse of the neighbourhood as a segregated space for people who are 'identified' and/or who identify themselves as Muslims, but also to discover how the city simultaneously confines and 'gives space' to the residents of Jamia Nagar and other segregated enclaves.

Segregation and Built Environment

The segregated enclaves are fast reaching points of saturation but more are pouring in—to study, find jobs, educate their children, and set up enterprises. With the increased in-migration and the growing

aspirations, all the large segregated concentrations of Muslim population in Delhi are experiencing some form of the business of real estate.
Jamia Nagar, especially, is experiencing intense construction activity.
Undoubtedly, this is also a great opportunity for some circuits of
capital to encourage Muslim investors to invest such that while the
profits are maximized in the short run, the segregated topography of
the city remains undisturbed.

People who invest in the construction activity do so because this
is recognized as a method of investment which is legal, secure, and
sanctioned by the faith as legitimate. In other words, it is not so
much that homes are needed but that financial opportunity is created
by this need. Such market being profit driven caters to consumption
of those who can afford it either through purchase for their own use or
for earning steady rents from tenants. Harvey's analysis (2003) fits our
purposes aptly:

> It would be difficult to argue that during this period the surplus of capi-
> tal arose out of the tendency to overaccumulate as we have specified it.
> The latter is, strictly speaking, a phenomenon which arises only in the
> context of the capitalist mode of production or in capitalist social forma-
> tions which are relatively well-developed... [but] The role of 'fictional
> capital' and the credit and money supply system has always been funda-
> mental in relationship to the various waves of speculative investment in
> the built environment.

Even though speculation is frowned upon under Islamic principles of
economics, the investment in the built environment in Jamia Nagar
is largely speculative in nature, and like everywhere else in the city of
Delhi, fuelled by over-accumulation. Just as Harvey (1978) indicates
for developing economies in transition from feudalism to capitalism,
investment in the built environment was largely fuelled and financed
by overaccumulation such as Haussmann's project for the urban renovation of Paris in 1853.

The overall logic of capitalist investment in built environments
in Delhi is also a result of a search for secure investment of capital
accrued by over accumulation, rather than any interest of either the

state or private developers in the use value of the buildings. Speculative activity undergoes almost periodic and cyclic crises which ensure that most investment will take place in building infrastructure that have productive use like malls, office spaces, freeways, and airports, among others, rather than housing units that only have a use value. Harvey (2009) further argues that often the working class is made to bear this burden but big investors are not totally immune from this process. Built environment as devalued capital actually leaves the city often with physical environments that have greatly reduced earning capacity but still some use value.

In an ideal capitalist analysis, the finance circuit should not be interested in the nature and location of the buildings; financial institutions should fund these projects based on their assessment of the builders' potential for profit-making; and builders should sell their housing units to people without bothering what their identity is. But while scrutinizing a minority, assumptions regarding 'ideals' have to be set aside. The identity issue in housing and segregation does not simply stop at the issue of intolerance and prejudice, but has a material consequence. The owners of property want their investments to multiply and would not favour anything devaluing their investment. This is the reason why Muslims cannot buy a property in certain neighbourhoods that would like to maintain Hindu exclusivity. This, in turn, is the reason why developers and builders in Muslim areas are doing roaring business, because it provides them an excellent opportunity to sell their wares at increased profits to a niche market that has little choice. But developers and builders in these areas are also Muslims who must manoeuvre in the limited segregated spaces because they cannot operate in non-Muslim areas largely because of a prejudiced market environment, and also because they are small players whose economic worth is of no real consequence in the larger order of things. In some cases, it was found that the Muslim builders had Hindu Gujjars as their partners, who are still connected to and interested in this niche market because they continue to own large landholdings even now. This is also because of their rootedness in the area and already existing social relationships. Their familiarity with the area and its people makes them confident of building and maintaining business relationships with well–to-do Muslims in the area. More importantly, having studied in Jamia, they are most likely to be classmates and good friends with their Muslim partners. But these partnerships remain tacit, informal, and largely unacknowledged publicly.

The mechanisms of making profits in construction projects in Muslim neighbourhoods are also fraught with numerous other constraints and peculiarities. Being self-employed, or in services in the unorganized sector,[3] Muslims also usually do not have such large disposable incomes (NCEUS 2006, 2007). Financial institutions would not either give them credit *per se* because of prejudice and discrimination, or because properties in these neighbourhoods are ineligible for home loans due to unofficial redlining policy, and special assistance schemes for housing loans are inaccessible due to difficult rules (PMHLC 2006). To add to this, many Muslim localities in Jamia Nagar and elsewhere are not regularized for housing. Interestingly, all this combined proves to be an opportunity for developers to make profit, if they have the capacity to take risks. Innovative collaborations with landowners are the order of the day. A builder enters into collaboration with an individual who owns a property but lacks the means to develop it. The agreement between the two involves typically cash payment by the developer and a share in the housing units developed on the property. After making an initial and only partial investment in the property, the developer proceeds to enter agreements to sell with various prospective buyers, who are required to pay in instalments. The size and frequency of the instalments may be irregular and decided based purely on mutual 'goodwill and trust' between the parties.

---

[3] Ninety-five per cent of all working Muslims are engaged in occupations in the unorganized sector. In 2004–5, 13.3 per cent Muslims were in the middle-income group—an increase from 11.1 per cent in 1999–2000, and 1 per cent Muslims were in the high-income group—an increase from 0.9 per cent in 1999–2000 (Sengupta et al. 2008).

There are two ways to scrutinize these processes, which are not contradictory explanations but are rather complimentary. This informal solidarity economy works not just because it helps Muslim families to avail decent housing and own flats that they would otherwise not be able to procure given their position in the market economy, but *more importantly*, also because it enables the developers to raise money that entails no tax liabilities, and from that part of market, that is utterly at their mercy. They are required to reinvest a very small portion of their surplus, mostly for short periods of time, and whether the property values in the area appreciate or depreciate, the developer never stands to lose. Even when business is down, the speculative activity on the built properties keeps the profit-making enterprise of investing in real estate in Muslim neighbourhoods lucrative.

NIZAMUDDIN

Nizamuddin is among the oldest continued settlements of Muslims in Delhi as a *basti* (literally, 'settlement'; connoting an urban neighbourhood) surrounding the *khanqah* (a place for Sufi gathering) of the Sufi Saint Hazrat Nizamuddin. Many of the old residents are attached to the *Dargah* (mausoleum) for their livelihood and can trace their lineage for centuries, living in the same area. The place has an immense religious importance for Muslims, both due to the dargah of Sufi Saint Nizamuddin and many others Sufis of lower order. Nizamuddin being in the same Sufi order as Moinuddin Chishti of Ajmer, all pilgrims to Ajmer must come here to pay their obeisance first to the disciple before they go to his master in Ajmer. Interestingly, the Basti also houses the international headquarters of the Tablighi Jamaat,[4]

---

[4] Tablighi Jamaat is a revivalist movement of the Deobandi stream that stresses on proselytising trips and gatherings among Muslims, with a professed aim to bring them closer to the practice of Islam. Tablighi ideology draws eclectically from diverse Islamic theological schools, and especially renounces any local customs that do not have the sanction of the religious scriptures (Hasan 1997).

popularly called the *Markaz* (literally, centre). Between the Dargah and the Markaz, Nizamuddin Basti probably receives more Muslim visitors through the year than any other Muslim locality in Delhi. Since this is the area where Muslims come to 'learn to be a Muslim',[5] this is also where lots of other visitors also come to see and experience things 'Muslim'. Restaurants and joints selling food abound here as do publishers and book shops of Islamic books. The Basti, similar to the walled city is a 'museumized' space for curiosity. In fact, the entire area has been handed over by the civic authorities to the Aga Khan Trust for 'preserving its heritage'. The trust is running various programmes for architectural 'renovation' and 'preservation' of various big and small historical monuments in the locality, including the UNESCO world heritage monument, Humayun's Tomb. Along with this, they also have a community development and welfare initiative, which takes up interventions for children, adolescents, and women on issues such as life skills and health, among others. One of the initiatives was, for example, to develop a park which was reserved for women and children only. It received a lot of coverage and attention in the print news media and online forums (Ramachandran 2012, April 12; Kumar 2012, June 13; Humayun's Tomb—Nizamuddin Urban Renewal Initiative 2016, March 9) for creating a 'breathing space' for Muslim women in midst of the 'congested' locality with 'backward practices' such as purdah. Several other NGOs intervene with their education, health, and youth development projects in the area, and the small locality is seeing their busy activity with alternating interest and apathy, depending on the frame and limits of their agenda. A resident of Basti Hazrat Nizamuddin told me that even though Nizamuddin East is also as close to Humayun's Tomb, and dotted with other small monuments, the residents of this area are not subjected to displacement and relocation that these 'developmental' initiatives entail. A public private partnership Humayun's Tomb-Sunder Nursery—Nizamuddin Basti Urban Renewal Initiative was

[5] This refers to the Tabligh's popular slogan which translates as 'O Muslims! Become Muslim!'

signed in 2007 between the Aga Khan Trust for Culture (AKTC) and Aga Khan Foundation (AKF); and the Archaeological Survey of India, Central Public Works Department and the Municipal Corporation of Delhi. While the AKTC is an expert agency in heritage renewal with experience of working in various historic heritage cities, AKF is responsible for community co-operation. AKF has an especially crucial role in Basti Hazrat Nizamuddin because the neighbourhood sits cheek by jowl with the monuments in the vicinity. From the very beginning some residents, researchers and culture enthusiasts have been suspecting displacements (http://mail.mail.sarai.net/pipermail/reader-list_mail.sarai.net/2007-April/009041.html).

In 2008, when a wall adjacent to a step-well (Nizamuddin baoli) collapsed, the trust and the foundation cajoled 18 families with their houses next to the baoli to relocate. They were able to relocate 17 of these (Mathur and Ray 2014). The project's discourse of 'urban renewal and heritage conservation' can be read along with 'beautification' discourse of the city administration and its usual lack of sympathy to housing rights of the poorer inhabitants of the city who are aware of being referred to as blight on the city. Aga Khan Trust has had a substantial, regular and positive media coverage of their work in which the neighbourhood is repeatedly invoked as dirty and backward. For example, one such article says, 'The area is rich with culture, music, art, architecture and poetry. Yet, to an ordinary visitor in Delhi, this is just another minority community ghetto seeped in poverty, dirt, filth, crime, drug peddling and so on' (Basu 2016). People's fear of displacement arises from their experience that an improved space will necessarily be an exclusionary space. In this light, it may be argued that Aga Khan Trust's initiative is one of eventual gentrification of the neighbourhood.

My study area, Nizamuddin, is also peculiar in the clearly polarized contrast that one sees in its two distinct parts. The Basti is a very old settlement with winding lanes made narrower by the businesses and households spilling out of the shops and houses, respectively, while the contiguous Nizamuddin West has comparatively much larger houses, broader roads, and more affluent residents. While the Basti is exclusively Muslim, the west is now predominantly Muslim but still has many Hindu residents who are old owners. Since the Muslim population became sizeable, the Hindus have been selling off their properties and moving out.

Mr Qamar, whose daughter is a newsreader on a TV channel and lives in Nizamuddin West, says that now the locality does not have any Hindu families moving in or purchasing houses. This trend is worth noting, because Nizamuddin is an illustration that spatialization of discrimination depends largely on where people can buy and rent property over and above the factor of whether they can afford it. A Hindu locality that has proximity to some poor and/or Muslim area has a higher probability of slowly being sold out to Muslims, if they desire the purchase and are willing to pay higher prices than the going market rates in the area. The first few purchases will be the toughest to bring about, but subsequent transactions will be easier as the speculation would have pushed up the prices in the vicinity to an extremely profitable level, and readiness to leave the area to Muslims would increase because their numbers would have reached some arbitrarily perceived but crucial threshold of tolerance. In other areas such as Seelampur, Jaffarabad, Ahata Kedara, and Beri Wala Bagh, where there was or is a sizable Hindu population the trend is of Hindu families moving out to better areas. Since Muslims cannot operate from other spaces, they pay attractive prices for space needed for their businesses.

This is an analysis that finds credence in many observable instances in the experience of the participants of this study. As mentioned in the previous chapter, after Partition, many Punjabi and some Sindhi refugees from the Pakistani side were given properties in areas like Karol Bagh, Ajmal Khan Road, Bada Hindu Rao, Beri Wala Bagh, and Model Basti, among others. Okhla had a sizeable population of local landowning Hindu Jat, Gujjar, and Yadav residents. Seelampur had many poor non-Muslims who were resettled there along with the Muslims who were displaced from their original houses in the aftermath of Emergency. In most of the areas, where fieldwork was conducted for this study, and where people reported there were many

Hindu families residing along with Muslims, the Hindus sold off their houses and bought properties in 'Hindu-only' areas. The 'Hindu-only' areas maintained (and continue to maintain) their exclusivity by refusing to sell to Muslims. Mr Azeem Akhtar mentions the experience of his neighbour, who was a well-to-do publisher who lived on the 'Muslim side' of Daryaganj. A tutor used to come to their house to teach his grandchildren every day from the 'Hindu side' of Daryaganj in the 1980s. One day she mentioned that she may not come to teach the children after a couple of months because her father-in-law had decided to sell their house. Mr Azeem Akhtar's neighbour was intrigued and asked the tutor to tell her father-in-law that he would pay INR 200,000 more than whatever was the highest price that he was getting in the market. She promised that she would let him know. After that day, the tutor never came back. A few weeks later, they happened to meet by chance in Chandni Chowk market. The woman was embarrassed. She said that when she told her father-in-law about the offer, he was very angry with her for not even knowing better than asking him to consider the offer. He said he would gladly give the house away in charity than sell it to a Muslim, and from then onwards forbade her from giving tuitions.

TAJ ENCLAVE

While some more affluent among the residents of the segregated enclaves sought to make their surroundings more to their likeness, many affluent Muslims are put off by the idea of living in a 'ghetto' enough to build an entirely separated gated community for themselves. Taj Enclave and a few other such gated housing societies of affluent and elite Muslims are interesting spaces because they are microcosms that are fraught with all kinds of contradictory processes that Muslims are subject to in the global urban. Taj Enclave is near Gandhi Nagar in Trans-Yamuna about 4 kilometres away from Seelampur metro station on Geeta Colony road, but its residents virtually eschew any contact with Seelampur on an everyday basis. According to the president of the residents' welfare association (RWA), the society was registered in 1972 but the allotment of around 6 acres of land took place only in 1988; by 1992, the members of the society were given possession of the flats. The residents are proud of living in a colony of 'educated, intellectual and professional' Muslims. The heavy tall gate is guarded by private guards, the lawns are well manicured, and generators are available for power backup. The RWA is responsible for all kinds of maintenance in the premises. There is a mosque, a general store, and a greengrocer's shop inside the compound. The old residents and most educated elite ones vehemently deny ever feeling any threat of violence. They feel, as Mr Jaffrey puts it: 'Violence happens where lower classes live, at the slightest commotion they get agitated that Islam is in danger. We, here, are educated... We understand... We keep quiet... We've never experienced anything...'

The participants here all report that they have spent 20 years, 30 years, in government colonies being the only Muslims, but were never made to feel as if they were any different. They assert that communal violence and discrimination is a thing of the past and perpetrated only by illiterates. There is an apparent anxiety in their strong assertions that 'anyway, these issues are like natural disagreements in a large family', and that if the 'head of the family is responsible, then nothing could ever happen'.

Among these assertions, the family interview with Mohd Naim and Nisha is an anomaly. The couple with their two children shifted here in 2003, from Sarai Khalil near Sadar Bazaar. Naim has a shop in Gandhi Nagar. The flat has been renovated recently, and is decidedly more lavishly decorated than the other flats I have visited in Taj Enclave. They now have four children, who, Nisha says do not have many friends as other parents do not want their children to mix with children from Delhi-6. A housewife, Nisha does not feel welcome among the women in the neighbourhood, most of whom are working women. Naim says that though the neighbours do not say anything openly, he is aware that his family is thought of as uneducated and uncouth. He still wants to live here, because he sees this as a fresh chance for his children. In Taj Enclave, he says, 'the children come out to play in the lawns for a fixed limited time and ride their bicycles only for an hour in the evening'. Nisha says that earlier most residents were older people retired from government services. Now, most occupants are young families of doctors and engineers. Naim effectively sums up when he says, '*Mussalmanon mein bhi yeh hai... Ke aap Dilli-6 ke ho, aap Seelampur ke ho, aap Zakir Nagar ke ho... Thappa lag hi jaata hai*' (Even among Muslims it is like this... You are from Delhi-6, you are from Seelampur, you are from Zakir Nagar... Branding does happen.) He is also the only resident who does not seem as confident as to the threat of violence, and says it is a real possibility. He tells me the residents of Taj 'work hard at forgetting Ehsan Jafri'.[6]

In the end, it can be said that contemporary processes of segregation are variable, but durable. Notwithstanding the homogenizing tone and tenor of hegemonic discourses, not all Muslims are discriminated against in the same manner; they are not all segregated in the same way. As a result, everyone aspires more to become the kind of Muslim who would be less discriminated against. Like a chimera, segregation is a strange animal. It buys complicity of its subjects by discriminating between them. The degree and effects of the segregation varies according to its material purpose. These material purposes are defined with a cool and calm capitalist rationale but infused with deep vitriolic prejudice and hatred. The seemingly increased flexibility of the boundaries may enable people to push these, but the same flexibility and elasticity ensures that the confinement cannot be shattered.

---

[6] A former Congress member of parliament (MP) and resident of Gulbarg Society in Ahmedabad, which was devastated by murderous mobs in the 2002 Gujarat pogrom. In an investigative report in *Tehelka*, Khaitan (2007) reports,

> For over five hours, about 30 Muslim families in the society prayed and hoped that they would be rescued. Along with them were many Muslims from the adjoining slums who had taken shelter in Gulbarg, thinking that a society housing a Congress leader would be an unassailable refuge. Finally, at around 2:30 pm, the mob stormed into the society and killed whoever they could lay their hands on. The official death toll was 39. But the survivors claimed that a far greater number were killed. Jafri himself was burnt alive. The remains of his body were never found.

In the next chapter, this exploration continues by shifting the focus of enquiry and analysis to the issues of globalization and urban governance. While in this chapter, we saw how capitalism impacts production of space, in the next, I explore how practices of governmentality aid and abet accumulation of not just capital, but also of political clout by the already affluent. This clearly results in the weakening of claims for equality and justice by the 'undesirable' populations in the city. Muslims' disadvantaged positionality is a further impediment in their claim to space and to an equal footing in the political community.

SECTION B

Discursive Bases of Segregation

CHAPTER THREE

Muslims in Delhi

The Normative Non-Citizens of the Global Urban

. . . .

I have established thus far that the city is not a cauldron that brings all the constituent ingredients together; it is rather a multilayered sieve segregating people in a process that is, paradoxically, at once quite subtle and also coarse. I have also shown that the roots of the processes that have an important role to play in maintaining and reproducing this segregation lie in material causes, and that these processes are geared towards capital accumulation. In this chapter, I turn my attention to the multiple discourse-weaving processes that are influenced by the 'official' state-recognized version regarding which labels to apply to whom. I contend that there are important and devastating consequences of how these labels manifest in the daily life of Muslims in Delhi—mainly that the spatial relegation of all-of-a-kind is based on the worth of the 'city-zen', judged by the discourses regarding their lumped up identity labels, and activated by various facets of the sovereignty of the state as exercised upon the Muslim subject.

I begin with a compelling question, 'Where does the often invoked idea of "Muslim alienation" stem from?' An allegoric reference to 'alienation' in this regard is hard to resist here. Very simply put—relationships of production in a capitalist structure alienate workers from their own produce. In other words, surplus in one place is bound to produce deficit in another. It would be interesting to scrutinize other similar processes that permeate *everything* in a given social structure and alienate some people within it. For example, gender relations in a patriarchal structure disempower women. I propose that it is the systems and institutions of governance, in which the Muslim experiences a deficit in citizenship and alienation in the political community. A state relates to its people by a social contract which is operationalized in the citizenship granted to its subjects. The Indian reality as experienced by Muslims falls far short of the understanding of 'citizenship' in a structure of governance, where the state makes a *legal promise* of equality and full integration in the political community. Habermas (1994) opines that this promise is to be realized via writing a constitution and building requisite institutions. Given Foucault's views on norms based on some objective, decontextualized, and universalized notions, it is not surprising that according to him, this view is deeply 'utopian'. He exhorts us to focus on the study of how a constitution is interpreted and practiced in institutions in reality, and emphasizes transgressing the view of writing a constitution as an effective way to empower a citizen (Flyvbjerg 1998). In reality, citizenship as experienced by all the legal citizens is not an equalizing *status*—'a full and equal membership in a political community' as mentioned in a commonly cited old definition by T.H. Marshall (1992 [1950]). It is rather an *asset* that is inequitably distributed with some among the 'legal citizens' experiencing a deficit in citizenship, and others enjoying citizenship in surplus.

Directed thus, let us turn to examining citizenship 'as experienced' not *legally* but *normatively* by Muslims, through a close examination of the history of their relations with the state, and contemporary contestations and negotiations of Muslims with the mechanisms of governance in Delhi through the practice of everyday.

DELHI: A BRIEF HISTORY OF THE RELATIONS OF MUSLIM CITIZENS WITH THE STATE

In this part of the chapter, I argue that the citizenship deficit that confronts Muslims in Delhi at present has at its foundation, a long history and the colonial 'legacy' of a strained relationship with the state. Here, it is the 'historicity and the embeddedness' of citizenship and the national state that is under scrutiny, rather than their legal–formal features. Gramsci (1971: 52) asserts that the state is a realization of historical unity of the ruling classes, and it is their history that is the history of the state. On the other hand, 'the subaltern classes, by definition, are not unified and cannot unite until they become a "State". Their history is therefore intertwined with civil society, and thereby with the history of States or groups of States' (Gramsci 1971: 72). Gramsci then goes on to lay down methodological criteria for a subaltern reading of this history, which include among other things looking beyond the immediate in the story of domination, covering all repercussions of domination, conceptualizing the subaltern globally, and studying the development of parties that include elements of the hegemonic group. It is in this *spirit of Gramsci* that I move forward with my analysis in this part and those subsequent to it.

Spivak (cf. De Kock 1992) points out that in Gramsci's original covert usage, subaltern signified 'proletarian', whose voice could not be heard, being structurally written out of the capitalist bourgeois narrative. She asserts that in postcolonial terms, *subaltern* is not just a fashionable synonym of deprived or oppressed. It signifies the space inhabited by those who have limited or no access to the cultural imperialism—having been systematically written out of mainstream discourses. Such a reading exposes how colonial English writers—bureaucrats and missionaries, presented a convenient image of the Muslim rule, to legitimize the British seizure of India from the remnants of the Mughal Empire. Indian historians and writers uncritically borrowed these colonial narratives on the 'Hindu' India and 'Muslim' ruler—despotic, foreign, and imperial—as authoritative statements about India's past (Bharucha 2003). This discourse weaving can be traced back to the events that took place during and after the revolt of 1857 ('Sepoy Mutiny') and the role played by Muslims, especially artisans, during the revolt (Chandra 1979). As I have discussed earlier in the book, after the British crushed the revolt and regained control of Delhi, they judged all Muslims to be rebels and went after them ruthlessly. The distrust of the state meant that Muslims were edged out of both land and employment. In fact, all Muslims were evicted from the walled city in Delhi and their properties confiscated (Khalidi 2006). During the course of my study, many old residents of the walled city recount hearing stories from the elders in their families about Muslims having been required to get a permit issued from their Hindu employers in order to gain entry into the city to work in those days. This obviously took a huge toll on the community, from which it took a long time to recover. When the anti-Muslim sentiment in the British colonial state ebbed, the walled city slowly became home again to a sizable community of Muslim small manufacturers, shopkeepers, and artisans (Gupta 1981). At the turn of twentieth century, Muslims constituted 32.5 per cent of the total population of Delhi (Khalidi 2006), but the distrust and suspicion remained. Distrust between the colonial Indian state and its Muslim subjects, as also between Hindu and Muslim communities marked all negotiations for a standing in social and political space in the country. This continued even after the British rule in India ended with the division of India and Pakistan in 1947 (Hasan 1990). In fact, it was this distrust on which the foundation stone of the Muslim state of Pakistan was laid.

Muslims in Delhi experienced independence as rioting, looting, and stabbings. By September 1947, 60 per cent of the Muslims of Old Delhi and 90 per cent of those in New Delhi had fled their homes. Between 20,000 and 25,000 were said to have been killed. Towards the end of October, about 150,000 of Delhi's 500,000 Muslims remained

(Pandey 2001). From the other side of the newly crafted border, Delhi received the highest number of refugees for a single city. The population of Delhi grew from under 1 million (917,939) to a little less than 2 million (1,744,072) in the period 1941–51 (Census of India 1941, 1951). The creation of Pakistan reaffirmed in many complicated ways a concept rooted in the colonial discourse and highly embroiled with the politics of communalism in India even today—of Islam as a foreign imposition and Hinduism being a 'natural' condition of Indians. Over the years since after the partition and independence of India, classifications and exceptions have been introduced to the conception and definition of citizenship, which reflected the communal fault lines (Jayal 2013). Tracing the history of construction of Indian citizenship as a legal status, Jayal (2013) discerns that a 'long shadow of Partition' loomed over it. The partition of India and creation of a 'Muslim' Pakistan also proved a fertile ground for the idea that Indian Muslims are less inclined players in the cause of the nation and nationalism and, by the extension of the deductive logic, inadequately committed to the value of participation in the Indian polity.

And thus begins a new chapter of Muslims in India as lesser citizens which still continues in Muslim localities in various parts of the country being called 'mini-Pakistans'.

Post partition, the affluent and educated Muslims had almost all left Delhi for Pakistan. Those who did not leave were mostly poor artisans belonging to 'lower' castes—their claim to normative citizenship of independent India weaker than ever. Such was the fear and threat perception that many participants of this study report that it appeared unthinkable in the days immediately following Partition that Muslim youth could visit Connaught Place at leisure while that was the common activity among the youth in pre-Partition Delhi. People report being afraid to move about anywhere in the city freely, except the walled city. Mr Qamar says,

A Muslim boy or a man, especially a bearded man dared not venture to Khari Baoli … Paharganj, Connaught Place. It was considered very

dangerous… If someone did go… we would wonder oh! He has gone
to Paharganj, God knows if he'll return or not… The environment was
such… What would a person do, if not be confined to only their own
neighbourhood?

Having lost lives, property, livelihoods, and being suspected of being
disloyal, many among those who had remained began wanting to
leave the country, if they could afford to. The Indo-Pak war of 1965 hit
some of these aspirations but only after the creation of Bangladesh in
1971 did the last ones hoping to go to Pakistan settle down finally to
the status of normative unequal citizenship in India.

The next brush of Delhi Muslims with the state came during the
period of Emergency, in 1975, when many parts of the walled city
were bulldozed after forced evictions of mostly Muslim and poor
residents. This has been charted in detail in the earlier chapters. In
the present analysis, this episode is important because it presents
itself as the first mention of areas where a predominantly Muslim
population resided as dirty blotches in the urban landscape. Post
Emergency, the Muslim population was living scattered in pockets in
and around Old Delhi, Okhla, Basti Hazrat Nizamuddin, Mehrauli,
and Seelampur. These pockets got consolidated into segregated
Muslim areas.

Segregation of Muslims in specific areas is a characteristic of Delhi's
spatial–demographic profile. To be fair, segregation per se (on class
or regional identity lines) is a characteristic of Delhi, but I argue that
involuntary segregation poses serious challenges in front of anyone
concerned with the notion of citizenship as membership of a political
community. Independent India extended a legal citizenship to all in its
vast multitude through constitution writing with only a minimal distinction as part of the 'adult franchise' doctrine. Muslims who stayed
behind in India after the partition for various reasons have found
that mainstream discourses continually equate them to Pakistan. The
representative democracy required them (like other citizens) to be
participative in actual processes of political governance in a limited
sense of electing their representatives only. While formal inclusive-
ness was guaranteed, their marginal status in the hierarchy of Indian

polity was pronounced and continued to be that way by way of denial of equal normative citizenship, which was not just a formal status but an enabling condition. In whatever limited way, the 'duties' that the state requires its citizens to perform mark the idea of citizenship in a way that citizenship denotes activity or, at least, 'capacity' for activity. People are thus liable to be judged for their worth as citizens based on the development of certain characteristics displaying civic virtue ('virtue' derived from the Latin *virtus*, which means manliness in the sense of performing military duty, patriotism, and devotion to duty and law). Apart from other social disadvantages, from the point of my interest in this inquiry, segregation of Muslims away from largely Hindu-only city neighbourhoods prevents optimal collective participation and spins off into a vicious cycle of decreased partici-pation and consequent representations of Muslims as a community of people with devalued civic virtue as contributing, willing, and loyal citizens. This, in turn, becomes one of the covert justifications of segregation.

L.K. Advani, Leader of the Bharatiya Janata Party, began his motor-ized *rath yatra* from Somnath on 15 September 1990, which was to reach now demolished Babri Masjid in Ayodhya on 30 October. In the towns all along the route of the yatra, and in many other loca-tions across the country anti-Muslim violence was enacted for over two months even as Advani was arrested in Samastipur, Bihar, on 23 September. Beginning with this event, the decade of the 1990s saw a relentless, violent, onslaught on Muslims in India culminating in argu-ably the most devastating and ferocious episode—the 2002 Gujarat pogrom. The pockets of Muslim population got consolidated (some even expanded) after each communal riot in the country, especially the post-Babri-Masjid-demolition riots in 1992 and Gujarat pogrom in 2002.

This part of the history of communal violence coincided almost perfectly with the initiation and pursuance of neoliberal 'reforms' in India (Chatterjee 2009). It is also interesting to note that both these processes show a good congruence with the trends of global Islamophobia in the post-9/11 world, and the swiftly accelerating economic 'globalization' project the world over. This is an opportunity for me to position my perspective or researcher's gaze at Delhi as a city in the *Global Urban*. Saskia Sassen (2010) cajoles us to engage with sociological methods, concepts, and data on a global analytical landscape, even though they may not have been chosen or created to address a global phenomenon. One of the ways this can be done, she further argues, is by conducting research, especially ethnographies, of the multiple processes that may be operating within national boundaries, but are most often either global in nature or at least are engaged by the global processes. She emphasizes that such processes may be embodied and experienced in the local, but they accommodate and enable global dynamics.

What exactly are the factors in Muslim marginalization in Delhi (indeed, in India) is a complex question that has been answered variously. We have seen in the exploration in the Introduction, of how the overarching allegations of Muslims as irrational, backward, and anti-modern people have often been used to 'explain' their predicament. Yet, there can be little denying that large-scale poverty, the activities of the far right, and Islamophobia have impacted the way the word 'Muslim' becomes configured. All the three components of this configuration are simultaneously, 'national'—specific to India, and 'global'. Thus, I locate the examination of this configuration of the word 'Muslim' in the decade of the 1990s in Delhi, as the Global Urban. And, since the trajectories of the neoliberal policies of the state and communal politics gaining legitimacy are intricately intertwined, I direct this examination now at the subsequent fortunes of the 'reforms' in India for some clues as to the fate of the Muslim community and insights into the issue of citizenship.

DELHI: A CITY IN THE GLOBAL URBAN

The way globalization is often spoken about in mainstream discourses makes it appear a fuzzy (and warm) concept, engaging with which we may find it easy to forget that it is simply the name of a process within which large corporations make quick profits because they have now an enhanced freedom to move their operations from one location to another in a quest for cheap labour, raw materials, markets, and concessions from national governments and local administrations. Finance capital moves easily from one national economy to another, unencumbered by any state and societal regulations, but movement of people chasing capital flows across national boundaries is tightly regulated (Stiglitz 2002). And often, the movement of labour even within national boundaries can be fraught with extreme distress and disadvantages, and be circumscribed by markers of identity and class. Increased communications of people, cultures, and ideas across boundaries (especially the boundaries of nation states) is definitely also a feature, but this freedom is limited and available only to a small minority on the right side of the economic and digital divide (Sassen 1998). 'Globalization' in terms of uniform/equal access to opportunities, ideas, and lifestyles is truly a phenomenon of the 'global' elite. The globalization project clearly leaves out the agendas of the people, while catering to the warm and fuzzy wishes of the elite.

From amongst the various much-discussed and well-documented features of globalization, I turn my attention towards one of its core premises, which is that the state cannot deliver and must not intervene in market-driven processes. The receding of the 'inefficient' and 'corrupt' state is proffered as a panacea for all the ailments that plague the masses in developing economies. In the first decade of the twenty-first century, the neoliberal 'reforms' of the 1990s assumed a 'missionary' zeal in urban India, à la the Jawaharlal Nehru National Urban Renewal Mission (JNNURM). This essentially envisaged expansion of the neoliberal agenda to many more sectors of engagement of the government in urban India. One of these is privatization of public utilities and welfare services (electricity, water, education, among others), along with deregulation of markets. In substantive terms, the Government of the National Capital Territory (NCT) of Delhi displayed its own 'missionary' spirit by introducing schemes like Bhagidari and Samajik Suvidha Sangam (SSS or Mission Convergence), that are a part of its 'commitment' to the 'convergence of urban management functions with urban local bodies' as stated in the Checklist for Mandatory Reform Agendas in the JNNURM Memorandum of Association (JNNURM Delhi, Checklist for Mandatory Reforms

Agenda, delhi.gov.in/wps/wcm/connect/... /Checklist.doc?MOD=
AJPERES&CACHEID.).

The RWAs of the Bhagidari programme are associations of people
that are already segregated on the well-charted topography of
identity and class, and the Delhi government's Bhagidari programme
incentivizes an exclusionary view of communities. The 'active' and
influential RWAs in the programme act as elite pressure groups to make
claim to benefits exclusively for their members, who are also members
of the powerful economic elite (Ghertner 2011). They influence the
government and bureaucracy at the cost of the welfare of *less active*
citizens, who do not have the time or the funding at their disposal
to sustain such pressure group tactics. Solomon Benjamin (2010),
investigating similar tendencies in the city of Bangalore, explains that
the trajectory of corporate-funded, and sometimes even explicitly
corporate-governed civil society is on the upsurge, in view of the consuming potential of this *active citizen* in the middle of media hype. He
argues that this has 'thrown off course and left confused urban progressive activists and many academics who cling to the idea of partici-
patory planning, good citizenship ... ' (Benjamin 2010: 94). Benjamin
points out that while marginalized groups have traditionally mobilized
local political power circuits comprising local politicians—grassroots
party workers, corporators, and members of the legislative assembly
(MLAs), among others, for attaining and accessing services, these are
the very realms that elite circuits of NGOs, self-professed activists,
and progressive academics shun from their vision of participation.
Benjamin further argues that considerable influence of urban elites
is exercised outside the confines of the mainstream political contests,
which may be the only arena where masses can disrupt neoliberal-
izing influences that have financial power, media hype, and corporate
influence. Ghertner (2011: 523) agrees when he says, '[i]n addition to
strengthening RWAs, incorporating their problem definitions as part
of the "mentality" of government, and giving them privileged access
to upper- and lower-level state workers, Bhagidari's second effect is the
weakening of the electoral process and forms of bureaucratic "fixing"
upon which slum dwellers have historically been dependent.'

Programmes and 'Missions' such as the JNNURM, Bhagidari, and Mission Convergence are being run either with funding and directives from international monetary and trade agencies like the World Bank and the World Trade Organization (WTO), among others, or are being run in conjunction and 'partnership' with corporate-controlled civil society organizations such as corporate social responsibility (CSR) initiatives and corporate-funded NGOs. Thus, the phenomenon extends itself to governance by corporations or those entities that are being controlled by corporate capitalism. The government is downsizing in the name of modernization and efficiency, and creating an illusion of filling the vacuum created thus, by symbolically emphasizing 'participation', 'active citizenship', and the role of 'civil society'. Paradoxically, the RWAs and 'civil society' organizations are in the thick of this movement of downsizing of government and erosion of democratic citizenship.

In such a scenario, the state seems more concerned with the *management of inequalities* rather than endeavouring towards progressive attainment of equality for all its subjects. Urban governance in India includes no attempts at spatial and social integration, and on the contrary, as a diversionary tactic, encourages segregation. It need not require much elaboration then, how this would impact the already marginalized and *lesser citizens*, Muslims.

Despite this kind of citizenship deficit, it would be fallacious to say that the state is absent from within these segregated Muslim localities. In Delhi, the state has in fact a deep presence and penetration in these marginalized localities via NGOs that are co-opted into garnering complicity of the masses towards the receding welfare state, and collecting data ostensibly for disbursing public welfare services and programmes through administering and monitoring the Gender Resource Centres (GRCs) of Mission Convergence. The harvesting of biometric data for Aadhaar cards was pursued most aggressively in slums, resettlement colonies, and Muslim localities by agencies that are not answerable to any democratically elected representative body. During the course of my research in Muslim areas of Delhi, photocopies of the Aadhaar registration form were selling for as much as INR 50. I could see the scramble of poor and rich Muslims alike to get themselves registered for Aadhar cards because the public campaign mounted it almost as the last opportunity for them to claim citizenship. The contradiction inherent in these processes is that governance functions in the city are being fragmented territorially, while on the other hand, political concerns of unequal groups that need to be addressed differentially are seeing a strange kind of 'convergence' entrepreneurial management. I contend that this is contributing to fortifying the segregation and surveillance regimes, instead of integration and inclusion. The state receding from its welfare functions but stealthily strengthening its surveillance functions, both impact the citizenship experiences of Muslims in the city, as they constitute what is the city's marginal population both socially and territorially. Further, this amounts to the neoliberal state making a deliberate attempt to not only slowly erode democratic citizenship but also to push the discourse of hiding disparity. This is in line with Saskia Sassen's (2002) assertion that citizenship in the global city is a mix of distinct elements in contrast to being a 'unitary category or a mere legal status', and that these elements can be even be contradictory. An important and useful viewpoint in this regard is that of Arjun Appadurai (2006) who says that the violence that minorities are facing across the globe is intrinsically linked to and is a manifestation of the processes of globalization. He opines that the exploitative relationships that manifest in globalization when coupled with its amorphous and slippery nature, evoke what he calls 'fear of small number'. Using illustrative examples from India and abroad, Appadurai says that even though there may not be clear-cut patterns regarding which communities are targeted in which context, what is clear to him is that, 'rather than saying minorities produce violence, we could better say that violence, especially at the national level, requires minorities' (2006: 45–6).

CITIZENSHIP AS CLAIM-MAKING AND POLITICS OF SOLIDARITIES

Another example that illustrates this point is the civil society initiative by a network of NGOs called India against Corruption (IAC).

The supporters of IAC and those mobilized in its protest gatherings were predominantly the middle class that vehemently painted
all political parties in the same hue, regardless of the differences in
ideology, because they 'are all corrupt'—corruption being defined in
strictly monetary terms and not as a moral prerogative (Chatterjee
2012; Shah 2012). The vision of this 'movement' was shown to be
tinged with authoritarian ideas, which were criticized on the one
hand for their implicit links with the Hindutva groups and trying
to give a clean chit to Narendra Modi for his developmental work in
Gujarat; on the other hand, it was also critiqued by many for its views,
ideology, methods, and demands (Sharma 2011). The leaders of the
mobilization made their contempt of democratic processes public
and were supported by people who were equally contemptuous of
these processes that they alleged are 'dirty', 'vote-bank driven', and
'corrupt'. It was argued both by the agitation's leaders and supporters
in the progressive circles that the passionate sentiment of a large number of people by itself sufficiently justified whatever demands they
were making. This implicitly would amount to justifying the large
mobilizations of anti-Mandal campaigns, the Ram Janmabhoomi
campaign and, the passionate *and* violent Bajrang Dal and Akhil
Bharatiya Vidyarti Parishad (ABVP) mobs imposing their version
of 'Bhartiyata' on streets and university campuses across India (Jha
2011). Extending this Hobbesian logic would also mean that it would
be possible to justify (as there have been not entirely unsuccessful
attempts) the 2002 Gujarat pogrom, which saw the majority organize
in large attacking brigades and kill Muslims to punish them in a state-
legitimized twisted version of communal relations. In subsequent
elections, Gujaratis have turned out in large numbers to reward Modi
and vote him to power.

Clearly, the implication of this vision was that the space for
Muslim participation in IAC mobilization was fairly limited. The
saffron tinge was obvious in the non-cognizance of the leaders of
the other sense of corruption—that of the executive, bureaucracy,
police, and judiciary literally not doing anything for the victims
of Gujarat 2002, and other earlier pogroms against the Muslim

community. In addition, the IAC rhetoric that all political parties are the same, rung hollow to the Muslims. As any minority that has been under attack from a political ideology in power knows, Muslims too, know the difference between the BJP and other political parties in India. Quite simply put, it can be the difference between life and death.

The mobilization also brought forth an extremely important aspect of power that a community can muster to launch a contestation of rights for its members in the public sphere. It is that historically Muslims are required to leave their own issues and questions behind when their participation is solicited by any movement. Movements, political parties, and NGOs often resort to the symbolism of includ- ing Muslims, but only to add numbers. A real or even strategic soli- darity is never sought to be built. The burden of building solidarities always lies with the most marginalized within the margins. In her book *Recovering Subversion*, Nivedita Menon (2004) discusses how the mainstream women's movement in India has been opposing res- ervation within reservation for OBC and Muslim women. 'Why?', she asks, '[a]ren't OBC women "women"?' (Menon 2009). Muslim and OBC women have never been afforded much space within the mainstream women's movement in India, which remains a largely upper-caste, upper-class north Indian Hindu women's movement. Muslim women keen to build solidarities with the 'mainstream femi- nists' are asked to jettison their fears, suspicion, and issues which are never addressed beyond the personal laws discourse vis-à-vis them. This is not to say that there are no 'Muslim' feminists within this mainstream, but they are well assimilated into the dominant discourse and oppose the 'division' of their movement solidarities on caste and religious lines. When the elite women's mobilizations contest their right to go freely to pubs and wear whatever they want to wear without fear of violence and harassment, the feminists from 'backward' classes feel obliged to support them, but the feminist movement in India has never raised the issues that confront Muslim women in their daily lives that do not invoke their Muslimness explicitly.

Interestingly many other bills, apart from the Lokpal Bill, have also been delayed in the parliamentary procedures because of being mired in controversy such as the bill against communal violence, and the one on social security for the unorganized sector workers. These have failed to find comparable support among the elite circuits. The elite circuits and their new found candlelight political activism has shifted the scale of political contestations in the public sphere. Maverick ideas, skills, and competence to attract the media gaze ensure that certain groups are needed only to pad up the protesting crowds, if at all. Nationalist discourses are the staple of these 'modern' elite mobilizations, and thus any critical engagement is disallowed. For the elite, security of their person, property, and their lifestyles is the major preoccupation.

POLITICS OF LIFESTYLE AND BIOPOLITICS OF STATE

Anthony Giddens's (1991) interest in what he called 'reflexive modernity' or 'late modernity' led him to explore the questions of security and lifestyles or 'life politics' as he calls it. He does not see the concerns regarding 'security' as a symptom of the postmodern age and end of modernity. Rather, he proposes that the practice of reflexivity in modern practices actually opens the possibility of change and improvement, but, he claims, that it also leaves a gap that may potentially house the fear of change, scepticism, and feelings of insecurity. It is also as if to a modern, liberal, reflexive individual, everything is changeable, interim, and anything is possible. The challenge to tradition presents itself as a human problem and late modernity exacerbates this insecurity to all-pervasive levels. Giddens actually claims that this reflexivity pervades even institutions and the conceptions of knowledge and possibilities of intervention by institutions in conceptions of the human body and life. Giddens juxtaposes the 'emancipatory politics' of the modern to the 'life politics' of the late modern. While the former is more familiar to us social workers as that politics which aims at freedom from exploitation and coercion, the core concern of 'life politics' according to Giddens is 'politics of lifestyle'. It is the politics that is geared towards fashioning and expressing a self-identity and self-actualization, and is based more on personal ethics. We can see the operationalization of this kind of politics in that of the new social movements such as the feminist movement and LGBT (lesbian, gay, bisexual, and transgender) movement. Giddens further asserts that this has been made possible because of the 'end of nature' (1991: 224), by which he means that even the human body is no longer seen as an unalterable physiological entity, but as a site open to the practice of 'reflexive modernity'.

The central insight offered here is explosive. The marginalization of class discourses by identity laden discourses is a phenomenon that does not need much elaboration. But it bears pointing out that identity discourses of the reflexive late modernity are severely limited to the articulation of aspirations regarding lifestyle choices, and find it difficult to intertwine within their discourse, a concern for emancipation from systems of power and dominance, especially class. Although it is possible to discern the strains of what Giddens describes in the contemporary, his 'life politics' is inadequately and disappointingly centred only on individual self-actualization and does not adequately lend itself to enabling a comprehensive understanding of the interplay of power relationships in a larger social canvas. To comprehend those, I turn to Foucault (1990 [1976]) and Agamben.

In classical philosophy, the Greek words *bios* and *zoe* are used to distinguish between two conceptions of life. While the meaning attached to the word *bios* refers to human life circumscribed by notions of good and bad, proper, and improper—unlike any other living being, *zoe* refers to the simple fact of a human being existing just like any other animal. Thus, *bios* stands for 'political life' and *zoe* stands for what Agamben (1998) has called 'bare life'. Within classical political philosophy, the ultimate end of politics is to ensure a just and good life for human beings. Foucault recognized in his work the *History of Sexuality* (1990), the conception of a new and distinct form of political rationality of state that centred on viewing its population as resources to be managed in the pursuit of power rather than the utilization of power in pursuit of freedom and a good life for the citizen. This wish for management required that the state developed knowledge about its subjects as human bodies whose capacities can be developed and who can be disciplined. This then is the purpose towards which, for example, the GRCs of Mission Convergence are geared. The state relates to its subjects not in terms of their specifically human life but in an abstract aggregated statistical way. Foucault termed this political rationality *biopower* which, when exercised, reduced *bios* to *zoe* for all practical purposes. The conception of biopower also includes the use of technology to exercise power over bodies. Agamben further elucidated the concept of bare life as that which has been exposed to a state of exception. In simple terms, it takes exceptional circumstances to collapse the difference between *bios* and *zoe*. For a human being, his or her life to be reduced to bare life effectively means that though the biological existence is given, there is no concern for the *humanity* in existence. Needless to say, the consequences for a population to find themselves in these circumstances can be alarming. Agamben, in fact, uses an analytical device afforded in a conceptual category of people in Aristotle's conception of polis—*homo sacer*, to grasp Nazi state's sovereignty over its subjects in extermination camps. These were those populations (mostly Jewish) that the sovereign state created only to strip them of all political rights and discard them to the margins, while they were simultaneously being included in spheres of state power that wielded control over their right to life.

A useful starting point for my purpose in using this framework appears to be Agamben's (1998) assertion that a close scrutiny of the figure of *homo sacer* of archaic Roman law is valuable in any attempt to unravel the codes of political power and sovereignty in modern times, in which *life itself* has become the principle object of state power. Talking of Nazi concentration camps, Agamben focuses on the 'paradoxical status of the camp as a space of exception' (1998: 96), and the fact that those excluded by the sovereign into the camp are taken into account (included) by the very act of exclusion. What they are included into is a juridical order of the 'state of exception', which in Agamben's words is 'the extreme form of relation by which something is included solely through its exclusion' (1998: 18). In a theoretically parallel analysis but one in which Agamben's analysis is rooted, Foucault explored questions of power and war. In his book, *Discipline and Punish* (1979), Foucault expanded the conceptual scope of 'war' as a paradigmatic device to ask deeper questions on power as it is exercised within the modern political arena. One of the things he proposes be done is to introduce historicism (archaeology) to achieve an alternative reading of the history of, what he insists is, a secret discursive war that operates in societies. This may be the pathway that leads to a better view of a continuous coding and recoding of power relations that do not follow any unitary order but are haphazard.

When the state wills to exercise its sovereignty and doles out death summarily to a life, that by its own definition qualifies to be 'killed without the commission of homicide (and that is, like *homo sacer*, "unsacrifice-able," in the sense that it obviously could not be put to death following a death sentence)' (Foucault 1979: 94), it does so in a new juridico-political paradigm in which exceptions (extra-legal killings) become normalized. The normalization of exceptions ensures that they are never questioned. Agamben (1998) persuasively argues that in a camp-like situation, the sovereign power does not limit itself to *defining* the situations in which the 'exceptional' will be exercised, but effectively *produces* the situation of exceptions, which is the reason why raising the question of what is legal and what is illegal in a concentration camp makes no sense whatsoever. At this point, Agamben credits Hannah Arendt (1951) with the insight that totalitarianism exists on this very principle that people suspend their common sense to believe that *anything is possible*. To understand how Agamben uses the concentration camp as the '*nomos* of the modern', it bears quoting him at length:

> Insofar as its inhabitants were stripped of every political status and wholly reduced to bare life, the camp was also the most absolute biopolitical space ever to have been realized, in which power confronts nothing but pure life, without any mediation. This is why the camp is the very paradigm of political space at the point at which politics becomes biopolitics and *homo sacer* is virtually confused with the citizen. The correct question to pose concerning the horrors committed

in the camps is, therefore, not the hypocritical one of how crimes of such atrocity could be committed against human beings. It would be more honest and, above all, more useful to investigate carefully the juridical procedures and deployments of power by which human beings could be so completely deprived of their rights and prerogatives that no act committed against them could appear any longer as a crime. (At this point, in fact, everything had truly become possible.) (1998: 97)

Technologies of governmentality produce inequalities and the state is not oblivious to its role in the same. In fact, as stated earlier, the state also equips itself with those technologies that enable it to possess deep knowledge of these inequalities. Foucault (1990 [1976]) clearly identifies that biopolitics can be said to be operationalized in situations when biological features of individual persons are measured and recorded, such that population profiles may be aggregated from the 'biometric' data so collected. These processes enable the state or make it possible for the state to establish standards and norms in the public sphere according to which human lives are valued differentially. Life, then, can be treated as a mathematical entity that can be measured, compared, added, averaged and, therefore, also 'separated'—both epistemologically and practically—from real human beings. Those systems of knowledge and discursive practices that contribute to or form part of the biopolitical processes do not exist autonomously and inform the governmental action or practices but rather depend upon the practices of the state itself. Census surveys, research committees, and photo and biometric identity proofs 'produce a population' that may subsequently be managed.

In this context, Foucault differentiates between 'sovereign power' and 'biopower'. Since there is an agreement of sorts that Foucault did not develop the concept 'biopower' fully and deeply, there is a controversy regarding the framework in which he conceived it. Agamben takes it that when Foucault (1990 [1976]: 180) says 'one might say that the ancient right to kill and let live was replaced by a power to make live and reject into death', he is contending that sovereign power has transformed itself into biopower in the modern 'liberal' security regimes. Certain commentators on Agamben's work like Tagma (2009) point out that Foucault does not mean that these are two forms of power that lie in different temporal zones—one developing into the other—but rather that they coexist.

The question that occupies most authors is whether biopolitics is different or can be distinguished from more familiar or traditional forms of political activity. For this study, I also examine how this difference is important for explicating on contemporary experiences of political representation and political articulation.

The domain of the state's biopolitics is presumably not new, but in the pre-9/11 world, it was becoming increasingly too narrow for the states in the 'democratic' world to manoeuvre legitimately in the matters of the life and death of their subjects. The 9/11 attacks mark many landmarks in recent history, and it does seem to several authors such as Butler (2004) and Žižek (2009) that among other things, it gave the state a new leash over the life and death of all kinds of *homines sacri*. For example, police in various states of India felt free to go about dispensing 'justice' in what are essentially extra-legal killings but 'popularly' called 'encounters'. It is in this death dispensing posturing that the state truly reveals its absolute sovereignty over a subject—suspending their constitutional rights ostensibly to protect the rule of law.

RE-IMAGINING POLITICAL CONTESTATION AND DEATH

In the case of Muslims in India, the findings of the state-sponsored Sachar Committee report are being continuously used to legitimize the (seemingly benign) reasoning that acute deprivation and communal attacks/violence are causes enough to turn Muslims into terrorists. It is then only reasonable that all Muslims are suspected as potential terrorists. Even those Muslims who are not poor and/or do not live in Muslim neighbourhoods believe that poverty, deprivation, and 'ghetto' living are conditions enough to turn Muslims into 'Islamist terrorists', as evident in articles such as the one by Nomani (2008) which appeared in the *Los Angeles Times*. But those who are directly impacted by this logic obviously do not find it easy to buy. Revelation of 'fake encounters' such as that of Ishrat Jahan, or more recent killings in Bhopal of SIMI members who had allegedly escaped prison, also plant suspicion regarding the veracity of these encounters in people's minds (http:// www.firstpost.com/politics/ishrat-jahan-the-inconvenient-story-no-one-wants-to-tell-867173.html; http://www.thehindu.com/opinion/ op-ed/Seeking-truth-victim-number-two-in-Ishrat-Jahan-case/ article14140187.ece.; http://www.dailyo.in/politics/simi-bhopal-jail-break-encounter-inspector-yogesh-chowdhary-bhupendra-singh/ story/1/13750.html). The Batla House 'encounter' is one such example, regarding which the prevalent Muslim belief is that it was pure fabrication by the Delhi police—part of a bid to brand them all terrorists.

I contend that the extra-judicial killing of students of Jamia in Batla House rewrote the profile of Muslims as potential suspects for acts of terrorism. Not only the Muslim, who had experienced communal violence or structural violence of poverty and discrimination was a potential terrorist, but so was a young student, or educated professional resident of middle-class Muslim neighbourhoods. Jamia Nagar and Jamia Millia Islamia were labelled in the public sphere as spaces that gave birth to and harboured these cold-blooded, scheming terrorists who had the technical knowhow and resources to be well connected with global Islamist terror networks. Being made to feel guilty for the partition of the country, represented as irrational fundamentalist fiends, loathsome and polluted, disloyal normative non-citizens, and potentially dangerous terrorists, Indian Muslims were thus fashioned as *homines sacri* in the public sphere.

As the thesis, on which this book is based, was being finalized, Mumbai saw a protest organized by a Muslim group against killings of Muslims in violence between Muslims and Bodos in Assam and Rohingya Muslims in Myanmar. A section of the crowd went on a rampage targeting media OB (outside broadcasting) vans and the police. Police Commissioner Arup Patnaik, who has since been transferred, was much lauded for the 'exemplary restraint' that he showed in not giving shooting orders to his subordinates on duty at the site. But he was also criticized by many for being 'soft' on the Muslim crowd and for 'growling' at his own forces. Patnaik's response to this allegation is telling not of just what was at play on that fateful day when despite his 'restraint', two Muslim men died in the firing, but also how certain situations and people are perceived in the 'normal' functioning of the state. He said: 'When I came in, I found my entire force running helter-skelter. They had guns ... SLRs and hands on the trigger. Had they fired, 200–300 people would have died. My entire aim was to stop my people from firing because I had handled the 1992 riots as DCP... What happened? 188 people died on the first day' (*Outlook India* 2012).

In an article about political pressures on police officers handling riot situations, written in the context of Patnaik's role in riot control in Mumbai, a retired IPS officer, B. Raman (2012), said, '[n]ot infrequently, situations get out of control not because of the violent mobs, but because of over-reaction by the police in dealing with the mobs and disproportionate use of force by the police'. In another opinion piece carried by the news daily, *The Hindu*, Jyoti Punwani (2012) raised questions regarding the lack of action by the state government and Mumbai Police against blatant violence and rioting by the Shiv Sena and the Maharashtra Navnirman Sena (MNS)—both parties belonging to the Hindu right—which has become a regular occurrence in Mumbai targeting workers and taxi drivers from Uttar Pradesh and Bihar, couples on Valentine's day, and South Indians, among others. Punwani claims that the Shiv Sena and the MNS's violent posturing and the lack of will of the state to bring them to book has become an accepted part of the city, and that the Muslim youth that protested violently probably took it that they can expect the same treatment from the state. Punwani opines that not only were the Muslim rioters mistaken that *anyone* can get away with violence in Mumbai, but the entire Muslim community in Mumbai and elsewhere in India was left apologizing copiously for a protest that was ill conceived.

An important example that effectively illustrates the preceding analysis is the case of the 'Sealing Drive' in Delhi in 2006. Political assembly and protest are also performances of citizenship status and claims. While enactment of violence by protesting publics with non-Muslim identity markers are considered routine and normalized, an assembly of protesting Muslims is potentially just another site of their fatal targeting. Another important example that effectively illustrates the preceding analysis is the case of the 'Sealing Drive' in Delhi in 2006. The importance of this instance in the recent history of Delhi unveils complex dynamics of the political economy of built environments, the material logic of segregation, contestations, and negotiations of elite circuits with the unorganized sector in claiming their vision of the city, and biopolitics of the state.

The case exemplifies a tussle between big capital and elite networks represented by RWAs on the one hand, and traders and small manufacturers on the other. Elite RWAs insisted in getting this case filed at the High Court of Delhi that their sense of security, peace of mind, tranquillity, and aesthetic sensibilities were being offended by business establishments within residential areas (Ghertner 2011; Bhuwania 2016). An appeal for preventing mixed land use was in line with the vision of the Delhi Master Plan, and on the agenda of previous Delhi state governments headed by the BJP and the Congress. The judge presiding over the case, Justice Sabharwal showing keen interest in the case passed a verdict which effectively read as a mass eviction notice to lakhs of establishments which were 'illegal' (Mehra 2012). Allegations of misconduct on the part of Justice Sabharwal came to light later, illuminating the nexus between big capital and the judiciary (*Mid-day* 2006; Roy 2007). Justice Sabharwal's son owned a real estate firm that gained substantially from an instance of demolitions as a result of the implementation of the court order by civic bodies.

The traders in Delhi have mainly been Punjabi Hindu–Sikh but many small traders and small manufacturers belong to various diverse social backgrounds too. Diya Mehra (2012) points out that the movement run by the traders' association employed Partition rhetoric profusely. While on the other hand, they used the daily wage workers associated with their businesses to pitch up the protest against a judicial order which was anti-poor, anti-worker, and anti-unorganized sector.

During protracted protests, in which the traders associations were reluctant to go to the Supreme Court because it could have also given a judgement adversarial to their interest, the traders' associations continuously negotiated with the state and Central Governments, the municipal corporation, as well as the Delhi Development Authority (DDA). Violence and rioting was also used strategically as a final device of pressurizing the state and elite networks. There were many incidents of rioting and damage to public property such as state transport buses. Eventually the government informed the court of its inability to implement the order as it would give rise to a law and order situation.

Ovais Sultan Khan, a participant of this study gave me an account of the occurrences that led to the shooting. This foretold law and order problem took place when the police opened fire at a protesting crowd in Seelampur on 20 September 2006.

> (OSK) I was in the twelfth standard then. Like many other boys in the neighbourhood, I went out to see what would transpire. The call for demonstration against sealing was given by Mr Masood Ali Khan, who has contested municipality elections twice, but lost ... But soon there was a crowd over which neither Mr Masood nor anyone else had any control. Most of them were labourers and even rickshaw pullers. There were no traders ... nobody whose business actually faced any threat of sealing.
>
> (GJ) So... What precipitated the situation?
>
> (OSK) It is impossible to say with any certainty. But apparently someone threw a stone at the policemen ...at the DCP's car. The police commenced *lathi* charge and immediately started using tear-gas also on the crowd ....After that there was confusion ... total chaos... then the DCP ordered to open fire. Official figure is three but five people died. I was there ... I saw it happen. Police did not even let the family members of the dead bring the bodies to Seelampur, citing further violence.
>
> (GJ) Are you sure about that? Because I read in a news article that police requested but the families did not agree...
>
> (OSK) Hundred per cent sure ....They were buried in Bihari Colony graveyard near Shahdara under police *bandobast*. No one from Seelampur even went for the *janaza* (funeral).
>
> (GJ) Then what happened?

(OJK) Nothing ... I wrote a representation to the President of India and led a delegation to give him the memorandum. Abdul Kalam was the President then ....He heard me silently and did not say anything... nothing at all ....We did not even get any reassurance from his office. We came back empty handed. Nothing happened. At least in the Batla House encounter, there have been demands for judicial enquiry ... Delhi traders and the BJP used the Seelampur shootings to bolster their protest, but not once did they, or for that matter anyone else, demand a judicial enquiry into the incident.

While the traders' association and the government used the deaths to further their argument that the issue could escalate into large-scale violence, the traders were also quick to dissociate themselves from alleged 'Mohammedan' violence. Mehra (2012) marks the death of Muslim men as the final turning point in settling the deal with the state. The government passed a bill in Parliament conceding to the demands of overturning the High Court judgement, and the Delhi Master Plan 2021 came into force allowing mixed land use in certain areas of Delhi.[1] According to her, the traders' association leaders were relieved that 'somebody had finally died' (Mehra 2012: 87). She says,

> In Seelampur, local retailers-cum-manufacturers reacted by stone pelting to what they saw as yet another attempt at their closure, having already experienced eviction in the case of small-scale industries. After relentless closure and sealing, it appeared that both the small Muslim manufacturer–trader and the large wholesale Baniya trader seemed to know, despite their vast sociological and physical distance, that what was required was a politics of *irrational excess or urban violence*. (2012: 87, emphasis mine)

At the end even Mehra, who effectively established the frequent recourse that the traders' movements took to Hindutva rhetoric, succumbs to the stereotype of the irrational, violent Muslim and fails to recognize why the spectre of the final violent turning point

---

[1] Delhi Laws (Special Provisions) Bill 2006.

in the culmination and success of the movement would be located in Seelampur. This is the only logical explanation to why when violence and rioting had happened elsewhere too in the city by protestors, firing and killings took place only in Seelampur. The logic from within the mainstream discourses makes it seem but natural that the *irrational excess or urban violence* would take place in a space that was already and conveniently stigmatized for the same. Even though the issue at hand, around which the crowd had been mobilized, had no connection with the 'Muslimness' of the protestors, eventually, imageries employed by the police to open fire were that of 'Muslim' violence. In the neoliberal India, where citizenship is increasingly a function of the capacity of a people to collectively make claims, Muslims find that their capacity to claim equal normative standing as citizens of this country is severely limited by their effective normative status of non-citizen, *homo sacer*. Every act of criticism of the state can potentially attract the refurbishing of the 'anti-national' allegation, and consequent stigma. The only form of public voice that was still available to them collectively could be put to use only to claim that their sentiments and sensibilities as Muslims had been hurt by some act, or speech, or text, because this was the only claim that fitted their image of irrational, infantile, backward people. Thus, their critical speech and their right to protest also stood forfeited *de facto*.

Judith Butler concurs in contending that public sphere is not defined only by the content of what is being discussed, but also 'in part by what cannot be said and what cannot be shown. The limits of the sayable, the limits of what can appear, circumscribe the domain in which political speech operates and certain kinds of subjects appear as viable actors' (Butler 2004: xvii). Butler (2004) further argues that this limit of what can be seen or not seen (in terms of acknowledgement of its existence) in the public sphere has implications for perpetuation of violence against people, who according to her become 'faceless' or represented as 'faces of evil'. Because of this reason, their lives can be eradicated and 'public grieving' for the loss can be 'infinitely postponed'. Butler (2004) concedes that not getting any acknowledgement of their grief in the public sphere, some people may turn to political rage and get trapped into a never ending cycle of loss and grief for loss of 'precarious life'. But she makes a very fine and nuanced point that all forms of mourning may not lead to the inevitable conclusion of justifying violence. In the case of Muslims in Delhi, the frequent victimization by the police (read state) and condoning of the patterns in processes of representation has largely lead to a feeling of despair and a suspicion of all forms of discourses about them emanating from the state as well as other discursive practices such as journalism and even social science research. This results in further alienating them from the public sphere—effectively precluding any possibility of expressing meaningful critical dissent.

The matter that bears serious consideration in the final analysis is asking, would a people who have been rendered stateless—by virtue of their effective exclusion by the state—necessarily want to transcend the state? The desires of those who live in a state of exception are strangely most often to be included in the political community as an equal. In so many instances around the world, a large number of people alienated by the state aspire to citizenship of the same state. It cannot be overstated that alienation by the state is not a sufficient condition for people to turn against it. It is a paradox of modern democracy that the people who extend the nuanced, informed, albeit qualified support without succumbing to blind nationalist rhetoric, are actually those who are at its periphery and do realize that the state and its machinery are frequently anti-people regardless of the political hue of the party in power. Those who have suffered the oppressive and exploitative functioning of the state do recognize that often the last recourse and only avenue of hope (however bleak) for the excluded, is within the juridico–political set-up of the state.

Further, we should recognize that though Indian people, media, and even intellectuals, often find it easy to blame political parties for playing caste politics, abetting communalism and communal violence, and preserving corruption, among others, it is the sections of 'people' themselves that are communal, casteist, and corrupt. Foucault (1979) constantly alludes to the local and diffused nature of disciplinary power, which is embedded in the entire society as opposed to

Agamben's centralized sovereign (1998). It is this diffused disciplinary power which makes people believe that the state of exception is the norm. An account of state power may begin to read like an exercise in conspiracy theory, only if we do not realize that the decision regarding who gets designated as 'not fit to be an equal human' is not a top level decision. For Deleuze and Guattari (cf. Tagma 2009: 416):

> [S]overeignty is not a force operating at the top level but is supplemented by: 'rural fascism and city or neighborhood fascism, youth fascism, and war veteran's fascism, fascism of the Left and fascism of the Right, fascism of the couple, family, school, and office'. Fascism works at the micro level in the actions of soccer hooligans, nationalist militias, trigger-happy Blackwater mercenaries, racist bartenders, and bigoted party leaders. What goes on in prison camps, understood in this sense, is not just the product of a pure and simple Schmittian decision; instead, prison camps are spaces that are constructed and maintained at the micro level. Prison camps are 'legitimated' by a regime of truth and classification intrinsic to biopower, which provides petty bureaucrats, border patrol agents, intelligence interrogators, and so on, with the authority to implement sovereign violence on physical bodies.

It is some sections of citizens who consistently thwart the claim of 'others'—such as Muslims— to equal citizenship calling them foreigners, infiltrators, or Pakistanis. It is the people who discriminate with prejudice or with rational calculations against Muslims in opportunities at policy formulation, opportunities in education, jobs, and welfare services. Too often elite mobilizations form a symbiotic relationship with forces that go on passionately in their relentless persecution projects in different parts of India, while youngsters are growing up in segregated enclaves feeling that they are second-class citizens of the country.

As for the earlier mentioned confusion of the progressive intellectuals who fail to acknowledge the contradictory role of the state and people, *both* acting their part in enforcing disciplinary and affinities to authoritarianism within democracies. They often resort to the essentialist binary of state as unadulterated evil but 'people' as essentially 'angelic', forgetting that the phenomenon 'people' consists of not just a plurality but of fractured diffused parts of a system of dominance itself. Much of the brutality, injustice, and oppression in this country happens because of the laws, and the fact that state machinery tends to be more concerned about protecting private capital; and much of it happens not only because of the absence/presence or strength/ weakness of laws. It happens because prejudice, discrimination, and oppression are deeply and intricately woven into our social fabric. The onslaught is so aggressive and violent that it incapacitates people from even coming together to voice their interests and opinions.

The above reasons put together form the narrative of why Muslims in India have no movement to articulate and contest for equality, despite such acute levels of marginalization, oppression, and poverty. At the ground level, Muslims do participate in other move-ments (including the IAC campaign) but all these movements have accorded the issues of Muslims in India a secondary status, if they are considering them at all. The leaders and the participants both in fact emphasize 'assimilation'. When Muslims do raise issues specific to them, they are told that they have a problem of dragging religion into everything. Yet the probability of raising general issues of livelihood and class dominance, among others, are silenced, when the issues of Muslim are frequently reduced in research and journalistic writing to issues of personal law, fundamentalism, and terrorism, among others. For example, because of the 'legitimacy of large numbers', implementing the Sachar Committee's recommendations is alleged to be appeasement. In fact, Muslims have all but been told to forget about it. Salman Khurshid who owes his career to being a Muslim leader in the Congress party, told Muslims that the 'Sachar committee report is not Quran' that it must be followed (Chishti 2011).

Though within dalit and feminist movements, Muslims have still negotiated for and have been accorded relatively more space, the violence of caricaturing and stereotyping of issues goes on at differing degrees in all progressive movements, which solicit Muslim par-ticipation to pad up their crowds but never highlight the priorities of Muslims, never address them directly, and make no attempt to provide them any succour. Within the dalit movement, 'dalit Muslims' must prove that they are dalits, and treated discriminatorily *as dalits*. In the feminist movement, Muslim women must assimilate in the womanly 'sisterhood'. The identity 'Muslim' has no use-value whatsoever.

In such a situation, laws are often (whenever they are available and usable) the only tools of accessing protection and justice. The process is not flawless but it is the only one that allows for any hope of safeguards to a fully human existence. While I try to utilize Agamben's theoretical formulations, I shudder at the memory from elsewhere in the world where some people have been reduced constitutionally to a second-class citizenship. I shudder to imagine that such demands are made by elites and justified by the legitimacy of large numbers through media-hyped, self-styled mobilizations. Of course, following Agamben and Arendt, we know that such events are entirely possible in democracy as it is a system that is obliged to override its basic postulates in order to legitimize them. It is not then an entirely unbelievable contradiction that the most vulnerable on the margins appear to defend the state—affirming and reaffirming their faith in its supremacy. They are only defending what may be the last straw that will break their back that is already overburdened not by the abstraction that is the state, but by the atrocities of those who exercise the diffused disciplinary power in working the state mechanisms, institutions, and processes to reduce people to bare life.

I quote at length, an extremely ominous and captivating discussion by Agamben while discussing the limits of exceptions within the Nazi concentration camps.

> Now imagine the most extreme figure of the camp inhabitant. Primo Levi has described the person who in camp jargon was called 'the Muslim', *der Muselmann*—a being from whom humiliation, horror, and fear had so taken away all consciousness and all personality as to make him absolutely apathetic (hence the ironical name given to him). He was not only, like his companions, excluded from the political and social context to which he once belonged; he was not only, as Jewish life that does not deserve to live, destined to a future more or less close to death. He no longer belongs to the world of men in any way; he does not even

belong to the threatened and precarious world of the camp inhabitants who have forgotten him from the very beginning. Mute and absolutely alone, he has passed into another world without memory and without grief. For him, Hölderlin's statement that 'at the extreme limit of pain, nothing remains but the conditions of time and space' holds to the letter. What is the life of the *Muselmann*? Can one say that it is pure *zoē*? Nothing 'natural' or 'common', however, is left in him; nothing animal or instinctual remains in his life. All his instincts are cancelled along with his reason. Antelme tells us that the camp inhabitant was no longer capable of distinguishing between pangs of cold and the ferocity of the SS. If we apply this statement to the *Muselmann* quite literally ('the cold, SS'), then we can say that he moves in an absolute indistinction of fact and law, of life and juridical rule, and of nature and politics. Because of this, the guard suddenly seems powerless before him, as if struck by the thought that the *Muselmann's* behavior—which does not register any difference between an order and the cold—might perhaps be a silent form of resistance. Here a law that seeks to transform itself entirely into life finds itself confronted with a life that is absolutely indistinguishable from law, and it is precisely this indiscernibility that threatens the *lex animata* of the camp (1998: 103–4).

* * *

Finally, I contend that we may conceptualize the residents of Muslim neighbourhoods (of Delhi) as subjects of a governmentality that solicits their political participation only through communal polarization, and who are treated normatively as non-citizens at the minimum, and as *homines sacri* in the extreme. The process that fashions Muslim subjects in contemporary India unfolds via, first, a very real threat of violence by communal forces and segregation that the state seems not to do much about and often directly abets; second, via an intense activity of the state to collect information that seeks to identify Muslims minutely, but, this deep knowledge acquired by the state rarely results in dispensation of welfare; and third, through the state's biopolitics of controlling life and death directly with the constant threat of Muslim young men being labelled 'potential' terrorists, arrested without due process to spend several years in jails contesting lawsuits that have no substance in a majority of the cases, or summarily killed in extra-judicial 'encounters' (Jauregui 2011; Ramachandran 2016).

In the next chapter, I direct the enquiry towards one of the domains, where these imageries of essentialized identity are continually reproduced—the Media. The news media and Bollywood cinema in India carry representations of Muslims for consumption of the wider society, and in their function of mass communication, these are the most prevalent form of constantly refashioning and forging these stereotyped representations that serve the purposes detailed in the earlier discussions. The narratives of media regarding Muslim identity and Muslim spaces are put through a discursive scrutiny for hegemonic texts and subtexts.

CHAPTER FOUR

Media Representations

Providing the Discursive Logic

. . . .

REPRESENTATION OF SPACE AND IDENTITY FORMATION

This chapter explores the issue of representation of Muslims and urban segregated spaces. At the outset, one very simple way to understand representations is to see them as allegorical or metaphorical presentations of things, people, processes, and spaces. They may also be understood as models of what they represent. They make it easy for people to understand what they seek to represent by scaling down (architectural models of buildings, among others), presenting them as codes, symbols (images, music, or other kinds of texts), or by converting them to a different but more tame and tangible form (such as a globe or maps). But in scaling down or coding, distortions or caricaturing are bound to occur. In this process, it is also perhaps inevitable that certain features of the represented will be highlighted, and others will be downplayed, depending on the use or consumption of the outcome of representation. If we see a human being as a *whole*, her identity may be seen as a representational model that presents her by highlighting certain of her features. Different identities of a person may then be seen as ruptured pieces of the whole, but the whole—the human being—is always something more than the arithmetic total of all the identity pieces. Social relationships, interactions, and experiences form the very substantial and critical glue that holds the whole together, the lifeblood that makes this whole—a person.

Within the layers of identity formation, there are people who have the power to compose identities more or less at will. For example, at a given instant of time, the upper-middle-class youth may project themselves as 'responsible citizens' at a candlelight protest, but in the next instant they exercise their choice and can be devil-may-care party hoppers. Bauman has captured accurately the predicament of the marginalized and excluded people—like Muslims in India—when he points out in a different context that at ....

> the other end are crowded those whose access to identity choice has been barred, people who are given no say in deciding their preferences and who in the end are burdened with identities enforced and imposed *by others*; identities which they themselves resent but are not allowed to shed and cannot manage to get rid of. Stereotyping, humiliating, dehumanizing, stigmatizing identities ... (2004: 38)

Drawing from the preceding discussion, I assert that each of a person's identities has a material function. I contend that an understanding of identity also as a political (and not merely as a social–psychological) construct would help us to complete this examination of the roots of discrimination and prejudice. An aspersed identity has a distinctly oppressive and exploitative material function. The tangible and intangible benefits to be accrued out of discriminatory behaviour make it worthwhile for a system of dominance to resist any changes and maintain itself. This fits very well in the Althusserian account of the ideological state apparatus in which individuals work on their own to reproduce class relations, which may not have any immediate consequence for themselves, but in the long run maintain the relationships which they have come to see as the actual, natural condition of their existence. In his book *For Marx*, Althusser (1969 [1965]) asserted that while in the last analysis, economic relations determined the political and ideological levels of the society, the three levels also had a certain degree of 'relative autonomy'. While it is true that the process of defining, redefining, and forging new identities is always carried on differentially, it is almost an aphorism now that people have multiple identities. One identity may be operationalized in a given context over others, while in a different context some other identity of the same person may prevail. The process is quite dynamic and often it may be so that the individual herself has no control over which of her identities is interpellated (Althusser 1969 [1965]) or called into action at a particular moment. People exercise agency in whatever limited scope available to them in proportion to their power through a play of comparisons, contrasts, and identifications. It would be a travesty to consider any one identity as the original or foundational identity of the person, especially when identities tend to be given ('gift'?) within the ideological constraints of society. This is why lumping together of people because they are Muslims does not make them stick together as Muslims *only*.

For example, in a hostile situation, people sometimes may try to activate those of their identities that are less stigmatized or even try 'passing' as the 'other'. The act of exercising agency in determining our identity in most cases is constrained and defined by our subjective knowledge of the perception of the 'other'. A Muslim subject strives to 'give up' a part of his or her identity so that a new identity is 'returned'. The 'gift' sought is a more favourable subjectivity (hence, socio-political agency) of the Muslim as reflected in the gaze of those who are capable of branding this person with an aspersed identity. This is what Muslims seeking to be recognized differentially as 'educated', 'moderate', 'progressive' are attempting. These contestations of Muslim people with their 'given' and 'assumed' identities in different contexts inevitably reshape their spatiality as we have seen in the preceding chapters.

It is in this framework of ideological obfuscation of distortions that I see identity and representation of Muslims while analysing media discourses (Van Dijk 1985, 1993). It would also be prudent to remind myself at this moment that Althusser does not see ideology as insubstantial and imaginary, but as existing in material and real actions of individuals even though these actions may not reflect the real nature of relationships. Since ideology is eternal, analysis may not take us to some 'truth' that has been 'corrupted', but it can definitely lead us to understand the dynamics of the exercise of power and the means people employ to make sense of the world around them.

Portrayal of Muslims in films and news media is a much-explored aspect in academia (Benegal 2007; Chakravarty 2011; Farouqui 2009). In this chapter, I take a fresh look at understanding the portrayal and representation of Muslims in congruence with the methodological choices in the rest of this work. I attempt what is called in the Marxist tradition an *engaged* analysis—which is a form of analysis that aims at emancipation and not just describing. Continuing from the conclusions drawn from the analytical discussion of observations in the preceding chapters, I stress that uncovering discourses and their ideological content can have emancipatory impact. This is done in consonance with the thread of concern that runs through the entirety of this book, which is space and Muslims, while also exploring the content of some of the prominent identity constructs prevalent in mainstream media including the aspersed identities. It is in this light that I shall undertake, in this chapter, a semiotic approach to analyse the mainstream media discourses. Thus, the concern here is not just with the contents of a text, but also the meanings and implications that readers derive from the signs appearing in a text, so as to discern the conventions that direct the discourse in media texts (Chandler 2002). What is being studied is not whether an article appears in a text and how frequently, but, what is the meaning of its appearance or non-appearance, and how do these meanings get shaped. One of the central concerns is to discern what are the assumptions in the given text, and how do these influence the narrative in the text. The issues of assumption directly relate to perceptions, and thus to identities.

ON 'READING': CONSCIOUSNESS AND IDEOLOGY

Critical theory's approach on this matter, drawing from Marxism, postulates that the modern technologies of material culture and cultural reproduction are but only the manifestations of fake beings— who are reified, inauthentic, and alienated. Thus, cultural theory largely aims at emancipation or freedom, which is understood as escape from reification. How is this possible? If all ideas of a time are contingent upon the relationships of production characterizing that society at that time, then, reification of the material, and alienation of life are inevitable in our times. Terry Eagleton (1989) explains that this is a case of much prevalent understanding based on a misreading of Marx. He contends that Marxian understanding actually sees the counter-hegemonic processes as an intrinsic part of the hegemonic processes. Marx himself spoke of the potential in art to develop disproportionately to the 'general development of the society, hence also to the material foundation, the skeletal structure, as it were, of its organisation' (quoted in Eagleton 1989: 9) and thus, art has the potential too, to act as a vehicle of counter hegemony. However, Eagleton cautions us lest we veer towards the other extreme, that art can transcend ideology, completely. Here he brings in Althusser who argued that while art is neither mere ideology nor completely free of it, it actually has a particular relationship to ideology. Eagleton(1989) contends that ideology is often mistaken as amorphous, unconnected free-floating ideas; he asserts, instead, that ideology of a time has a certain structural coherence, which is also what makes it suitable to be subjected to systematic analysis to discern the principles which bind it together, and point where these principles falter.

For my purpose, the preceding discussion of the uniqueness of art and artistic texts points towards a direction where we can get to a closer understanding of how ideology functions, and how it may possibly be transcended. Literary criticism has actually contributed much to the social scientific understanding of these discursive processes. Semiotic tradition in this context is the one that critical theory and Marxist approaches owe much to. In Saussure's semiotic framework (2017[1913]), language is the basic structure which orders, divides, and shapes the world—that is the phenomenal world. His contribution to structural analysis was that language is not a system of signs whose meaning is 'inherent' and 'obvious', but is rather 'produced' by the internal logic of structures of difference. In other words, it is our language that enables us to see 'differences' between 'our' culture and that of the 'other'.

Building on Saussure's work (2017[1913]), Lévi-Strauss showed that structural analysis is applicable to not only written texts but to myriad other textual practices. He stressed that even though the various forms of social life such as language, art, law, and religion seem to be different from each other, it is possible to see a basic similarity between all these forms by extricating and analysing the structures which communities use to constitute themselves, such as 'customs, institutions and accepted patterns of behaviour in addition to the written text' (Lévi-Strauss 1963).

Roland Barthes (1993) contends that in a narrative the codes[1] that enable its coherence are also the very codes that divulge its limits. It is by analysing the very structure or ordering of these codes that they can be transcended. In this context, for example, if the discourses regarding Muslims rely and revolve around the figure of violent, irrational being, then the structural analysis of this narrative would not

---

[1] Codes are points that define a network of meaning that shapes a narrative. Barthes defines them rather ambiguously but the definition could be discerned from his typology of codes. He says that codes may take the shape of voices, characters, events that take the narrative forward, sometimes giving it an unexpected twist. 'Code' may also refer to the structure of meaning inherent in a text. All in all, Barthes probably refrains from defining 'code' because of his view on the possibility of multiple readings of the texts. It is the specific, unique, combination of codes in a text that a reader reaches that makes an alternative reading possible.

just confirm the structure of meaning that the narrative gives rise to, but would also challenge these codes. The practice of emancipatory reading of the discourses which aims at discerning and divulging the meanings behind a hegemonic discourse must then focus on the contradictions, the inconsistencies within the meaning which produce a conflict in the narrative between a central figure confirming the codes, and a figure of the 'radical other'. An emancipatory reading does not attempt to resolve or harmonize the conflict but to display it.

Emancipatory reading leads me to 'deconstruction'. Derrida's 'deconstruction' is important because he conceives it both as an approach to enquiry and a political strategy. Derrida distinguished between 'deconstruction' and 'destruction' from the point of view of the philosophical tasks the two verbs involve. By his own admission, Derrida's deconstruction project has an interest primarily in radicalization in 'a certain spirit of Marxism' (1994: 92). It is essentially a *reading* that demonstrates inherent elements of a position that undermine the very position that contains them. Derrida said that deconstructionist reading is a 'gesture', rather a 'double-gesture' in which the first 'move' consists of inverting the hierarchy of opposition, and the second 'move' consists of displacing the system in which the hierarchy operates. This kind of reading requires a readiness to give full attention to the complexities of all the elements of a text, or an idea. It requires a special eye for contradictions and paradoxes. Derrida uses 'différance', a term he coined by combining the words in the phrases 'to differ' and 'to defer', to indicate that each 'sign' or idea contains within itself, its own absence. If it signifies deference to its own meaning, it also signifies its difference from that idea. It is this state of affairs in the use of language that Derrida calls 'play' and uses it to bring in a 'playful' form of reading.

Derrida's playful reading is not too far away from Lévi-Strauss's 'The Structural Study of Myth' (1955). 'Myth' in this usage is a unique way of producing a combination of ideas that are similar in form and are universal. Myths, according to Lévi-Strauss are ahistoric but also claim historicity. In his book *Imagined Communities* (1991), Benedict Anderson's discussion of 'Nation' is a discussion of exactly such a myth. The way national communities are imagined across cultures and the tropes that are used to prop up these imaginations in different languages are strikingly similar, while in reality 'Nation' as a concept is a recent invention. Finally, like all good myths, discourses of a Nation are nationalism performed. The performative nature of myths is what renders it the strength of a political position and also a political strategy.

Barthes (1993) further worked on the idea of myth as something so widely accepted as truth that it goes without saying—that which need not be said, because it is so well understood and widely accepted. He further elucidates that this happens through well-orchestrated ideological stage-management.

For analysing media discourses, Barthes's idea of 'myth' (1993) is important because according to him, the core competency of myth is to transform history into nature. He theorizes myth as a coded form of communication; it is a form of signification that is subject to history. Thus, myth again is performative and processual rather than an object, or an idea. The claim to historicity of myths requires that they depend upon rehashing old material and recycling it, and Barthes claims that while myths may be universal in form, they are specific in content.

In his conception of myth, Barthes was aided by his engagement with the theatre of Bertolt Brecht (Jameson 1998). Brecht used a technique called estrangement-effect in which he would deliberately stage his plays in such a manner that the experience of the audience is frequently interrupted by techniques that remind them that they are watching a performance rather than experience the performance as 'natural' or 'real', suspending their faculties. We know that cinema screenings in theatres today actually use strategies exactly opposite to this—known as alienation-effect. For this purpose, various tropes such as the dark proscenium and surround sound, among others, are used to draw the viewer 'totally' into the narrative—to the point that they forget that it is not a natural experience but a performance. In this sense, media stands in the modern society as a powerful tool of myth making. In fact, Frederic Jameson (1992) goes so far as to say that this realist 'performance' as a 'natural' quality of Hollywood cinema, enables it to be 'read' as depicting 'real problems' and proposing 'symbolic solutions'.

In his book titled *The Political Unconscious: Narrative as a Socially Symbolic Act*, Jameson (1981) talks of a 'political unconscious' which refers to underlying political and social assumptions in all cultural works and texts, including of course, popular cinema, but also architecture, space, and economics. As mentioned earlier, according to Jameson, cultural texts contain symbolic solutions to real historical problems. He further asserts that in the cultural texts of its time, each society is confronted with an image of the society that it has no vision to see. Extending this understanding further, Jameson (1991) refutes the idea that inherent contradictions of capitalism have been harmonized in the contemporary. He also rejects that postmodernity heralds the exhausting of the 'modern'. According to him, famously, it is only the cultural logic of late capitalism.

In other words, what is explained as the postmodern situation of the post-industrialist society, is merely a cultural explanation for a situation when capitalism has deeply permeated all aspects of life including consciousness (Jameson 1991). Understandably, it is an explosive argument that has altered the manner in which the humanities were charting the course to find ways to grasp the present realities. Jameson elucidates certain features that are symptomatic of the social shift to late capitalism or full-blown postmodernity (1991). Among other things, he mentions a 'geopolitical aesthetic'—a controversial concept according to which, representations of people and communities now have to contend with their linkages to the interrelationships between nation states, and what he calls 'a mutation in built space', which is now interfering with people's ability to produce a cognitive map of situations they are in.

MUSLIMS AND MUSLIM SPACES IN CINEMA

Cinema's potential for reproduction of human experiences and a realist representation of the same, have been the cause of much of the fascination surrounding it. Representation and interpretation, like the broader culture, arise in specific historical contexts to serve specific social functions and economic interests. In this way, it is easy to see how films are performative political events, and form part of the superstructure in the Marxist materialist theory. Critical theorists alerted media analysts to the impact of consumer capitalism (Horkheimer and Adorno 2007 [1972]) and global or late capitalism (Jameson 1991) on mass society and culture, connecting culture and media to the political economy. Because no representation is absolutely accurate, it needs to be understood by a conceptual framework that orders the impressions and assumptions of individuals. As such, cinema is also a myth in the sense used by Claude Lévi-Strauss and Roland Barthes (Nichols 1976).

A key question in any act of representation is with regard to who is representing and who is getting represented. The first question is in fact the question that forms the foundation of film theory. *Auteur* theory sees a film as a work of art, authored by a writer, and suggests that we look into the stylistic sensibilities of the author of the work in order to understand what he or she may be attempting to state (Wollen 1976[1972]). In *genre criticism*, recurrent themes in a genre are discerned and analysed (Tudor 1976[1974]). My efforts in analysis in this part of the work are a combination of Marxist criticism and semiology in film theory. These are characterized by a study of the ideological nature of interceding social and historical factors, and the 'formal properties of image as sign' (Nichols 1976: 1).

Studies of Hindi films are mostly marked by genre criticisms, which have also paid some attention to signs and symbols that are recurrently used in a genre. A genre that has had a major presence and significance in Hindi cinema is the nationalist film, within which not only the content but the practice of filmmaking was deemed to be a nationalist enterprise (Rajadhyaksha 1987). The other themes that are often studied and invoked are the portrayal of women, families, mental illness, and Muslims and other minorities. M. Madhava Prasad (1998) contends that the journey of Indian cinema in the international history of theorization of films began only in the study of realist cinema of the masters like Satyajit Ray. The cinema of fantasy or religious themes was regarded as 'not-yet-cinema' in film theory. Thus, Indian films become 'Indian Cinema' only as the brilliant *auteurs* begin representing and being lauded for representing 'Indian culture' in as realistic a way as possible. Moreover, Prasad points out that some theorists even went so far as to utilize the psychoanalytical conventions of Sudhir Kakkar and Ashis Nandy to associate popular Hindi cinema with the general masses, and thus equivalent to trash in artistic terms. In both cases, it was thought to be possible to say something meaningful about Indian society and culture (both high and low/popular culture) by studying its cinema. In the final analysis, it consisted of two kinds of audience—a refined audience that was capable of analysis and enjoying realism, and the mass audience that could not discern between 'myth' and 'fact'. These boundaries in understanding the difference in the degree of representation of 'reality' in films and assessing the capacity of different kinds of viewers are not static. They are being frequently redrawn and repositioned.

Another framework pertains to the development of aesthetics of Hindi cinema, whose co-ordinates are *frontality* and, again, *realism*. Both frontality and realism are a function of the relationship of the performers to the spectator. There is a sense of reciprocity in a film with frontal aesthetic sensibilities—the spectators face the performers and the performers also face the spectators, just as in theatre performances. In frontality as a mode of representation, the cinematic image is not just a 'capture' of reality, but a performed narrative which is addressed to the spectator and offered to them as an object for their gaze. Interpretation of the representation by spectators involves a complex interplay of aesthetics, technology, narrative forms, and conventions such as framing, editing, and mise-en-scène[2] (Prasad 1998).

For critical acclaim, Indian cinema contrives hard to portray 'reality'. Celebrated Bollywood filmmakers like Vishal Bhardwaj, Rakeysh Omprakash Mehra, and Madhur Bhandarkar have been actually lauded for presenting versions of 'reality' that are celebrated not for

[2] The way a scene and everything contained in it is set up—lighting, makeup and costumes, sets, positions, and entry and exits, among others.

their accurate portrayal, but for the rare insights that they provide into 'reality'. These filmmakers present an analysis of reality that is not cryptically hidden in the narrative but quite frontal. Their films offer the viewers a picture of 'reality', which makes them appreciate it and think of themselves as a refined audience—different from the masses. This kind of cinema provides a more nuanced motivation to the audience to suspend their belief. The more they believe the 'clever' narrative, situations, and characters as 'real', the better they can think of themselves. Žižek (1989) points out that no one believing in an ideological position considers that they are being deceived because of the pejorative connotations of 'ideology'. According to him, the Marxist notion of ideology stands compromised today because everyone agrees that there cannot be a singular truth that is obscured by the hegemony of the powerful. But, he says further, that this under-standing does not mean that we have seen the end of ideology; rather, this feeds into a situation he calls 'archideological fantasy' (Sharpe and Boucher 2010: 44), which refers to a situation when we know that a portrayal is not true but we pretend that we *do not know*. Archideology is more effective than ideology, because it means that people do not believe an idea to be a representation of truth but *behave as if it was anyway*.

In her classic article, 'Visual Pleasures and Narrative Cinema', Laura Mulvey (1975) brought forth the concept of 'gaze' to cinema in the context of the portrayal of women in Hollywood cinema and the male gaze. She drew her conception of 'male gaze' from the Lacanian and Foucauldian notions of gaze, and employed psychoanalytical techniques to discern the ways in which it shapes representation. My interest here is in the Lacanian conception which, unlike the all seeing, collective, internalized, and anonymized panopticon gaze, is hinged at an object which does not see you at all and therefore, induces shame and anxiety. This anxiety-inducing 'look' does not originate in an eye nor in a mirror, it is rather, 'a point of failure in the visual field' (Krips 2010: 93). In this understanding, 'the gaze' is in the mind of the one who is being looked at. This is the conception of gaze that is really relevant to the representation of Muslims in Bollywood cinema. It is not so much an all-seeing eye that deliberately misrepresents, but a point of collapse in sensory faculties that does not see Muslims at all in its portrayal of their image, and thus deeply humiliates them—shaming them into discipline. The failure in the field of vision that sees Muslims as the aspersed 'Other' is the precursor to the suspension of faculties. We suspect that this might not be true but we lose nothing in behaving as if this was the truth. This is a position which is obviously more effective than the position that 'people do not know'. It is effective in a situation when people do not know their own position and they define it as opposed to the position of what Žižek (1989) calls the 'big Other'. The tag 'Indian'—the master signifier without a signified—is substantiated by the decentring of portrayal of Muslims as 'big Others'.

Even when the representation is subject to political contestations and calls by minority and marginal groups which are routinely represented negatively, to be exposed for their hidden manipulative content, Žižek contends that this does not mean an end of ideology. In Althusser's idea of interpellation, when the person hears 'hey you' called out by a policeman, he turns into a subject. In his book *The Sublime Object of Ideology*, Žižek (1989) claims that this process is also not perfect. When the person who is being called out responds by turning, he is not turned into a perfect subject inside of ideology. There is always a leftover, a residue, because the person being called outturns around and asks, 'why am I what you are saying I am?'

> Althusser speaks only of the process of ideological interpellation through which the symbolic machine of ideology is 'internalized' into the ideological experience of Meaning and Truth: but... that this 'internalization', by structural necessity, never fully succeeds, that there is always a residue, a leftover, a stain of traumatic irrationality and senselessness sticking to it, and that this *left over, far from hindering the full submission of the subject to the ideological command, is the very condition of it*: it is precisely this non-integrated surplus of senseless traumatism which confers on the Law its unconditional authority: in other words, which—in so far as it escapes ideological sense—sustains what we might call the ideological *jouis-sense*, enjoyment-in-sense (enjoy-meant), proper to ideology. (Žižek 1989: 43–4, emphasis original)

These are the discursive considerations that frame my analysis of the film narratives and content for representation of Muslims. The questions being asked here pertain to assumptions regarding the attributes of society that are supposed to define the collective identity norms, the conventions and devices used to differentiate between identity markers—'us' and 'them', and the changing nature of the discourse regarding identities itself in relation to the political economy of culture.

FILM NARRATIVES REGARDING MUSLIM IDENTITY

Films included in this section of the chapter are popular Hindi films from among those that were released in a period of roughly two years between 2008 and 2010. This period is interesting because it saw many mainstream Hindi films with themes that spoke of Muslims and/or terrorism. For an easy categorization, I differentiated between the films that had the theme of terrorism woven into the plot, and other films in which there were Muslim protagonists but no references to terrorism. I selected films with their narratives placed in the contemporary context and times. Therefore, even though *Jodha Akbar* was also released in this period and has interesting references to Hindu–Muslim relationships in the historical context, I decided to exclude it.

* * *

Among the films with terrorism references, *Aagey Se Right* (Nattoji 2009) is unique in having a narrative that has a satirical and comedic take on various contemporary realities. For example, it makes a very astute and amusing comment on the corporatization of the 'underworld'. The film also makes interesting comments on several other issues, such as corruption in the corporate world, police, and bureaucracy. *Aagey Se Right* is a comedy of errors of a new Mumbai police recruit and a terrorist who lands on the Mumbai shoreline from Pakistan with a plan to engineer a bomb blast at a Mumbai Police function. Because the plot makes a fervent attempt at humour, it succumbs to exaggerated and stereotyped stock situations and stock characters.[3] The Pakistani terrorist and his bosses in Pakistan keep talking about *jang-e-azadi* (war for freedom), but never elaborate whose freedom (*azadi*), and how they zeroed in on a Mumbai Police event as the target which will ensure the attainment of their goal. The 'South Indian' gangster who invites him to collaborate in the blast is clear that it will help him establish his supremacy in the Mumbai underworld. While there is a parallel of Jai Singh inviting Babar to 'invade' India, the situations in the comedy never get really menacing. Within the first 15 minutes of the film, the terrorist renounces his mission after a 'love-at-first-sight' situation with a svelte bar dancer. The Mumbai 'Don' never quite becomes a 'traitor'; he too renounces his dream of reigning over the Mumbai underworld to tutor the terrorist on how best to pursue his love interest.

What is of interest for the present analysis is the film's take on the politics of language. The Don is a stock 'South Indian' character. He has no 'place'—we do not know where exactly in South India he is from, but he speaks in a Bollywood version of Mumbai *tapori*,[4] with a 'South Indian' accent. Right through the film, he delivers funny one-liners. His mission undergoes a change, but not his language. For the terrorist, on the other hand, only a change of heart is not enough. He must undergo many more changes. He begins by vocalizing the ferocious mission in chaste Persianized Urdu, and when caught staring at the bar dancer, he touches his ears in a gesture of reparation (*tauba*) and says, '*jang-e-azadi mein ye sab haraam hai...*' (All this is

---

[3] 'Stock' Situations and Stock Characters: Stock characters and situations are those that involve using stereotypes as a short hand to move the story forward in a cinematic narrative. Stock characters are remarkable for their lack of nuance and depth. Stock situations move the story forward because they can be read by the audience as a general comment characterizing a type of thing that happens in a type of situation to a kind of people, rather than a particular experience of a specific individual.

[4] *Tapori*: A Hindi dialect with Marathi words and slang, typically spoken in Hindi popular cinema by the Mumbai working class and underworld.

forbidden in the war for freedom), only to be reminded by the Don that '*haraam ke bad harem bhi kartey hein*' (*Harem* can be done after the forbidden). The Don is punning on the words *haraam* (forbidden) and *harem* alluding to the orientalist stereotype. Within the short span of the bar girl's performance, interrupted by a disturbance by another spectator and then an early closure by a police raid, the terrorist has undergone a complete change of heart. When everyone runs from the police, he miraculously acquires a burqa for disguise! In a scene resonating with reminiscences from *tawaif* (courtesan) films, he must stop the bar girl's auto to ask her what were the next lines of the interrupted song she was singing. Bhaskar and Allen (2009: 46) opine that,

> [T]he Islamicate idioms of the Muslim Courtesan film locate[s] the *tawaif* and her art forms and values in the historical imaginary of *nawabi* Lakhnawi culture, and conceive[s] the figure of the *tawaif* as a repository of social and cultural forms and values of this imagined world as they are expressed, and also transformed, in spaces other than Lucknow and in times other than [the] nineteenth century.

Thus, the narrative partially inhabits this imaginary space, and it is not surprising that in this transformation, the terrorist's interest in Urdu poetry surfaces.

Later he requests the Don to help him with winning his love who retorts at the poetry sprouting chap, '*Tum to maar kaat karo, tumko wahi shobha deta hai*' (you kill and maim, that alone suits you). On being pressed further, the Don relents and diagnoses the problem—which is that he speaks in Urdu! To make the transition from a terrorist to a lover, he must lose Urdu. This is a curious statement for a Mumbai film to make, where Urdu has long been the primary language for the expression of love. The identification of Urdu poetry with the expression of love is reiterated by the mastermind of the terror group in Pakistan, who regrets having sent a 'poet' for a 'job' such as this one. We can argue that even though Hindi and Urdu are identified as different languages with distinct scripts, it is still difficult to ascertain where one language starts and the other ends. The basic structure, the grammatical sensibilities, and even the vocabulary are shared to such an extent that a boundary between Urdu and Hindi is virtually non-existent. This fact is apparent even in this film which tries hard to label Urdu as the language only of Pakistan and the language of antiquity, and anti-modern, if not the language of terrorists. In one of the opening scenes, when the terrorist lands on the Mumbai shores, he asks the Don if the people accompanying him are loyal, using the word *wafadaar*, and the Don apparently not understanding the word because it is in Urdu replies in the negative. '*Wafadaar nahin*', he says, '*bharose ke hein*', using the word *bharosa* for trustworthiness. It would be difficult to argue which of these words, *wafadaar* and *bharosa* belongs more to Urdu and which to Hindi. Later, when the Don hands over a pistol to the terrorist, he says, '*Hifazat ka waastey*' (for protection), which is again an expression which traverses the non-existent Hindi–Urdu schism.

An important aspect in the film is that even though it indicates that terrorists are made not born, it articulates a hierarchy of intent behind acts of terror. If the intent is rooted in alleged 'Islamic fervour' as that of the terrorist—it is dangerous—portrayed through menacing and frightening body language, makeup, and costume. On the other hand, the intent of the South Indian Mafia Don planning an act of terrorism is shown to be merely criminal intent—portrayed as if it is a project of a bumbling fool.

The Muslim practice of purdah is represented as being rooted in an essentially patriarchal Islam. A Muslim woman's body that is cloaked by 'patriarchal' Islam is derided and resented, at once. Kay Kay, playing the terrorist, falls in love with a 'fallen woman' but he then has to immediately slip into the 'protective' possessive patriarchal role. Mixing patriarchy with terrorist violence, the terrorist mission is portrayed in historical terms as a 'Muslim' project by invoking the viewers' memory of Mughal king Akbar portrayed by Prithviraj Kapoor in *Mughal-E-Azam*. On hearing of Kay Kay's having forsaken the mission, his boss, the mastermind of the impending terror attack, vows to kill the bar girl and roars, '*Jang-e-azadi ki zamin par ek laundi ko naachne nahin denge*' (we will not let a servant girl dance on the land of war for freedom). *Laundi,* of course, is the epithet with which Akbar had derided Anarkali in *Mughal-E-Azam.*

Mumbai Meri Jaan (Kamat 2008) is a collage of stories of seven protagonists living their lives in different milieus in the aftermath of the 2006 bomb blasts in Mumbai. The film narrative reads like a complex comment on the impact of terror on everyday lives of people. It details how terror becomes almost a part of modern contemporary urban life. It also highlights the sensationalization and commodification of news, and its increasing inability to say anything meaningful about human existence. Rupali, a TV news reporter played by Soha Ali Khan realizes this only when her life is the one that is being commodified for the consumption of the masses. In the face of death and fear for life, Madhavan's character becomes aware of the increasing futility of his youthful nationalistic optimism. He is derided for being a 'proactive citizen' who cares for the environment and the phenomenon of the so-called brain drain, but by the end of the film when he is ready to revise his utopia, he must also confront his yearning for 'security', which seems to elude globalized spaces all over the world.

What comes through the dialogues of Paresh Rawal, who plays a police constable who is soon going to retire, is the sagacity of being an ordinary—inactive spectator because little else makes any sense. To a rookie police officer—Kadam, who is agitated at not being able to do anything of significance in life, he says, '*Tere man mein na ek art film chal raha hai ... Sirf picture dekhne ka, acting nahin karne ka ... Man ke ek kone mein kursi pakadne ka, aur picture dekhne ka ...*' (There is an art film running in your mind ... You must only watch it, don't start acting in it ... Prop a chair in a corner in your mind, and just watch the film). Here I am reminded of Žižek's take on Hollywood films, which according to him stage...

> a semblance of real life deprived of the weight and inertia of materiality—
> in the late capitalist consumerist society, *'real social life' itself somehow
> acquires the features of a staged fake,* with our neighbors behaving in
> 'real' life as stage actors and extras ... Again, the ultimate truth of the
> capitalist utilitarian de-spiritualized universe is the de-materialization of
> 'real life' itself, its reversal into a spectral show. (2002: 14)

But Rawal's advice for inaction extends to proactive inaction, which stretches into an explanation of the futility of retributive discourses of 'action and reaction'. It is this that is seen as having the ability to reason with the fanaticism of Hindu nationalism, which is portrayed as being reproduced in the life of Suresh, a computer hardware seller by bigoted narratives of a primordial *Akhand Bharat* (Unified India), and expressed in the everyday domestic sphere. This proactive inaction is also seen to be complimented by global capitalism. While the disruption of everyday life arouses in the police officer and Suresh the hysteria of impotence and paranoid scapegoating, respectively, it is the need for money to continue consumptive life that keeps them both from tipping over. Wads of notes are received by both with gratitude, and concerns of legality are brushed aside with a 'resourceful' logic of what is 'fair'. It is only fair to take bribes for letting illegal businesses operate or to use pirated software because these are making a lot of money in any case, and would continue regardless of one individual's position in the matter.

In a very interesting sequence in the film, Suresh and his friends are hanging out near a roadside tea stall. They are recounting the horrific scenes and devastation they witnessed in the aftermath of the bomb blast. While the friends talk, the camera focuses on Suresh who seems to be getting angrier with each description and stares ahead towards the deserted road. As if in answer to his prayer, an old man appears pulling his bicycle. He is wearing a *Lakhnavi* cap and sporting a white beard. Suresh begins to harass him, when the two policemen—Rawal and his rookie colleague appear on their bike. Rawal calls out to him *'kya ho raha hai?'* (what is happening?). Suresh is undaunted and says, *'Dekho saab kaun hai…'* (Look sir, who is here). The expression on his face is one of complete self-assurance. Rawal retorts, *'haan, toh?'*(Yes, so what?). The expression on Suresh's face now turns to one of surprise and incredulity. Clearly, he did not imagine that a Muslim could also be considered a citizen by a policeman who would actually act to protect him; rather Suresh assumed the complicity of the police in his harassment of a stranger for no reason but that he is a Muslim. In his surprise, Suresh forgets his original victim. He gets into a scuffle with Rawal and has to flee the scene after pushing him to the ground.

In another sequence, Suresh is convinced that Yusuf, who is also a regular at a restaurant where Suresh usually hangs out with his friends, is somehow involved in the bomb blasts. He decides to investigate himself and forces one of his friends to take him to Yusuf's house. Until this event, we have little idea where Suresh is from except that he sells computers and is not doing well in his occupation. At some point in their walk, the two friends reach a place where Suresh visibly winces, and hesitates to continue walking. Clearly, Suresh does not belong to the Mumbai slums. The camera zooms out and pans low, foregrounding a cage full of chickens presumably to signal that they have reached a Muslim neighbourhood. As they continue, the lanes become narrower and Suresh looks up and notices a minaret, but the area is so congested that the mosque itself is not visible. This, of course, is a sure shot sign that they are indeed inside a Muslim local-ity. Along the way, they hear the wafting lyrics of the nationalist film song 'Kar chale hum fida jano tan saathiyon/ab tumhare hawale watan saathiyon' (Having given our life and being, we leave, comrades/now the nation is in your custody, comrades) sung by Mohd Rafi. The song and exchange of words regarding the religious identity of the singer is fully frontal, and is obviously intended for the benefit of the viewer of the film. At Yusuf's house, they are met by his mother who is a warm and talkative woman. The way she is shown to talk of her son's habits and schedules only confirms Suresh's doubts. We know that the space in which this conversation is occurring is a 'Muslim space', because throughout the conversation the sound of the *azaan* is playing in the background.

Suresh and his friend manage to find Yusuf and follow him. They find that he meets a burqa clad figure and rides away on his motorbike. Suresh is convinced that the person in the burqa is a terrorist. The friend protests it's a woman, evidenced from the gait of the person. Suresh says in a totalizing sort of way, '*Woh log sarey seekh kar aatey hein...*' (these people are all trained for this). It turns out that the burqa clad figure is Yusuf's girlfriend, whom he is meeting clandestinely and taking to Haji Ali *dargah*. Here too the hatred and envy of the Hindu patriarchal viewpoint on considering Muslim patriarchy evidences itself. The friend is given the task of keeping an eye on the lovers, but gets bored soon because he cannot see much of the woman because of her burqa! Suresh chastises him and adds wryly, '*Ye log aise hi hein sab kuchh chupate phirte hein, ek hum hi log hein jo nange ghoomte hein ...*' (These people are like this, they keep hiding everything; it is we who go around naked ...). Why Yusuf and his girlfriend go to the dargah is not clear. Probably the filmmaker thought it important to keep Muslims in 'Muslim' spaces. Somehow in Hindi cinema, lives of Muslim people are spent in spaces that are characterized by their 'muslimness'. These spaces are different from secular spaces. Secular spaces in Bollywood formulation are where *everyone else* conducts their everyday lives and Muslims just pass through, standing out and being noticed for their Muslimness. This act of passing through is meant to bring discomfort and aversion to everyone, while, by standing out Muslims bring anxiety and humiliation unto themselves.

In the film *Amir* (Gupta 2008), the protagonist is a young Muslim doctor returning from London. The film makes an explicit statement that he is inconvenienced and harassed at the customs solely because of his name which is a marker of his Muslim identity. When he exits the airport, for inexplicable reasons, he is informed over the phone that he must follow the orders of a mysterious person, if he wants to see his family alive. Thus begins Dr Amir's journey to various 'Muslim spaces' in Mumbai that *even he is completely unfamiliar with*. The film is extremely fast paced like one in the thriller genre, and moves from one space to another in quick succession. Somehow the logic of this imposed tour of Muslim areas is to convince Dr Amir of the legitimacy of the terror project because of the socio-economic positioning of Muslims in these dark, dense, and derelict spaces. While in *Aagey Se Right* the binary between good Muslim and bad Muslim was internalized into the metamorphosis within an individual, *Amir* makes it more a real world contestation between two categories of people. But there is a third category of Muslims whom everyone talks of but who themselves are only pawns in carrying the story forward.

The Bad-Terrorist Muslim and the Good-Progressive Muslim are in a tight faceoff with each other in *Amir*, but the silent multitudes are represented to be inhabiting dark 'ghettos' not even been given place to relieve themselves (*hagne ki jagah bhi nahin dete...*), as told to Amir by his mysterious caller. It is these people and their existence that is portrayed as making the terrorists want to unleash their terror over the innocent world, but these people and their situation only makes the progressive Muslim throw up in disgust. Amir tries hard, he empathizes but all he wishes for is to go back to his 'normal' life with his friends where small inconveniences (at airports, for example), may be the only forms of discrimination that he faces. In an extremely tragic end to the film, while Amir chooses to kill himself rather than become part of perpetration of violence on others, he dies not as a sensitive, caring, responsible citizen, but as a failed suicide bomber because as a Muslim of any hue, he has no option or opportunity to redeem his image in the face of such predicament.

This is the reason why in the media formulation of 'moderate' Muslim, the 'progressive' Muslim must get rid of all or most signs of their Muslimness. 'The progressive Muslim' is heralded for not *looking like a Muslim*. S/he does not invoke her/his Muslim identity in casual conversations. S/he must display that Islam plays no role whatsoever in her/his everyday life or even in major decisions. In fact, if they renounce Islam totally or some key (but arbitrarily decided) feature of it, that is even better. But s/he must be ready to serve up Islamicate culture for consumption of the mainstream—serve *sivaiyan* on Eid, biryani and qorma on other festivals, and recite Urdu poetry, among others. They must appear very keen to castigate Muslim fundamentalism and especially move around with a 'not in our name'[5] placard in their hands all the time to be put up for display in 'secular spaces' as and when required. But the bottom line is that a Muslim is a Muslim.

---

[5] This is a pacifist political slogan usually used against their elected representatives/governments to protest justification of wars and acts of aggression against other sovereign states in the name of security of their citizens.

The Muslimness represented by symbolic costume or signifiers of space may be discarded by people in their quest for more convenient lives, free from day-to-day discrimination. This may earn them a label of 'progressive Muslims' and exclamation of how they do not look like Muslims at all, but when the chips are down, these things are of little relevance. I connect this discussion to the one in the earlier chapters, and I contend that the notion of 'Muslimness' is not limited to the physical or symbolic attributes of a person or a space, but is a function of being understood and portrayed in the mainstream discourses as a distinctive political community with common political interests and aims. Mushirul Hasan (2008), in his recent work titled *Moderate or Militant: Images of India's Muslims*, investigates these discourses regarding the 'Muslimness' in the political participation of Muslims, and refutes the charges of homogeneity of Indian Muslims' political interests. He further explicates,

> Put briefly, a decidedly elitist discourse should not be seen as reflective of Indian Muslims or their so-called communal consciousness. Nor can the politics of Muslim identity be reduced to a mere rationalization of normative Islamic discourse. There is much variation even within this elitist discourse, not all of which is focused on electoral representation, and still [shows] greater evidence of Muslim willingness to differ from rather than defer to the consensus of the community, however construed, in the rough and tumble of practical politics. (Hasan 2008: 73)

The construction of 'good Muslim' and dynamics of appeals to his understanding of, or his inherent complicity with, the cause of the bad 'terrorist Muslims' can be seen in other films such as *A Wednesday*, *New York*, *Kurbaan*, and *My Name Is Khan*. In *A Wednesday* (Pandey 2008), the protagonist played by Naseeruddin Shah is portrayed for the most part of the film as a Muslim terrorist working to secure the release of four dreaded criminals involved in various cases of terror. In the end, it is revealed that his real motive was to kill them rather than to get them released. It is in this moment that the film takes a frontal position of not divulging his real religious identity. Writing on 'encounters' (or extra-constitutional killings) in Hindi films,

Anustup Basu (2010: 185) says, 'A "good" follower of Islam is also, by differential measures, a figure of vice; if one acquires urban chic beyond that, one stops being "Muslim" altogether, no matter what one's identity is'. Basu is emphatic that even though, the body on the receiving end in an encounter is that of a Muslim, the narratives are often careful in stating that this is not an all out undeclared war by the Indian state against Muslims. The killing of a Muslim by the state is always represented as a stray, isolated incident. According to him, this feat is achieved by the presence of a Muslim assistant to the Hindu encounter specialist. In *A Wednesday*, the last terrorist is killed not by the bombs set up by Shah's *aam aadmi*, but shot simultaneously by a Hindu cop and a Muslim cop. Casting of these characters is interesting as the Hindu cop is portrayed by a Muslim actor Aamir Basheer, and the Muslim cop is played by Jimmy Shergill. The curious thing here is that the 'good Muslim' in this film is not playing the second fiddle. Jimmy Shergill is portrayed as an overzealous cop, who is not averse to illegal and extra-constitutional methods to punish those whom he deems to be in the wrong. A lot of footage in film is used to establish this representation of his character through his modus operandi in other unrelated cases. This is also noted in several reviews of the film. Several blogs called him ruthless, violent. He is described as a 'volatile cop' in a review by Taran Adarsh (2008). In another review which describes this character as 'hot-blooded and impulsive', the reviewer Rajiv Masand (2008) further states, 'It's Shergill who shines in this film with a performance that is measured and meticulous. It's the most "showy" of all roles in this film and the other actors allow Shergill to steal the film.' Basu posits that these killings or 'encounters' are built into the narrative of Hindi films as an opportunity to the 'good Muslim' character to redeem his status as that of a loyal patriot. My contention is that this is actually a fallacious situation in which while the patriotic sentiment can be proved by the Muslim cop with his involvement in a concrete act of extra-constitutional killing, but the *killing itself* proves the Muslim character true to the stereotype of Muslims bearing volatile and impulsive personas, and not being averse to violence and killings.

In a long speech regarding his aims and motivations, Shah claims that he is an *aam aadmi* (common man) who is simply fed up of living a life constantly threatened by terrorists. Here Shah uses the analogy of 'cockroaches' for terrorists as infiltrators, who have 'invaded' and 'polluted' his 'home', and thus must be killed. The fascist analogy is tellingly similar to the one employed by the present-day anti-Muslim right and Neo-Nazis all over Europe, and by Sangh groups in India. The seamless collusion of everyone involved in the extra-constitutional killing of the last terrorist is a reminder of the discussion of Muslims as *homines sacri* earlier in this book.

New York (Khan 2009) has two 'good' Muslims Omar and Roshan. While Roshan is an FBI agent, he targets Omar for his friendship in the past with Sameer, who is suspected to be an operative of a terrorist group. The 'bad Muslim' in *New York* in fact is also a 'good Muslim' when the narrative begins, because as a student on the New York State University campus he has hardly any markers of religious identity on his person or in his outlook. The narrative in fact has a clichéd college life track of the protagonists, which serves to establish that Sameer is completely oblivious to his Muslim identity. The character's name, which is also ambiguous to identity naming goes great lengths to establish this. In *Kurbaan* (D'Silva 2009), even though the 'good Muslim' Riaz is not a cop, yet he does not find it too difficult to *shoot to kill* the 'bad Muslim' Ehsaan, when it comes to proving his good-ness. The message clearly is that all Muslims are prone to violence, and it is just a matter of when, and what triggers it. The symbolism of Shah Rukh Khan's character, Rizwan Khan, in *My Name Is Khan* (Johar 2010) as a person with 'disability' indicates that your 'regular', 'normal' everyday Muslim is, somehow, always complicit and thus, cannot be completely innocent.

I argue that Rizwan Khan having Asperger syndrome is part of the larger metaphor for being a misfit in the world of 'normal' people. The film's narrative engages in a fantasy of a Muslim being able to say 'I'm not a terrorist', similar to mentally ill persons being able to communicate to the 'normal' world that they are not lunatics. The allegations of 'madness' of an autistic person and 'unreason' of a Muslim are not completely disconnected. When Foucault (1973) challenged the formulation of 'madness' as 'mental illness', he was essentially challenging the use of this formulation as a legitimate reason for separating people 'displaying' signs of madness from the larger society. He was also indicating a breakdown of communication between 'mad' and 'sane' persons that was contingent upon acceptance of inexact and non-uniform language rules. Thus, 'mad' persons, now separated in asylums, cannot 'speak', because their language has been taken away from them, and we are left with only what Foucault calls a 'monologue' about madness. He does not dispute the existence of difference, but strikes at the logic of difference as moral error and unreason. The social forces that see the reason to confine the unreason of madness in order to control it are the same, in Foucault's (1973) view, as those seeking to control and regulate the other 'undesirables'. The differences of belief, behaviour, or appearance from the 'norm' can get any group tagged as 'undesirable', and this tagging may be utilized to control, regulate, or get rid of these.

Rizwan Khan is a curious character also because of his unmistakable 'Muslimness'. Rizwan is spiritually and emotionally attached to the scripture which he frequently recites unabashedly in situations where most Muslims would hesitate today—at the airport when he is apprehended after suspicion, and at a memorial service for 9/11 victims. He possesses a deep understanding of Islamic symbols—he carries three pebbles in his hands which he uses to hit at a hatemongering cleric in a mosque, just as devout Muslims hit Satan with three pebbles in a symbolic ritual during Haj. And he is able to challenge being tagged as an 'undesirable' successfully and 'speak' about his position as *a Muslim but not a terrorist* (literally, with US President Obama in the film). What makes this film a fantasy is that this cannot be done in reality within the original precepts of the debate that assumes the 'truth' of some predefined 'norms'. That Rizwan Khan is able to claim liberty in the film as an autistic person with his wife and with the State is a fantasy which can be made believable, only if Rizwan Khan is portrayed as having some extraordinary capacity that makes him unaware of the normalizing discourse (Tortured in an extremely cold room, he offers to repair the air conditioning). To make Rizwan appear a 'good Muslim', *My Name Is Khan* does not make him strip off or dilute his identity. Because his Muslim identity includes a pre-enacted judgement, autism or Asperger syndrome has to be added to it.

* * *

Among the films that were selected for this analysis because they had a Muslim protagonist but no reference to terrorism, I begin with *Aaloo Chaat* (Grewal 2009). In the film, Nikhil (played by Aftab Shivdasani) has just returned from America, and loves a Muslim girl Aamna. His Punjabi family lives in Lajpat Nagar, and came to Delhi as refugees after Partition. Right in beginning of the film, it is made known to the viewers that for the family, '*Batware ke zakhm bharey nahin hein*' (the wounds of Partition have not healed). He dare not tell anyone in the family that he wants to marry a Muslim girl. Nikhil can only tell his secret to an 'uncle' and ask for help. This is interesting because the uncle is a *hakeem*, who treats persons with sexual dysfunctions and is thus, privy to numerous confessions regarding another taboo topic. The film employs the character of the hakeem to present jokes with double meaning alluding to sex. But the character also serves as a device to indicate that a Hindu boy's wish to marry a Muslim girl is an 'unnatural' wish, as much taboo as talking about sexual dysfunction. The film's narrative moves forward using racist and cultural stereotypes, even though on the issue of religious communalism it tries hard to maintain a progressive stance. While Nikhil's parents still have no knowledge of his intensions, they set up a match-making meeting, with a girl and her parents. The families are obviously well acquainted with each other because when Nikhil's father asks the girl's father about someone, he replies, '*chachaji se koi relation nahin... Bete ki intercaste marriage jo ki hai*' (we have no relations with uncle... They got their son into an intercaste marriage), to which Nikhil's father says, '*matlab first class ticket hai par second class mein ghus rahe hein... Gori larki se shadi karta to ek darja upar to chadh jaata*' (So they had a first class ticket but are entering second class... Had he married a white girl he would have climbed one step up in status).

Inspired by *Dilwale Dulhania Le Jayenge* (Chopra 1995), Nikhil and his uncle hatch a plan of telling his parents that he wants to marry a white American girl, but call Aamna also to come home so that she may endear herself to Nikhil's parents, by her supposed cultural superiority compared to an American girl. The narrative constantly runs into and gets entangled in a complex matrix of superiority and inferiority. A white-skinned person is claimed superior to a brown and Indian person, but Indian culture is proclaimed as superior to Western culture. Still, for the family, marrying a white girl is seen as a symbol of social advancement. There is also an underlying anxiety regarding the changes in contemporary Indian society and the world, but the family does not wish to come across as anti-modern. Amidst all these anxieties, the anxiety of Aamna's identity in the everyday life of the family is dealt with by her willingness to be assimilated into the culture of the Hindu Punjabi family of Nikhil. Cooking their kind of food, singing Punjabi folk songs at a wedding function—Aamna is a perfect potential daughter-in-law bearing no reference to her real identity, except her name. In the film's narrative, there is no mention of where Aamna hails from or where her family is. Even when Nikhil's family comes to know of the truth in the end, no one bothers to enquire of Aamna's family and their views on the match. It is eminently convenient that Aamna is without a place and family.

This is typical of the patriarchal norms of Indian society where in interreligious marriages, the rarity that they are, it is the woman who invariably converts because of her subordinated position. While in reality there is enough reason to believe that interreligious marriages in which Hindu women marry Muslim men also exist just as vice versa, in Hindi cinema interreligious marriages are always between Hindu men and Muslim women. Sunil Menon (2012) says, '[t]he society of idealised Indian types on screen, thus, came about through exogamous marriage, in its virilocal form—the men stay where they are, the women move, shedding their origins, their language', and their religion, I may add.

The issue of inferiority of Muslims and undesirability of a Hindu–Muslim marriage is not addressed directly but resolved in a strange hierarchy of all kinds of crises posited in front of this family by modern times. Alluding to the 'worse' scenario of the son declaring himself to be gay, Hakeem sahab says, '*aaj kal ki duniya mein isse achchhi khabar hi samjho…* America *se ladka bhi laa sakta tha*' (consider this good news in today's world… He could have also brought a boy from America).

3 Idiots (Hirani 2009) is a comment on the education system, attitudes towards learning, and factors determining career choices. The protagonists are three friends who are classmates in an engineering college, college each contesting his own demons of the past, family expectations and responsibilities. Of interest in this analysis is the fact that like Aamna in *Aaloo Chaat*, Farhan Qureshi is also 'placeless' and shows no signs of the stereotypical 'Muslimness' in his personality and mannerism. But while Aamna's religious identity was a pivot to the narrative, Farhan's religious identity is not invoked anywhere in any manner in the film. Neither does the film raise any questions or issues that are of special or specific interest to Muslims. When the three friends visit his house twice, we look for any signs of the space being inhabited by Muslims. Even Farhan's parents do not express their anxiety regarding their son's education or career prospects vis-à-vis their identity. *3 Idiots* is probably one of the few films, one of whose key characters is a Muslim, yet only happens to be a Muslim. This is a deviation from the normal course of things in Hindi cinema, where a character is Muslim only when his/her Muslimness is of some consequence to the narrative. Alternatively, a Muslim character is sometimes inserted as a tokenism for diversity, even when he/she is not required to take the narrative forward. But this tokenism is also centred on the Muslim identity as a marker of difference. Since Farhan is neither in this film, his character pays by not being fleshed out as well as that of the third friend Raju. The film narrative contains a lot of information about the two other friends—Rancho and Raju who have their own story tracks—but hardly anything about Farhan, except a brief reference to Farhan's father's expectations, and the sacrifices he has made. Perhaps an acquaintance with Farhan at this level could not have been achieved without invoking some reference to the family's identity.

Delhi-6 (Mehra 2009) is another film that engages in some fantasizing just like *My Name Is Khan*, though it is not so much about Muslim identity per se. *Delhi-6* belongs to an older genre of films, namely Hindu–Muslim or communal relations in India. It is essentially an optimistic romanticized look at an imagined 'Indianness' from the unique perspective of its protagonist, who straddles many binaries without taking sides. Roshan, played by Abhishek Bachchan, is both Hindu and Muslim, he is both traditionalist and modern, and he is an Indian and an American. *Delhi-6* portrays the Old Delhi in contemporary times that is lurching towards a modern consumptive milieu, yet is held back by its rootedness in the old. The tussle is bound to give rise to trauma. An important feature of the film is that its narrative upsets the stereotype of Old Delhi as a Muslim locality. It meticulously shows the culture of the Hindu *Dilliwallah*s but portrays at least two generations of both Muslim and Hindu residents of the walled city as having been 'left-behind'. Both in their tradition and in their yearning for modernity, the characters that inhabit Old Delhi strike Roshan's sensibilities as 'unreal'. The film portrays the fantasmic *Kala Bandar* (black monkey) as the metaphor for communalism calling it a 'beastly' feeling. In the film (but also in reality, a couple of years before the release of the film), Kala Bandar is an urban myth spawned by rumours and outlandish media coverage—a hysterical reaction of people, caught in the demands of modernity but living in antiquity, who do not quite know which is which (Singh 2001). The film builds up to tension between Hindus and Muslims in the walled city that in reality has not seen any riots since after the partition of the country, and the horrific killings and looting in its wake. The appearance of the black monkey from the imaginary to the 'impossible real' can be interpreted in the Lacanian fashion, in a way, as a desire which is brought forth by naming it (Lacan 1991). Roshan, who chastised the Dilliwallahs to 'get real', in the end becomes the Kala Bandar, perhaps because, the myth of the Kala Bandar needed to acquire a material persona to be destroyed.

Whether in their portrayal of Muslims as terrorists, as loyal cops, or progressive 'good Muslims', the representation of Muslims in Bollywood films remains mired in the dominant discourse. This is true when the film narrative just echoes the dominant monologue. But even when the characters genuinely try to break the mould, they either end up being impetuous, interrupted, or mere apparitions. This is a reflective of the shatter-proof nature of the limits that form boundaries of the segregated spaces. While the nature of segregated spaces may change or vary between spaces, the logic and fact of segregation does not. Segregation is cast in the same mould—discursively, culturally, and spatially.

THE INDUSTRIALIZED MASS MEDIA

One way to see the preceding discussion is to understand how Bollywood cinema not only attempts to remodel the 'realities' it claims to represent, but also attempts to often frontally convey to viewers that a representation is 'real'. Muslims have been an intrinsic part of Hindi (Hindustani and Urdu included) cinema. This is also the cinema that hardly ever breaks the mould of dominant discourses, and gives expression to these. Fredrick Jameson (1979) acknowledges a tendency in academia to study popular and mass media as an exalted form of media, because it is thought to be the one that speaks to and is 'understood' by a vast multitude. On the other hand, the Frankfurt school, especially Horkheimer and Adorno (2007 [1972]) also advocate the study of media culture of the same stream, but stigmatize it by calling it 'culture industry'. Jameson points to the usefulness of the Frankfurt school's methods and their view of 'instrumentality' of culture. He elaborates how in contemporary times, because of a 'universal commodification of labour power', all forms of occupations which used to have different and distinct end uses are now suspended into different activities which are geared towards one end only, which is to become more and more effective (1979: 130). Thus, journalism or filmmaking, like agriculture or pottery or any other activity, are no longer about their unique end, rather all of these activities are now just means for a universal valuation in terms of money. He poignantly puts an example illustrating this process thus:

> The objects of the commodity world of capitalism also shed their independent 'being' and intrinsic qualities and come to be so many instruments of commodity satisfaction: the familiar example is that of tourism—the American tourist no longer lets the landscape 'be in its being' as Heidegger would have said, but takes a snapshot of it, thereby graphically transforming space into its own material image. The concrete activity of looking at a landscape—including, no doubt, the disquieting bewilderment with the activity itself, the anxiety that must arise when human beings, confronting the non-human, wonder what they are doing there and what the point or purpose of such a confrontation might be in the first place—is thus comfortably replaced by the act of taking possession of it and converting it into a form of personal property. (Jameson 1979: 131)

Most important in this quote is the 'image' which, according to Guy Debord (1983, cf. Jameson 1979), is the ultimate form of commodity reification. As discussed earlier, we consume not so much a commodity but *the image*—of us consuming the said commodity conveyed to us by advertising. Jameson (1979) uses the example of consuming popular pulp literature like detective stories that are read only for their 'end', to illustrate the supremacy in the contemporary world given to 'the end' compared to 'the value' that could be inherent in a non-commodified activity. It is in this light that Jameson asserts that 'popular' as opposed to 'high culture' does not exist any longer in the same way as it did when there clearly was a creation of organic 'popular' in unified social groups that were culturally specific like peasants or a medieval city, among others. It has been replaced by a new commodified industrial mass culture.

As far as the representation of Muslims is concerned, cinema and news media thus churn out 'commodity' images of Muslims distorted by their profit driven agenda, and the same are 'consumed' by the viewers who do not question their position in this industrialized mass media. The 'popularity' of a film, measured quantitatively by the box office collection, is ultimately about profit. The formulaic films that were loath to experiment, and the present day Bollywood with its claims of 'fresh' stories, look, and approach in a film, are both measured by the money the film makes. Efficiency may demand different means but the instrumental end remains the same. Similarly, a TV show continues to be judged for its popularity by its TRP (television rating point) and a newspaper by its circulation, and so on. This is also because as a discourse gains currency, its hegemonizing potential also increases. Hegemonic discourses that fall out of favour (reduced 'popularity') due to demands of being politically correct thus have to rehash themselves so as to appear to have undergone a transformation. While Bollywood cinema is understood to be only a re-presentation of reality, people trust the news media to give them truthful accounts of events.

I alert myself to Edward Said's (1998) cautionary discussion of orientalism, and how media images distorted by it continue to be presented as authentic and believed by the viewers also to be the same. In this regard, continuing from the story of built spaces in Jamia Nagar in Chapter 2, and drawing on the discussion on the representation of Muslim identity and Muslim localities, I take up an example of reportage in the print news media to analyse and illustrate the instrumentality of representation in the media. Within this frame of reference, I invoke the usefulness of conceptual frameworks in media studies, such as the agenda-setting theory and cultivation theory (West and Turner 2007). Both these frameworks point to repeated news coverage so that an issue assumes importance; also that the repeated messages within an agenda cultivate in people's minds a given viewpoint (Severin and Tankard 2000). Van Dijk (1991) also discusses the role of the media in prioritizing which news is worthy of public attention, and also in 'suggesting' rather emphatically what views people must adopt in discussions so propped up. George Gerbner, who along with his team of researchers pioneered the development of the cultivation theory, found the more time people were exposed to a particular view on television, the more their perceptions and attitudes were affected (Gerbner et al. 1994). The agenda-setting theory also has a conception of 'gatekeepers' in the news media, who decide what finally makes the news, in what sequence, and with how much priority (McCombs and Shaw 1972).

PRINT NEWS MEDIA: REPORTAGE ON TERROR

On the evening of 13 September 2008, five bomb blasts at different locations rocked Delhi. The death toll reported by the police was 20, though some newspapers reported that in all 30 people had died—some succumbing to their injuries later. On the morning of 19 September 2008, the Delhi police raided a flat in a building numbered L-18 in Batla House, Jamia Nagar. Two boys alleged to be terrorists who made and planted the bombs were killed in an 'encounter', two others were arrested, while according to media reports, one 'managed to escape'. One inspector, Mohan Chandra Sharma, received bullet wounds and died later in hospital due to a heart attack induced by excessive bleeding. Sharma who had killed 35 terror suspects in his career, was hailed by the media as 'brave heart' (Singh 2008) and 'winner of 75 odd-encounters' (Sengupta et al. 2008). His exploits as an 'encounter specialist' had received state recognition in his 150 medals and four gallantry awards.

The boys who were killed or arrested were students of Jamia Millia Islamia, almost all aspiring to be computer professionals, and studying or getting trained for the same. More arrests followed and the same trend was seen. Newspapers went agog with stories with details of the courses they were studying, their hometowns, and conditions in which they lived (*Hindustan Times*, 21 and 22 September 2008). Prominent space was given to minute details of the interactions of the alleged terrorists before and after the blasts—including the jokes they allegedly cracked amongst themselves. *The Times of India* and *Hindustan Times* (22 September 2008) printed photographs of the arrested suspects with their faces covered in red *kafiyeh* scarves that were originally used by Arab men to cover their head and are popular among Muslims all over the world.

The newspapers also carried many stories giving details of an intricate network of spaces from different neighbourhoods within Jamia

Nagar and Sangam Vihar in Delhi to Mumbra and Cheetah Camp in Mumbai, and Sanjarpur village in Azamgarh (*Hindustan Times,* 24 September 2008; *Times of India,* 25 and 29 September 2008). The group was linked to blasts in Mumbai, Hyderabad, Bangalore, Varanasi, and a failed attempt at Surat. The university—Jamia Millia Islamia was portrayed as having a link with all these 'operatives'. Police rounded this off with claims, at first that the money came from 'a gulf country', and later mentioning Western Union transfers from Riyadh. There were also many reports that dwelled on the fact that many of these 'terrorists' were educated, techno-savvy individuals (Tripathy 2008). They were represented as consciously creating and being affected by their own history. Their connection with larger political processes and the material logic of their condition was often brought into the picture to legitimize prejudice against all Muslims. Their religiosity was also brought into the picture as an explanation of their 'irrational attitudes' and 'dangerous behaviour'.

The contradiction here is that detrimental material socio-economic conditions and violent oppression of Muslims in various parts of the country was invoked as a cause for 'Islamic terrorism' in these discourses. Not a single story questioned why, if such deep rooted oppression is being faced by Muslims, there are no stories in the media reporting the same. Both the cautious educated progressive Muslim and the supposedly more volatile, orthodox backward illiterate Muslim were portrayed in the media as drifting into terrorism, as an act of resistance to this oppression, which had gone largely unreported. There were also sporadic stories (Khan 2008) regarding the Muslim discomfort and dismay at being portrayed thus but these were also written in a way that made their discomfort also sound suspicious. Broadly, the contemporary media discourses ascribe to the *entire community* conscious complicity with acts of terrorism of some Muslims.

Findings of the Sachar Committee report were also used to legiti-mize the (seemingly benign) reasoning that acute deprivation and communal attacks/violence are potentially potent enough causes to turn Muslims into terrorists. Following this logic, it was thus only reasonable that we suspect all Muslims as potential terrorists. This logic was bought by even those Muslims who are well-to-do, are not poor, do not live in ghettos. They found it easy to believe that poverty, deprivation, and ghetto living are conditions enough to turn Muslims into 'Islamist terrorists'. I reproduce one such feature article (Nomani 2008) that appeared in the *Los Angeles Times* and has been quoted in numerous academic and journalistic writings since then.

The Sachar committee report recommended creating a commission to remedy the systemic discrimination and promote affirmative-action programs. So far, very few of the recommendations have been put in place.

Since reading the report, I have feared that Islamic militancy would be born out of such despair. Even if last week's terrorist plot was hatched outside India, a cycle of sectarian violence could break out in the country and push some disenfranchised Muslim youth to join militant groups using hot-button issues like Israel and Kashmir as inspiration.

What has irked me these last years is how the world has glossed over India's problems. In 2006, for instance, former U.S. Defense Secretary William Cohen, whose Cohen Group invests heavily in India, said the U.S. and India were 'perfect partners' because of their 'multiethnic and secular democracies'. When I asked to interview Cohen about the socioeconomic condition of Muslims, his public relations staffer said that conversation was too 'in the weeds'. But, to me, the condition of Muslims needs frank and open discussion if there is to be any hope of stemming Islamic radicalism and realizing true secular democracy in the country.

India's 150 million Muslims represent the second-largest Muslim population in the world, smaller only than Indonesia's 190 million Muslims. That is just bigger than Pakistan's 140 million Muslims or the entire population of Arab Muslims, which numbers about 140 million. U.S. intelligence reports continually warn that economic, social and political discontent are catalysts for radicalism, so we would be naive to continue to ignore this potential threat to the national security of not just India but the United States.

Throughout my 2006 journey, I found the idea of India's potential for danger unavoidable. On one leg, my son tucked safely in bed with

my mother in our Taj hotel room, I went out to watch the filming of
A Mighty Heart, the movie about the murder of Wall Street Journal
reporter Daniel Pearl by Muslim militants in Pakistan. When the
location scouts needed to replicate the treacherous streets of Karachi's
militant Islamist culture, they didn't have to go far. They found the
perfect spot in a poor Muslim neighborhood of Mumbai.

I also reproduce extracts from other articles that attempt to understand the root cause of alleged 'Muslim terrorism'.

> That was the essence of SIMI. They didn't feel they belonged to India,
> or any one country, but to the global Islamic community. Their lives
> were ruled not by the Indian Constitution, but by the Quran. The fact
> that they lived in a country overwhelmingly populated by non-Muslims
> only strengthened their resolve to convert it into an Islamic State. Living
> in harmony with the non-Muslim majority, as their community had
> for centuries, meant abdicating their religious duty as Muslims. If, in
> working towards an Islamic state, they offended the sensibilities of the
> majority community or broke a law or two, so be it. The latter were kafirs
> anyway. (Punwani 2008)

In another article about Azamgarh, the writer refers to Shibli College
as being ineffective in combating 'Muslim backwardness'.

> Anil Gaur, a lawyer in Azamgarh district court, traces the spiralling
> crime to the administrative neglect. Muslims are vulnerable due to their
> economic and educational backwardness, despite the presence of Shibli
> College run by the minority community, which had secular credentials.
> Terror outfits are now trying to cash in on their ambitions and energy
> that lie largely untapped. (Mishra 2008)

Yet another article combines the techno-savvy image of the terrorist with the image of the 'boys-who-saw-their-relatives-raped-and-
murdered':

> Since terrorists are increasingly becoming tech-savvy and writing emails
> in perfect English, the theory that deprivation alone breeds terror does
> not apply any longer. Eminent journalist M J Akbar, in a recent column,
> beautifully explained the trend: 'The email (of the Indian Mujahideen

sent a few hours before the Ahmedabad blasts) destroys the subliminal connect we make between terror and deprivation. This is the work of someone who speaks English and therefore must be educated.' The terror outfits' increasing use of cyberspace (succinctly called a 'virtual caliphate') to spread the word is another disturbing reiteration of the fact.

Nothing makes a terror group's task easier than a deep alienation and a sense of victimhood among a section of the educated youth. Scholars point out that this alienation has steadily taken place owing to a stream of political events, beginning with the destruction of the Babri masjid and the subsequent Mumbai riots to the Gujarat pogrom of 2002. 'Those boys who witnessed the rape and murder of their relatives in the post-Godhra pogrom have now grown up. They are seething with anger and want to avenge the riots. Some of them could have been recruited by the terrorists,' admits Vadodara's scholar–activist J S Bandukwala. 'I have been appealing to the Hindus of Gujarat to publicly apologise for the genocide. This will help initiate a process of reconciliation.' (Wajihuddin 2008)

These articles get space not for their incisive journalism on discrimination and violence faced by Muslims, but for using the fact of this discrimination to imply that all Muslims are either potential terrorists or sympathizers. In my discussions with Muslim individuals from different classes and localities in Delhi, I observed that the sense of persecution that Muslims feel is more like a burden that they are keen to get rid of. The truth is that Muslims have far too much at stake, and terrorism—even as a desperate act—provides no way out of the deplorable conditions of existence. As shown in the earlier chapters, the conditions are made bearable by the efforts and contestations of people themselves.

The reproduction of the image of the Muslim community *as an entirety*, complicit in the terrorizing designs of the extremist outfits, is also a reproduction of an orientalist image of Muslims across the world. Like all other hegemonizing orientalist images, it is nothing but a part of the simulacrum in which the images are reproduced mechanically and repeatedly, while no original of the image exists. It is in Baudrillard's sense that the media (especially, the news media) has itself become a simulacrum, in which situations devoid of meaning are continually simulated and nothing is sacred—least of all the life of a member of an 'undesirable' group. But that makes a Muslim life profane and a Muslim body *homo sacer* in a process that voids and profanes other realities too. In such a commodified media, all reality is reified and no one can be sure what a thing means. After the Western world had watched 24×7 footage of the Gulf war, when Baudrillard (1995) questioned whether the 'war' had actually taken place, he was not deluded as much as he was questioning the meaning of the concept behind the word 'war'—whether the overwhelmingly one-sided and overpowering US aggression in Kuwait and Iraq could be called a 'war'. What the Indian media uncritically calls 'encounter' is not a case of a rose by another name. It is rather a case of truth being replaced by appearances repeatedly till all involved forget what the original looks like. Following Baudrillard's methods, I assert that while the Sachar Committee report becomes useful to justify the allegation of complicity of all Muslims in the so-called Islamic Terrorism, it is reduced to a pataphysical document (Bök 2001), because it is never used for purposes towards amelioration of Muslims; rather in an absurd (sinister?) twist to its intended meaning, it is used to eliminate the very need for amelioration of the Muslim population.

The stigmatization of Muslim neighbourhoods in Delhi as harbouring criminals and 'new age techno-savvy terrorists' has served to contain and control the Muslim youth that was finding space in computer-related professions. Jamia Nagar neighbourhoods that were being gentrified as middle-class neighbourhoods that gathered their own resources wherever possible, especially housing, were painted as hubs of illegal activities and irrational people. This is evidenced in an affidavit filed by an SHO (Station House Officer) of Jamia Nagar Police station during hearings of a case on unauthorized construction in June 2012.

> Highly sensitive from the point of view of law and order; residents have scant regard for the government and especially police; tendency to over-react and indulge in confrontation after getting united on communal lines; more volatile situation after Batla House encounter... Majority of the people are illiterate or semi-literate and they have scant regard for

the government, particularly the police. They have tendency to over-react and indulge in confrontation with government agencies even on petty issues.

The incident and the contents of the affidavit were reported in the *Indian Express* (Anand 2012). The article further reports that,

> This affidavit left Justice Kohli incensed. She described the comments against the minority community as 'uncalled for and without any cogent basis'.... The judge also refused to accept this affidavit saying this was not filed in terms of the court order. 'There are areas like Pandav Nagar, Govindpuri, Seelampur where residents belong to one community. How can the police have a different take on only Jamia Nagar?' it observed.

As this last report demonstrates there was, in 2012, a beginning in some parts of the news media (both print and electronic) to enthu-siastically report and question some instances of discrimination against Muslims, especially their persecution by law enforcement agencies. I posit that it is the material conditions of the position-ing of the specialized workforce in the Muslim areas that have probably given rise to this counter-trend in the media. Given the ideal–exploitative positioning of Muslim neighbourhoods in the network of relationships of production, it was hoped by scholars that that the communal conflict may not play out in future as was possible in the not so distant past, and that would prevent the kind of open instances of violence and riots that have destroyed trades that flourished among Muslims in Meerut, Moradabad, Aligarh, and Bhagalpur. We have seen in the last chapter that the most recent threat that happened was actually in Delhi at Seelampur, during the sealing drive against businesses and industrial units in residential areas by the Delhi government, in keeping with its urban plan vision of no mixed land use. I contend that, unfortunately, since these exploitative relationships of production are maintained to a great extent by the threat of communal and state violence, it would be wishful thinking that the outcome of the process would automati-cally root out its own foundation. It would be also useful in future enquiries to consider whether it also because of the onset of this curious change in the relationships of production, that we are encountering in academia the discourses that explain segregation of Muslims in certain neighbourhoods as being practiced voluntarily in an attempt to maintain their cultural distinction.

This chapter may be brought to a close by reiterating that Muslims are continually represented such that their own voices are silenced by the most outrageous claims handed out as the truth by industrialized media in the age of commodified culture and global capitalism. Indeed, what the entire discussion in this chapter clears is that the assertion that identities have a material function is not just an abstract theoretical position. In the context of the media industry, 'identity' is clearly ploughed to garner and accumulate profits. When cinema 'strives' to and the news media 'claims' to depict and report, respectively, the 'reality', it also becomes possible, according to Jameson (1992) to 'read' the 'symbolic solutions' being offered in the narrative. It is this that would enable the Muslims to re-imagine a form of resistance that will allow them to break the confines of their status as the new sub-proletariat of the urban.

In the last chapter, I charted out the traditional forms of resistance and claim-making that are available to other oppressed classes, but have been made unavailable to Muslims because of their unique positionality in the global capitalist economy and the practices of governmentality. In this chapter, I explored how the dominant discourses not only essentialize the aspersed identity, but also utilize this to rationalize the oppressive material conditions, and thereby accumulate more capital. In the next chapter, I take up an exercise in faith and optimism and explore how Muslims in Delhi have created spaces from which they may draw hope for emancipation.

Counter-Discourses

CHAPTER FIVE

Avenues of Hope and Optimism

. . . .

So far, I have described the material conditions that perpetuate and sustain prejudice against Muslims in Delhi, and how cultural industrialization as well as exploitative relations of production and accumulation 'produce' segregated Muslim neighbourhoods. I have also discussed how the familiar methods of resistance, protest, and claim-making that are accessed by other marginalized and subaltern groups like tribals, dalits, and LGBT (lesbian, gay, bisexual, and transgender) are unavailable to Muslims due to their peculiar and precarious position in globalized capitalist urban spaces. As norma-tive non-citizens, and *homines sacri*, they find themselves included in the political community only for exclusion and elimination. Their representation in dominant discourses of mass media as vessels of irrational, anti-modern, aggressive/violent ideology, plague and haunt almost all their endeavours. Admittedly, this does look like a picture where Muslims are doomed to flounder from one *faux pas* to another—some fatal, some humiliating, and others just gaffes of people caught in an absurdist modern conjecture. Clearly, there is a need to look for those spaces where, somehow, the contradictory logic of total dominance and the willingness of people to let them be defined by the symbolic markers of the same give way. Towards the end of the book, I employ the overarching framework in this chapter to explicitly examine the avenues that are sources of hope and optimism for the people who participated in this study.

Orthodox readings of Marxism have often charged that it is a unified position that aims at totalizing explanations. There has not been a worse misreading of any concept which has been as prevalent as this. Marxism is not above the historical processes that it seeks to understand, and it can hardly be accused to be a framework that has been static. From Foucault, Derrida, Gramsci, Althusser, Horkheimer, Benjamin, Lefebvre, Harvey, Jameson, and Žižek, the influence of Marxism and its own metamorphosis has been phenomenal (Daly 2006). On its own, but even when it infuses any other perspective, Marxism has a way of filling the view with deep insights, passion, and hope. Critical theory enters at a point when finding ways to resist the complete commodification by late capitalism becomes an imperative. With an insight into their experiences, I embrace critical theory's call for critical engagement, but refuse to share its enthusiasm for 'doomed' prophesies. While doing this, I am keenly aware of the deep prevalence of capitalist commodification of all forms of life. Be that as it may, this section has been not written as if there are some spaces that are immune to or even unrelated to the logic of capital accumulation. What is being evidenced here is that 'everything is pregnant with its contrary' (Marx 1978 [1856]: 577). What gives hope is that the hegemonic narratives are not seamless and that within them, people spawn their own counter narratives. They interpret their realities and respond to them in a way that may not amount to total liberation from all forms of subjugation and prejudice, but signal anticipation of definite amelioration.

Later in this chapter, I also deliberate on those avenues that have not yet been explored, but have an immense theoretical potential to assume such a position.

EDUCATION AND SOLIDARITY: A COMMUNITY HELPS ITSELF

Throughout my ethnographic fieldwork, a most striking attitudinal change that I observed was that *every single* participant of this study, without any exceptions, stressed that it is important for Muslims to get educated. This is a far cry from the laments heard around 10–12 years ago among Muslims—'what's the good of getting an education; it's not as if a job is waiting for us'. The examples that I recount in this section are representative of the intent and aspiration for education among Muslims in Delhi. These must be read with a caveat that these are avenues that help people keep their hope up in a larger reality, where the provision for education for Muslims made by the government educational institutions, and arrangements made by the members of the community themselves fall woefully short of the need. In most circumstances, it was a scenario in which the system made it easier for the young students to fail in their quest for education. The purpose of this exercise would be achieved if it can serve as an inspiration for improvement within the existing institutions, and initiation of new spaces where education can be fostered.

Mr Mohd Sadiq is an autorickshaw driver who lives in Jaffarabad. He can barely write his own name when a signature is required, and works all day long to make around INR 17,000–18,000 a month to support a family of seven. He has two sons in their late teens and a daughter. All of them go to school. I asked him if his sons are also apprenticing in some trade or skill together with their studies. He replied in the negative. He tells me '*hamne to kisi tarah zindagi guzaar li, lekin aaj kal bepadha aadmi to naa hone ke barabar hai*' (we spent our lives somehow but nowadays, an uneducated man is as if he does not even exist), and proceeded to ask me what kind of job his eldest son can get after he passes his class twelfth exams, and if it would be better to let him study further.

Ms Parveen Bano came to Jamia Nagar, Delhi in her early teens with her mother and seven other siblings, escaping starvation, from Dhanbad in Jharkhand (erstwhile Bihar). Her mother, she, and her four sisters have worked as domestic workers for the past 15 years, while her brothers have largely remained oscillating between periods of unemployment and underemployment as unskilled workers in the advertisement hoarding industry. Ms Parveen's husband is a cycle-rickshaw puller, and together they spend almost half of their total earnings to send their children—two daughters—to a local private English-medium school. Till last year, she lived with her mother in a shack put-up on a plot of land of a builder right next to the river Yamuna behind Batla House. During the rains, or when the concerned authorities decided to release more water in the river, her entire family would sometimes live in knee deep waters. For the most part of the rest of the year, this would leave the *kuchcha* floor slushy. She tells me she stayed because she did not have to pay rent, '*Aisi haalat mein kai saal nikal diya baaji, ke chaar paisa bach jaega to bachhon ko padhaenge. Magar jab Seema aur Saima log badi ho rahi, to padhai mein pareshani hoti hai. Sab kharcha ke liye mushkil se bachta hai par kiraya ka kamra lena hi pada...* ' (trans. In this state I passed so many years, sister, so that some money can be saved and the children can be educated. But now Seema and Saima are growing up, it was inconvenient for studies. For other expenses there is hardly anything left, but we had to rent a room...).

I met Dr Mohammad Kamran in a clinic attached to a madrasa in Jaffrabad. He has a BSc from Zakir Husain Delhi College and a BUMS (Bachelor of Unani Medicine and Surgery) from Tibbia College. He comes from family of *darzi*s (tailors) originally from Bijnor. His grandfather and two brothers were taken from Bijnor as children to work with reputed tailors in Lahore before Partition. Interestingly, immediately after the partition, the brothers came back to Delhi to live in the walled city, and started working for some tailors in Connaught Place. They later established their own shop called Iqbal and Brothers. Mr Iqbal was interested in education and always encouraged his children to pursue his dream. While Dr Kamran was still studying, he started teaching children in the vicinity wishing to study in the science stream. This effort grew so much that today he has coaching classes running for over 300 students of secondary and senior secondary classes. The coaching classes run on two floors of his small house. College students are employed as teachers and students pay minimally—INR 100 per subject every month, which also Dr Kamran is amenable to waiving off partially or fully, when petitioned by needy parents. The centre makes no profit and barely breaks even, though Dr Kamran does not have to pay rent for the space and teaches several classes himself without drawing any payment. The sight of teenagers studying in this coaching centre is moving. There are many more girls than boys. They sit on simple wooden benches. There are no desks to keep books or to write, and the students must make do with their bags on their laps. In a small well-lit room, but with barely any ventilation, 45–50 children are engrossed in studying. With the knees of children in one row touching the backs of children in the next, there is barely room for the teacher to stand. I visited the centre twice in the winter but found myself imagining what it must be like during summers. Dr Kamran says it gets pretty impossible sometimes with the power outages, but the children and the students carry on as best as they can.

The coaching centre invited me again to their annual career counseling cum felicitation ceremony for its students who had passed board exams of the tenth and twelfth classes. The children are keenly aware of the stigma their identity and their locality carries. They are also extremely upbeat about getting education, and dream of professions. None of the parents of the children in the ninth standard whom I spoke to had ever been to a university. No one had a working mother. When I asked them about what their father did, most said 'business' or 'job'. Dr Kamran later clarified that 'business' mostly meant a small retail shop of some kind or a manufacturing unit, and 'job' meant employment in a small manufacturing unit. He said that in the last seven years that he has been running the coaching centre, there is a great change in the children's attitude to studies. So many come each year that he can barely accommodate them. Among the parents, he complains, the change is there, but not as much as he would like to see.

… achchhe gharon mein aisa nahin hota… Bachchon ke paas choice nahin hoti… unko to padhna hi padta hai. Yahan toh agar nahin padhna chahtey,

toh parents *kehte hein theek hai... kaam pe baitha dete hein. Koi pressure nahin hai. Par tabdili hai... Pehle to school kya, padhai kya, kuchchh khabar nahin thi... Par agar ab bachha padh raha hai, to woh support karte hein.* (Trans. In well to do families, it is not like this... The children do not have a choice... they must study. Here if they don't want to study, parents say fine... and put them to work. There is no pressure. But there is a change... Earlier they used to not bother about the schools, education... But now if the child is interested, they support them.)

From what I learned about jobs in information-technology (IT)-enabled industries, it is no surprise that many children want to become computer professionals, but there is also a fair share of aspirations along gender lines—most girls wishing to be teachers and doctors, and most boys, engineers.

The Anglo-Arabic school is an old institution that has provided education to boys for generations in Old Delhi. One of my respondents, Mr Azeem Akhtar, who is an alumnus of the school and has been very active for years in the Old Boys' (alumni) Association, told me that the schools had its genesis in a madarsa started three hundred years ago in the 1696. It is in this madarsa that even Zakir Husain Delhi College had its genesis. In 2012, the Anglo-Arabic school started to admit girls as its students and is now a co-educational school. Other schools such as the Fatehpuri Senior Secondary School, attached to the Fatehpuri Masjid, and Shafiq Memorial School are also important in this regard. Boys from Seelampur localities also come and study in these schools. Rabia Girls' School in Daryaganj caters to Muslim girls' education. St Anthony and Presentation Convent schools are among other schools popular among parents who can afford to, and wish to send their children to these. In Old Delhi, there is also a school that is at once the symbol of the tragic and valiant state of Muslims' education. It is the school that runs inside the Shahi Eidgah near Quraish Nagar. Qaumi Senior Secondary School was originally located at Sarai Khalil, where its building was demolished during Emergency. The school was not given any land to rehabilitate but was asked to temporarily store their furniture and records, among others at the Eidgah. Later the school started its regular teaching at the same site, and continues even today in a makeshift state. Between all these schools and the several government schools in and around Muslim localities, the Muslim people strive hard to educate themselves.

Mr Azeem Akhtar told me that Hakim Abdul Hameed, who turned the entire Hamdard operations into a Waqf[1] is called 'Sir Syed-us-Sani' (the second Sir Syed) for his love of education and his keen interest that Muslims receive education. Even today, apart from the much respected Hamdard Public School, the Hamdard Waqf through the Hamdard Educational Society makes an important contribution in the management and running of many of these schools. The role of the Hamdard Educational Society to a large extent, and the involvement of functionaries of Jamia Millia Islamia in the schools run by Muslim bodies and societies are commendable, and must increase exponentially.

Early mornings near Zakir Nagar auto stand, and Ghaffar Manzil, Batla House, Okhla, and Abul Fazal bus stands look very busy with school buses and vans picking up children for school. Most children from middle-class families go to schools such as Hamdard Public School, Crescent Public School, New Horizon School, and MAF Academy, even though these are quite a distance away from the neighbourhood. These schools are being run by Muslim managements. Many also go to schools like Dev Samaj Modern School, Fr. Agnel School, and Mayoor School, which are in the neighbourhood, and open their doors to Muslim children. The upper-class Muslim families can manage to get their children into schools like Delhi Public School, and Sardar Patel Vidhyalaya, among others, only if they have any influence with a central government minister or cabinet secretary level bureaucrats. In addition, they have to *pay* exorbitant amount of money as 'donation' for the school. What makes the access to high profile schools more difficult is that even when a Muslim can and is

---

[1] Waqf is an Islamic concept of charitable trust that holds donated property or assets, income or profit from which is to be spent on welfare and charity while the asset itself cannot be sold.

willing to pay the 'donation', the schools practice fierce gatekeeping such that that only the very rich and politically powerful can even get information regarding how to pay such donations/bribes. Amir Ahmed is a travel agent whose father retired from a senior position in Air India. He was able to get his son admitted in a 'reputed' public school by paying a donation of over INR 100,000 to the school after they had rejected his application and the admissions had officially closed. He says, '*Aap donation dene ke liye tayyar bhi ho, to yeh kaise maloom hoga ke kisko kya dena hai? Paise bhi woh log har kisi se nahin lete. Koi source ho, to hi batate hein ke bhai itne de do to admission ho jaaega*' (Trans. Even if you are ready to give 'donation' how would you know who to pay how much? These people do not take money from just anyone. Only if you have a 'source', do they tell you that if you pay so much, the admission will come through).

The lower middle class sends their children mostly either to numerous Jamia schools or to the government schools in the vicinity. Like everywhere else, government schools are not parents' first choice because of the perceptions about their quality of education. Jamia is preferred because of the quality education it offers, and also the chance for students to become a Jamia Internal student which is a category that has reserved quota in seats in all the university courses. Once a child gets into Jamia, access to even higher education is assured. Also, the scale at which Jamia services the educational needs of the locality cannot be matched by any other institution. Jamia runs many schools inside its sprawling campus in shifts, catering to different needs. There is a very large and well-conceived, well-equipped, and staffed nursery school. There is a main Urdu-medium primary and middle school that also turns into English medium after the eighth standard; there is a second shift English medium self-finance school (but the fee is still much less than the public schools); and there is a school for girls who may have dropped out of school at some earlier stage and wish to study again.

A very large number of girls are also enrolled as private candidates, who cannot or do not wish to attend regular school and come to write only their examination. The option for women to study as private students continues well into undergraduate and postgraduate courses, which is often utilized by women who want to resume studying after their families move from other parts of India to Jamia Nagar. Ms Ranam is young mother of three children, whose two sons are now studying in Mayoor School in the second standard and nursery. Her youngest, a girl, has yet to start school. Her husband is a software engineer working with TCS. When their first son was born, they worried that in the point system[2] their son would lose out because Ms Ranam was only a graduate. She enrolled in Jamia as a private candidate to study for a postgraduate degree in Public Administration and by the time her son was three and half, and eligible for school she was also a postgraduate mustering a few more but precious points.

Mr Khalid Javed was a small vendor in Saharanpur, where he used to service the hardware needs of the local BSNL. When BSNL, as a matter of policy shifted from engaging with small vendors, and centralized the process with larger firms, he was unemployed for two years. He shifted to Delhi, and found a low-paying job as a hardware and networking engineer. His wife Ms Asma Javed shifted a year later with their three-year-old son. It was difficult to make ends meet. She started giving tuitions and enrolled in a post-graduate degree programme in Jamia as a private candidate. Today she has finished her masters in education planning and administration. She is enrolled in the B.Ed. programme of the newest of the Jamia initiatives—a Centre for Distance Education offering even professional courses. She also teaches during the morning in a neighbourhood private school, and continues to give tuitions in the evening.

---

[2] The admissions to school in the nursery class are governed by certain criteria. These pertain to the distance from school to child's home, whether there is a sibling already enrolled in the school, whether the parent have been alumni of the school, if the child is a single child or a girl child, and the education levels of the parents and any such criterion that the school and state education administration may decide. Each of these can get a child some points that are then added-up for a score. This score is used for short-listing for admission.

Ms Sabiha Ahmed is a software engineer who works in a small private firm that provides custom-made software to clients. The firm is located in one of the posh colonies near the Jamia Nagar neighbourhood, and the list of their clients reads like a who's who of the corporate sector in Delhi, Noida, and Gurgaon. The owner of the firm is a Hindu but the employees are mostly Muslims. Ms Ahmed has been working there for the last 12 years, and is the senior most employee, who is trusted by the owner with managing all the operations of the firm. She does not want to change her job because the daily commute is convenient, and it is important for her that she is available at short notice in case her two young children need it. Ms Sabiha says that the employee turnover at her office is high because they pay miniscule salaries. The business model of her boss is to provide cutting-edge software, and support for the same to his clients at very competitive prices. This he is able to do because he routinely hires employees who are qualified—BTechs or MCAs, but have no experience. These Muslim freshers find it difficult to get jobs partially because of, sometimes subtle, sometimes explicit, discrimination, and partially because their backgrounds have not allowed them to pick up the requisite communication skills and confidence. They are paid salaries that are sometimes less than even the minimum wages for skilled workers, but they are happy and grateful for the opportunity, because for them it is a rare opportunity to break into this industry, get on-the-job training, and precious experience with reputed clients. When they leave after a couple of years, their resumés are impressive with the names of firms that are leaders in their industry, and the jobs that they get pay them exponentially more. In the last 12 years, Ms Ahmed has trained so many of these youngsters that she has lost count. Her ability and willingness to perform this role as a mentor serves her employer well, and he compensates her comparably to industry standards in order to retain her. It is a situation that everyone involved sees as a win-win. But not everyone is this fortunate. There are many other firms that exist which hire freshers as trainees and do not pay them at all for a year, sometimes even for two years if they are still unable to find jobs elsewhere. It is a situation that gives us deep insight into the condition of capitalist accumulation and its conjunction with communal prejudice and discrimination, but it is also a process that enables people to escape worse forms of subjugation. It has to be recognized that these are the situations that make it worthwhile for youngsters and parents to make an effort towards education.

Similar to this situation is that of a large number of youth working in call centres. Just as one can see a crowd of school children going to school in the morning and coming back in the afternoon, one can also see a steady stream of cabs picking up and dropping smartly dressed call centre executives through the day, as well as late at night at various Jamia Nagar exit and entry points. Most of these youngsters are students studying for their undergraduate or postgraduate degrees and excited about making decent money alongside. The parents are happy too, to see their children earn money in a manner and at an age which was unimaginable even ten years ago. Some call-centre executives are also MCAs and MBAs, who are waiting to get more appropriate jobs. Although I did not meet any such person myself, but some of the call-centre employees told me that a small number of people have stuck in this field and made 'stable' careers within the call centre industry.

The manufacturers in Seelampur and Old Delhi extend credit to each other on the basis of little else but trust and solidarity. We have seen in Chapter 2 how this solidarity networking also enables capitalist entrepreneurs among Muslims to make profits in housing, but the process does allow people to possess affordable housing in the absence of any housing finance services from private or public financial institutions. Just as they are expending effort to educate themselves and their children, people are also investing energies in creating mostly informal networks for jobs, businesses, education, housing, and much else. In the hegemonic din of the market economy, an economy of solidarity is a humane but decidedly counter-hegemonic response. These processes and changed attitudes are not isolated from the larger structural scheme, but well within the logic of the globalized, neoliberal set-up. Muslims (who had lost their old-traditional skills which had become redundant) are gaining new skills that are saleable and required by the market. They are buoyed by the changed atmosphere that may not be just and inclusive, but is marked by a breathing space and a hint at dignified sustenance that has eluded them for long.

COUNTERING EPISTEMOLOGICAL ISLAMOPHOBIA

Another avenue for hope consists of works such as the one being presented in this book—ethnographic, narrative enquiries that become spaces/opportunities to give tongue to the language of the marginalized, and through this new articulation aim to give rise to a new political consciousness that brings change and creates new realities. Efforts must be made to study society from the perspectives of the periphery, and to strive to present these to the larger society. This is a task that would entail an exploration by people of their identity, and must end in the creation of a new altered identity for those who engage with the process. The primary aim here must be to support *knowledge creation by people* about themselves and the world they co-inhabit with other people and communities, and bring it to the fore, to the space where it can be used. Here language (or articulation) and the socio-political conditions shaped by it are the central theme since, through communication or an inability to communicate, specific ideas and interpretations of the world and how people behave in it are formulated.

We are confronting a moment of global proportions when merely bearing a 'Muslim' identity is aspersed as a political position, and 'muslimness' of a subject often brings in connotations of 'fanatic', 'irrational', and 'contentious'. In the orientalist tradition, Muslims have been portrayed in the present epoch as people who not only face a deficit in development, but also have no sense of the 'superior' values of modernity, rationality, and democracy. In this section, I engage briefly with an understanding of Islamophobia explored in more detail in the introduction. This relates not only to a broad fear of Islam and Muslims, but a phobic position that extends itself into the epistemology of Muslims, both globally and in India. 'Studies of

Muslims' abound measuring their socio-economic status, representation in various sectors of the economy and public service, and their attitudes to issues such as encounters and terrorism, among others. While these studies have their utility, it is pertinent to point out that what is also needed are studies from the perspectives of Muslims and studies that are useful for Muslims to understand their own situatedness in the larger political–economic paradigm. Genres such as studies of globalisation, urban studies, and labour studies, etc. have barely begun to make a mention of Muslims. This is a major impediment in the way of any genuine effort to eliminate 'Epistemological Islamophobia' from knowledge production/discursive processes and outcomes. This book sees itself as claiming the epistemological value of perspectives of Muslims per se, as well as the importance of putting forward this claim as a political strategy in the movement for justice and equality for Muslims.

As an illustration of the foregoing theoretical argument, I narrow my focus to argue that 'ghetto' discourses have long been employed uncritically (Jasani 2008; Susewind 2017) to spawn research and popular imagination of Muslim localities in Delhi as dense, congested hubs of criminal activity. Observations from within the Muslim clusters in Delhi show that these are contiguous or discontinuous but segregated areas that may or may not be poor and decrepit. But because all Muslim localities are labelled 'ghettos', it is difficult for them to be imagined by anyone as otherwise. The 'common sense' usages of the term limit the expression of the existing reality of these spaces. These limits are rarely, if ever, contested by researchers, journalists, or documentary filmmakers who are often Muslim themselves, but whose intended audience/readers are rarely Muslim people. In order to challenge the utility of the term 'ghetto' as a discourse marker, this work has provided thick descriptions of these localities and interactions with the residents that in turn challenge the view that involuntary segregation is an undesigned, uncontrolled, and ecological process as understood by the Chicago school, and shows that people clearly perceive it to occur with full complicity of the neoliberal structures (Wacquant 2011). Wacquant further asserts that the Jewish ghetto marks the 'inaugural' moment of the rise of the 'ghetto' as a socio-organizational device that employs space to unleash an oppressive process aimed at maximizing the material profits extracted out of the discriminated category, while at the same time minimizing intimate contact with its members to avoid an alleged defiling and contagion the segregated are believed to carry.

I assert that once a neighbourhood is branded a 'ghetto', it is imagined only in a certain way by the discursive practices. For example, while only a small area of Seelampur constituency comprises of squatter hutments/*jhuggis*, but this is the part of Seelampur that captures the imagination of the social workers, urban planners, and other people interested in 'slums', defining the entire locality by their myopic view. In another instance, during the course of my research, I was asked by a development consultant to meet a group of planning students and professionals from Barcelona, Spain, because of my familiarity with and work in Jamia Nagar localities. These students are working in a collaborative engagement with the School of Architecture and Ekistics, and the Sarojini Naidu Women's Studies Centre at Jamia Millia Islamia. The group was being facilitated by the consultant who, incidentally, is not a resident of this area. They had been planning and had designed a detailed project for building several 'gender resource zones', as they called them, in the area. One of this entailed a horticulture programme for livelihood and income generation for Muslim women of Shaheen Bagh and Abul Fazal Enclave. Considering that these are the most expensive and 'posh' areas of Jamia Nagar, I advised them to make sure that they have ample parking space and grow 'organic' vegetables because that might bring the women to their centre to buy the vegetables. For actually working in the fields, they would have to maybe get the women who are employed as domestic workers in the area and live in Taimur Nagar rather than in Jamia Nagar. The other parts of the project were also full of assumptions about the area that were grounded in the perception of the area as a 'ghetto'. When I said that Jamia Nagar is a hub of educated, professional, and white-collar workers, the consultant disagreed with me. But confronted with the same opinion by an ecological scientist (and male, I must point out), who is a resident of Shaheen Bagh, she relented. Later she told me that she had thought the area residents to be poor because she had found out that it had no drinking water supply by the Delhi Jal Board. She based her opinion entirely on this, having little clue that the residents of the area are serviced by private pumps for drawing out groundwater, and huge overhead tanks to store it just like other posh areas of Delhi. For their drinking water, there is an elaborate network of private players supplying bottled water to each individual household according to their requirement and collecting payments from them.

For example, the discourses that paint Muslims as reluctant and disloyal citizens, prone to violent behaviour and irrational outlooks, as dirty and polluted, etc. are efficient because they generate the possibility of occurrence of events that fit to these self-fulfilling prophesies (fantasies), thus maintaining themselves. The 'encounter' also marks a new low on the residents' relationship with the state. In the Muslim clusters, the state appears so eager to deliver penal justice without due process and paint the people criminal, but when it comes to the delivery of welfare services and facilitating integration with the rest of the society, polity, and economy, it marks a naught. Even the most progressive and sympathetic groups and people succumbed to the epistemological Islamophobia that has permeated deeply into all public space discussions relating to according Jamia, the status of minority educational institution. These mostly point out to an understanding of all Muslims as fundamentalist and parochial, whose presence in larger numbers enforced through reservation would rob Jamia of its 'cosmopolitan' atmosphere.

In the analysis drawn from the narrative of this study, I am not merely claiming that residents of Muslim enclaves in Delhi are experiencing a deficit in welfare benefits and governance in the urban set-up. The making of the normative non-citizen is a much more complex process that has historical content related to the material forces and relationships of production, as well as content stemming from contemporary discourse-weaving practices such as the news media and films. In Delhi, apart from the mainstream media, social science researchers, urban planners, social work field trainees and supervisors, historians and/or intellectual celebrities guiding 'heritage' tours and walks, journalists, bloggers writing food columns on Ramzan delicacies, 'secular' feminists, and 'progressive-liberal' Muslims, all contribute to discourses on Muslim areas. These numerous and diverse disciplines or practices nourish on spatial segregation and churn out all kinds of representations of Muslims as a spectacle—outlandish and exotic, wretched and inert, irrational and dangerous. In turn, these representations discursively feed the logic of othering and segregation, fortifying around the marginalized people a sort of discursive fencing or trap which is tough to escape from.

Traditional activities that seek equal status for Muslim citizens are located in the sphere of Muslim 'representation' (in the sense of presence and participation) in processes which influence public policy on issues concerning the Muslim community. Nancy Fraser (1997) designates this as an 'official-political sphere', and it involves, for example, demanding legislative support or affirmative policy measures regarding development and welfare allocations and equal presence in the social, economic, and political arena by way of reservations, among others. Countering epistemological Islamophobia would entail changes in the other sphere which Fraser calls 'discursive-political'. These lie in those realms that are mostly perceived as apolitical— culture, conduct, and other manifestations of everyday life. Activities belonging to this sphere, she explains further, involve transformative political practices that reveal the 'contingent and socially constructed' nature of what is portrayed as 'necessary and natural'.

RE-IMAGINING RESISTANCE

I have now amply demonstrated in the preceding chapters why we need to re-imagine resistance by Muslims from their constraining, subjugating, and degrading position. In order to be able to do this, let us revisit the earlier discussion briefly. As discussed earlier in the book, identity has a material function. In this understanding, it can also thus assume both 'use value' and 'exchange-value' and act as a 'thing', a commodity in the real world. Any exchange, any bartering between various facets of identity may seem to be an individual, internal, symbolic act, but it is never uninformed by the surrounding society. In a social structure where 'Muslim' identity comes along with many negative aspersed characteristics, it becomes difficult for a person to exchange it with any of their other identities that has equivalent value in this arbitrary system of valuing or devaluing identities over one another. The subjective internal and social agency of a Muslim person is almost always subordinated to the communal codes located in relation to the gaze of the Hindus, which reflects those ideas that paradoxically produce Muslims as inferior objects of suspicion. In Hegel's words, '[s]elf-consciousness exists in and for itself by virtue of the fact that it is in and for itself for another. That is, it exists only in being recognized' (quoted from Rauch and Sharman 1999: 20).

Yet, self-avowed Marxist Žižek alerts us to an innate knack of systems of dominance of co-opting and, indeed, drawing legitimacy from acts of resistance and transgression. I am reminded of the reaction of Barack Obama to protestors outside the North Atlantic Treaty Organization (NATO) summit in Chicago in May 2012, 'That is what NATO is here to protect… that's what America is all about…' ('NATO Summit' 2012). Žižek (1997) points out that the ideological limits of a system of domination are around the edges of the questions that are never asked. Indeed these limits themselves must not ever be revealed or articulated so that a notion of the fantasy as reality is sustained. Just as in the movie *Truman Show*, teenaged Truman theoretically has a choice (which even he recognizes as a fantasy) of leaving the island—a choice that must never be made. According to Žižek, when the system accommodates resistance, true resistance can only be through making those choices that are theoretically available (fantasies) but are forever unavailable through unwritten limits. How are these choices to be made? One of the characteristic ways these choices are made is what Žižek calls subversion-through-identification: 'sometimes, at least—the truly subversive thing is not to disregard the explicit letter of Law on behalf of the underlying fantasies, but to *stick to this letter against the fantasy which sustains it.*' (1997: 29).

This kind of resistance is seen, for example, being enacted by the 'untouchable' castes in asserting their subordinate—dalit (literally, oppressed) identity, which itself is grounded in the very system of caste domination that it aims to oppose. We know historically that this can be an effective political strategy. Gyanendra Pandey suggested, in answer to a question at a lecture[3] I attended, that in a movement for equality, there is a political moment when those who have been victimized must defensively assert their subordinated position and say that the 'other' would 'never understand'. A parallel may be read in the example of a woman whose right to equality and liberty a state professes to protect such that she legally has a choice regarding who to marry, whether to work, and what to wear, among others. But the unwritten rules of a patriarchal society limit for individual women the choices that may be made. It is through demanding that the state stick to the letter of its promise precisely in each of the circumstances, that effective resistance in Žižekian terms can be offered. Perhaps, this is what the woman who chooses to don any form of *hijab* is asserting symbolically, just as the woman who participates in a 'slut walk' is doing—asserting her freedom as a woman to resist the unwritten rules that seek to regulate her body and clothing choices. I speculate theoretically that this may also be the essence of exercising the 'choice' of living in a Muslim neighbourhood. Although the act of defensive assertion of a subordinate identity may possibly be a powerful political strategy, I contend that it addresses the system of dominance only partially, and never effectively challenges the limits of pre-existing suppositions regarding these identities.

But clearly, in the case of Muslims in Delhi, the resistance that can be provided to the spatial fantasmic unwritten law which states that Muslims must not live alongside 'others', either through juridico-legal action or via subversion-through-identification is grossly inadequate in challenging the structures that reproduce segregated, representational spaces. Why may that be so? For example, Muslims as reluctant and disloyal citizens, prone to violent behaviour and irrational outlooks, as dirty and polluted, among others. These discourses are efficient because they generate the possibility of events that fit to a

---

[3] Gyanendra Pandey, 'Un-archived Histories: Reflections on the Struggle against Caste and Race in India and the USA', Public lecture organized by the Nehru Memorial Museum and Library, 19 December 2011.

T as self-fulfilling prophesies (fantasies?) that maintain themselves. In the last analysis, it appears that identities may indeed be used as a tool for subjugation in maintaining and reproducing the oppressive relationships of production lucratively. This normalizing power of identity calls for a relook at both methods of juridico-legal resistance and resistance-through-identification. It seems logical to resist identification as this or that per se, but this may not be enough. The requirement is to foster a new kind of subjectivity which is empowered to transform the very content of self-representation.

Because some individuals manage to avoid experiencing one form of dominance, say being targets of communal violence or prejudiced and discriminatory behaviour, they may easily be deluded into thinking that they have attained true liberty. But to individually avoid subjugation, many Muslims abrogate the power to craft a new critical subjectivity that problematizes the prevailing identity stereotypes of Muslims. Foucault calls into question this tendency of the contemporary systems of domination to simultaneously individualize and totalize. He points out that,

> ... the task nowadays is not to discover what we are, but to refuse what we are. We have to imagine and to build up what we could be to get rid of this kind of political 'double bind', which is the simultaneous individualization and totalization of modern power structures... We have to promote new forms of subjectivity through the refusal of this kind of individuality which has been imposed on us... ' (Foucault 1982: 216).

The moment of problematizing a prevailing discursive content of an identity is defined not by some altruistic or divine intervention, but is indicated by a combination of events or social, political, and economic processes occurring together to throw light upon the system of subjugation and enabling people to see it as unjust. This is not to say that some kind of final unveiling and toppling of injustice would take place as a consequence, but that in the Foucauldian sense freedom is something that is exercised, rather than achieved, in a process that must run in tandem with the careful and creative exercise of power. This is the way in which we can effectively hope for the emergence of a capacity in people positioned adversely within a system of domination to seize the moment and draw the power to re-imagine themselves. Instead of seeing your own normalized reflection in the gaze of 'the other', resistance would involve saying 'I see you' without succumbing to feelings of shame and anxiety.

In the next chapter, I bring this book to a close by engaging in a critical exercise of recounting a complex web of problems which get into the very way of imagining Delhi as a city that may include all its residents *as equals*. The exercise, though critical, is not meant to be an exercise in cynicism. It is conceived in a way, however inadequate, to regard the problems of Delhi as a global urban and the Muslim residents of Delhi in a philosophical thread. The last chapter thus closes off with a brief statement of the core inferences drawn in the book in an attempt to respond to the problem of research that Horkheimer posed in his 1931 (1993: 14) address, as 'symbolic of the peculiar difficulty of social philosophy—the difficulty concerning the interpenetration of general and particular, of theoretical design and individual experience'.

CHAPTER SIX

Coda

*The Problématique of Envisioning
the Ideal Delhi*

· ·

A Coda to this book—this chapter is not a conventional conclusion, but it does aim to be a *gesture at closure.* Since the entire discussion brings to light so many problems in its analysis of Delhi's geography of discrimination (its material base and the discursive content of the processes), the coda seeks to recapitulate the structure of the argument with a closing comment that is not merely a repetition. In order to absorb and grasp the full thrust of the work, I attempt to reframe the discussion in terms of articulating a set of obstacles that arise in envisioning an image of Delhi without these problems—the 'Ideal Delhi'. While academic enquiries begin with a statement of problems that they aim to investigate, here I pose an additional but an inventive relook at *un ensemble des problèmes*—a set of problems with an outline of the interface between them.

The much prevalent view of a city as an evolutionary stage in the process of development leads to a difficulty in grasping contemporary globalized urban processes fully, because it fails to recognize the political–economic aspects of urban problems. In his book *Material Culture and Mass Consumption*, Miller calls material culture an elusive part of modernity which has 'consistently managed to evade the focus of academic gaze, and remains the least understood of all cultural phenomenon of the modern age' (1987: 217).

This was mainly because of academic anxiety to produce explanations of urbanization that show consonance between processes and practices. In this work, the task of envisioning the ideal Delhi actually involves highlighting and amplifying the tensions at the interface of the problems, rather than to deduce cause-and-effect relationships and come up with some 'remedial' and ready-to-use vision. In this chapter the task of envisioning ideal Delhi actually involves highlighting and amplifying the tensions at the interface of problems, rather than to deduce cause-and-effect relationships and come up with some 'remedial' and ready to use vision. This approach fits well also with the Marxist Urbanist analytical framework in this work. This view accommodates complexities and contradictions inherent in the processes of urbanization, because it understands *the urban* as a manifestation of capitalism.

From the discussion in the preceding chapters, it is clear that in the city, much has gone awry with the way spaces are produced and used. But, because of the rate at which urbanization of humanity is occurring[1] we shall have to consider that if we conceive urbanization as a progressive move for human societies, then urban spaces must contribute to realization of the human potential for creative existence and happiness. Horkheimer (1982 [1968]) asserts that in order to fully comprehend human reality, social philosophy must understand that life is marked by suffering *and also* the effort to surmount suffering. He says that 'striving for happiness is to be recognised as a natural

---

[1] More than half of humanity lives in cities; in 2008, the world's urban population crossed the halfway mark (UN Habitat 2008).

fact requiring no justification' (Horkheimer 1982: 44). An ideal Delhi then must give all its inhabitants space to build their happiness. But can a city bring people happiness? While the instinct for survival needs no selling, the desire for a lifestyle needs an elaborate market where it is sold sometimes aggressively and sometimes subtly. When people attempt to 'escape' the tyranny of rural hunger and/or rural parochialism, they probably do so with the belief that in the city they would be able to alter their lives. Between the two extremes, perhaps the lowest common denominator is the human conception of a good life. Whatever might be one's notion of a good life, it can be argued that once a person begins to lead this good life, he or she can be happy. In an ideal city, people may be able to build a good life for themselves and pursue their own happiness. This includes the ability and freedom to build a city in the image of their own happiness, not in the image of transplanted conceptions from someplace else. It is in this task of conceptualizing an image of *adequate* happiness that the problem in imagining an 'ideal city' lies.

Value considerations form a backdrop for the formulation and experience of happiness. I can be happy when I can pursue what *I think* makes me happy. But this enterprise is not as centred on the individual *self* as it might seem. Horkheimer (1982) suggests that personal happiness is connected to a moral sentiment of compassion. Human happiness is also an extension of self and a desire for happiness for others. For theorists of cities, a conception of a city that all must want has to be rooted in an implicit understanding of prioritizing what 'values' direct the pursuance of happiness of all urban collectivities—including Muslims. From the perspective of segregated and marginalized Muslims, I begin by asking, on what values should be based the conceptualization of the ideal Delhi? Susan Fainstein (1999) indicates that various urban theorists have considered *equality, diversity, and democracy* to be the values that govern the urban condition.

The treatment of minorities in democracies is of course, by far better than the treatment of minorities in autocratic states. Having said that, ample evidence exists indicating that experiences of Muslims as a minority in democratic India are far from perfect. Democracies are unfortunately often marked by a belligerent majority and populist tendencies in the state policy. Democracy as a value is a necessary condition towards a 'just' Delhi, but clearly it has not been sufficient. Advocates of diversity as the most important value are right in asserting that acceptance of diversity and difference is a prerogative or hallmark of the urban condition. Aristotle went so far as to say that, 'A city is composed of different men; similar people cannot bring a city into existence' (quoted from Balshaw and Kennedy 2000: 12). I assert that the availability of the option to individual citizens to obliterate any 'difference' that they may choose to, must also be a part of urbanity—that nobody should be burdened with identities or *expressions of identities* that are not of their choosing. The space to overcome or outgrow aspersed identities and labelling must be available to people. Diversity and difference, while desirable and unreservedly human conditions, are not to be espoused without any riders or qualifiers. Many scholars such as Varshney (2002) have suggested that diversity coupled with proximity fosters tolerance and harmony, but ample evidence and experiences also exist to show that diversity *per se* without equality ends up as a hierarchy of suspect 'lesser humans' and elite 'citizens'. A major factor in dealing with this kind of hierarchy may be state response. I am tempted to engage in what might seem (within the limited ambit of this study) a speculative exercise of imagining that instead of being concerned so much with categorizing, labelling, targeting, and eliminating various types of citizens from its 'welfare cover', if the state were to extend its generosity at least on counts of basic needs and services such as food security and housing to *all its subjects*, probably they in turn would be more tolerant of each other. Be that as it may, it is ultimately *justice* that comes up at the top of my list (as it does in other Marxist approaches to understanding urban), when we prioritize from amongst these three values. This is not to say that democracy and diversity are not important, but that practices of electoral democracy and mere existence of difference and diversity, devoid of political and economic justice ring hollow to minorities.

At this juncture, I put out three interfaces in which I have framed a problématique involved in envisioning the ideal Delhi. These have not been chosen for any verifiable importance and may appear arbitrary, but I chose these because while undertaking this research and writing it, these are the tensions that I found most challenging. In the following sections, I explore the tensions at these interfaces whose nomenclatures I have found in David Harvey's faith that, '[i]f our urban world has been imagined and made, then it can be re-imagined and re-made. The inalienable right to the city is worth fighting for' (2003: 941). Harvey (2003) insists that this cannot be done by just claiming rights and demanding a different ordering of rights, but by insisting upon different political–economic practices.

IMAGINING 'URBAN': STUFF OF DREAMS VERSUS EVERYDAY REALITIES

In a discussion regarding 'the ideal city', legendry architect Charles Correa (2010) says that cities are the spatial embodiment of the dreams and aspirations of a society. This is so today and it was thus even in pre-modern times. Correa mentions the mythical city of God—Jerusalem, the Islamic *Charbagh*, and Vedic *Mandala*, as prototypes of cultivated 'urban'. Yet, he laments, that contemporary cities are mired in everyday realities. The stuff that dreams are made of may not be referring only to the 'concrete' (or steel) or built environment of a city, but to the city as an image in the mind of its inhabitants. Like all images, this image has also succumbed to being a mythical image. Correa mentions how Kolkata may appear as a 'morass of chaos and decay' to visitors 'but to Bengalis, it is the stuff of which dreams are made of' (2010: 123). It is in the discussions of, let us say, Delhiites with Mumbaikars regarding 'their cities', that these dreams are articulated. It is the dream of the kind that allegedly 'pulls' labouring bodies to attempt to survive and become more human. It is this dream that brought Balraj Sahni's Shambhu Mahto in *Do Bigha Zamin* (Roy 1953) to the city of Calcutta. The dream of making enough money to go back to a piece of land they can call their own still continues in the lowest echelons of the city's labouring class—domestic workers, head loaders, waste pickers. Everyday realities of their utter dehumanization convey to them that their dream of becoming more human can never be fully realized in the city. Then there are people who are caught not so much in the struggle to survive but to become more like the image of *the person who is in their dreams*. The dream of a fresh Muslim BTech or MBA in Delhi is one of acquiring urbanity, modernity, and liberty. The everyday reality of their homes without ventilation and natural light, long commutes, and long working hours are disregarded in the pursuit of this image which is a mythical promise communicated to them from the advertisements and hoardings. The latter are also characterized by oblivion to their membership of the exploited working class. Boxed in the partition of their workstation in a corporate office chasing daylight timings of another time zone in the world, traversing the length of cities in cabs and cars, they too chase an image which they will never fully become.

In any case, it would be unfair to say that all these dreams are unreal. To a woman whose lot was slow starvation, a belly full of food for her children is the immediate dream. Once that is taken care of, procuring other requisites becomes the next dream. Many dreams are very real, at least to the one dreaming them. Only, the tragedy here is that what people see as their own dreams are only conjured up by the ideology implicit in media practices, urban architecture, practices of governmentality—such as zoning, urban planning, urban 'renewal', identification of people below the poverty line, among others. And, the fulfillment of some of their dreams is the ideological lure to continue to dream of the unattainable because all of it appears so near and so clearly visible. Thus, the city becomes the site where the dreams are continually *nurtured*, but the everyday thwarts the *realization* of these dreams. The communal politics of industrializing India in the decades of the 1960s, 1970s, and 1980s shook up Indian Muslims such that this kind of dreaming was not available to them. The slow turning up of modernist heat by the globalization of capital, spaces, and prejudice has put urban Muslims in a situation where slumber full of consumerist dreams induced by ideology is therapeutic by comparison.

'INCLUSION' AS 'EXCLUSION': CITY AS A SITE FOR DWELLING VERSUS CITY AS A SITE OF CONSUMPTION

The mainstream discourses referring to 'urban development' often offer a peek into the fetish of 'urban infrastructure development'. Urban planners speak of urban spaces and built environment as if these have nothing to do with the relationships of production, thereby giving a peek into the fact that the dominant conception of development of a city is all about the development of productive infrastructure and not about people. The role of human beings is limited in so far as their capacity to consume. The city is geared towards a new mode of production—at the centre is not the industrial production of goods (though that still has a robust continuity in Delhi), nor is it the service industry (very much evidenced by the advances in technology); it is rather, the culture industry which is geared towards creating a culture of new needs and then providing for the needs thus created. The paradox of this culture industry is that no one is left out of its ambit, *everyone* is included. Reality shows, daily soaps, crime news shows, downloadable ringtones, and innumerable other examples abound for the ways everyone is recruited into the city of consumption. For those of us in social work and the 'development sector' who have been agonizing and agitating about the exclusion of groups and communities, the task now is to comprehend this new form of exclusion by inclusion. Just as states have biopower over bodies, the culture industry has power over consciousness. This hegemonic thought-power working parallel to biopower, is advancing in the everyday life of Delhi residents by leaps and bounds. It has made people believe that they are not *entitled* to any welfare or security from the state, that welfare and security can only be *claimed* by those who can *pay the price* (literally in the 'free' market or to the state in the form of taxes). Dwelling as a prerequisite to human dignity does not even find an 'honourable mention' in the official narratives of the city. The homeless, the Muslims, the squatters, and all kinds of urban 'undesirables' are included by the state's biopower and the culture industry's thought-power, and this inclusion is leveraged to *exclude* them into segregated neighbourhoods, *harijan basti*s,[2] resettlement colonies on the edges of the city, and shelter homes for the homeless, such that the rest of the city may lose any cognition of their presence, and the 'undesirables' themselves lose the capacity to register their exclusion.

As it stands, the issue of happiness too is mired in the issue of consumption, and therefore, is completely entangled in the issue of relationships of production. It is the positionality of people in this entangled thread (web?) of production, consumption, and accumulation that becomes the function of happiness. A person likes to think of himself as a 'consumer' and forget that he is a 'worker', because while the worker 'serves', a consumer gets 'serviced'. 'Exclusivity' is for the prized few, and everyone else is included in the state of exclusion. Premium spaces in the city are those where only a select few live, or in which no one lives—everyone just passes by. Those spaces that are dwellings of the multitudes are spaces of exception. It is then easy for those who can buy and consume to think that *the product* they are buying and consuming is *happiness itself*. When happiness is reified like this, the 'ideal' city is easy to produce and construct in the image of dominant discourses—conceptualized by discourse-weaving practices such as urban planning and governance functions. These practices are the fountain heads of zoning rules, urban 'infrastructure development' projects, and urban 'renewal' projects that intensify the contestations for control over city spaces. And contestations are all about power and politics. The spaces that are required by the select few for their accumulative purposes become central spaces of the city, and the undesirables get thrown to spaces of exceptions. It is futile to hope that continuing on the same trajectory that it is being traversed

---

[2] Harijan Bastis: Settlement of dalits. *Harijan* (literally, people of God) was the preferred term of Mahatma Gandhi for people belonging to 'untouchable' castes.

now, Delhi can become an inclusive space where all its inhabitants can freely construct a true image of their happiness and *live in it.*

RIGHT TO THE CITY: INDIVIDUAL NEEDS
VERSUS COLLECTIVE RIGHTS

In the wake of the global spread of capitalism, Western liberal democracy and its intrinsic values have gained an unprecedented hegemony. This fact has been discussed in detail earlier in this book in the discussion of ideas proclaiming the end of history, and so on. I take the opportunity in this coda to reiterate that discourses asserting that *there is no alternative* to Western liberal ideas on economy, systems of governance, and rights of individuals, among others, which may be viable and acceptable, are hegemonic. Harvey uses Gramsci's formulation of 'pessimism of intellect and optimism of will' (quoted from Harvey 2000: 17) to describe the contestations that function within the discursive framework of hegemonic TINA—there is no alternative—to capitalism. I also emphasize following Marx that the notion of individual as a locus of claim-making in the Western liberal ideas, has been undermining the rights of communities. Various unlimited rights are being asserted by the liberals for individuals, which are testing the increasingly precarious conditions for co-existence of human beings. In Delhi, for example, claims to 'silence' and 'beauty' in 'residential colonies' wreaked havoc over the livelihoods of working-class people. Car owners claimed right of way when confronted with a BRT (bus rapid transit)-dedicated corridor for mass public transport (http://www.cseindia.org/content/brt-missed-bus-cars; http://www.citylab.com/cityfixer/2016/12/why-did-bus-rapid-transit-go-bust-in-delhi/510431/;http://www.thehindu.com/news/cities/Delhi/trying-to-run-delhis-brts-off-the-road/article3728091.ece). Liberals assert that the right of a community not to be offended does not exist, but the right of an individual to offend must be unlimited. Entire slum localities are dubbed as illegal squatters and denied the right to shelter, but maverick individuals get unlimited media attention when they assert their right to gratify their lifestyle choices that are in congruence with liberal values. It does not need another repetition in this book how Muslims fare in such a scenario. Designated official misfits in the Western liberal scheme of things, Muslims, as a community, are pitted in direct opposition to the liberal, modern individual. In a race where almost all identity groups wish to claim to be more 'modern and progressive' (read Western) than the other, Muslims have been peculiar in their 'represented' refusal to embrace individualism and capitalism as a community (whether this is the case on the ground is another debate). The Islamophobes transferred their hatred, and asked about Muslims in the language of fake naiveté, 'why do they hate us?', while leaving it 'thoughtfully' to be added by an oppressive environment that 'it must be because we are better than them'.

When the politics of lifestyle choices and individual rights is appearing to gain strength, Muslim individuals too are attempting to articulate their resistance in this language. A closer reading of the text of everyday is required to read what is actually not written in the transcript. Embracing a slur and claiming loudly what one is being ridiculed for, needs to be understood as a weapon of the weak. It would be a travesty to allege that 'everyday artful forms of resistance' (Scott 1990) by Muslims are only a matter of lifestyle choices. Muslim people who 'chose' to wear their identity loudly are taking a political position in the only language that is allowed to them. How do queers contest that they are no different than any human being, and must not to be treated differently by society? Paradoxically, by proclaiming and expressing their difference more loudly in events like gay parades. It is a situation that is symptomatic of fragmentation and individualization of collective and class-based politics. Individual Muslims can assert their 'Muslimness' through adopting certain life choices peculiar to them as much as they want in limited spheres, but any collective effort by Muslims is doomed to be reduced to a farce or a tragedy. Even in this case, the individual assertions are only a manifestation of the community losing ground in society.

SOME MORE QUESTIONS LEFT UNEXPLORED

This study raises a plethora of questions and makes assertions regarding issues that were explored. Almost all of these merit an exploration of a much bigger magnitude on their own. Apart from this, I encountered several questions regarding Muslims in Delhi, or more broadly urban Muslims in India which were not explored for paucity of time and limits of this endeavour, which was geared towards the award of a doctoral degree. A fresh concerted research effort is required to explore the existing prevalence of caste markers and their expression among Muslims. More concerted studies are also required of urban Muslim women, of the experiences of Muslims with the state agencies with special reference to the officially appointed commissions for enquiries and status reports, and of the conceptions mired in epistemological Islamophobia among civil society organizations and the academia. These are but a few indicators for an entire field of research that has been afflicted with the same ailment that has inundated the subjects of research. Research pertaining to Muslim people and localities has long been in a state of stagnation. If this book sparks off fresh frames of reference, that in itself would be a worthwhile contribution to countering the prejudice, discrimination, and violence experienced by Muslims in India.

Closing Gesture

A Vision for the Ideal City

. . . .

The Ideal City is made up of the stuff of dreams. All its residents can dream of a city which they can create in their own image of happiness, and live in everyday. In the Ideal City, the worth of human life is not measured by how much an individual being can consume. In the Ideal City, the residents are aware that they do not merely consume, but they also can and do create. The Ideal City comprises of persons and collectivities who share an inalienable humanity, and not just of people marked as 'islands' by their 'individuality'. In the Ideal City, differences do not need insularity and each dweller *belongs*.

Annexure
Brief Profiles of Key Participants

. . . .

Azeem Akhtar Azeem sahab was a senior officer in the Delhi Police. He has also served as the secretary of the Delhi Waqf Board, and the president of the Anglo-Arabic Old Boys' Association. He is a writer who has published extensively on Delhi in Urdu. Azeem sahab walked with me in Daryaganj and Chandni Chowk. He took me to meet several of his friends and acquaintances including his publisher in Kucha Tarachand. He now lives in Zakir Nagar after his retirement.

Dr Mohammad Kamran A Unani doctor trained at Tibbia College, Dr Kamran attends patients in a charitable OPD clinic attached to a Madarsa in Jaffarabad. In addition, he also owns and runs a coaching centre for school children from his home in Jaffarabad on a not-for-profit basis. Conversations with him took place at the OPD clinic and his coaching centre. Sometimes his teachers would also be present and participate in the discussions. I was also invited for the centre's function to felicitate its students after the board exam results were declared.

Haji Umar Haji Umar 'Lipstickwaley' owns a business manufacturing cosmetics in Jaffarabad. He is an old resident of the Seelampur area, having shifted here even before the emergency forced others to be relocated here. He is intimately familiar with the contemporary history of the area. I met him at his office in a group discussion with community leaders from Jaffarabad and Chauhan Bangar.

Jamshed Khan A small manufacturer, Jamshed sahab is Javed Khan's (see next profile) father. Despite not being educated, he set up his workshop from scratch and now employs 10–12 workers.

Javed Khan Javed has an MBA degree and (around the time the interviews took place) had just joined his father's workshop where denim garments are stitched. They employ about 10–12 workers. Javed has helped children in the neighbourhood with their studies for years. He is looked at as a role model by many of them. Conversations with him took place at his home and while walking through J and K blocks, New Seelampur.

Khalid Javed and Asma Javed (names changed) Khalid and Asma are a couple from Saharanpur. First generation migrants, they had to come to Delhi when Khalid lost his contract with BSNL Saharanpur for hardware and networking work. Asma is also pursuing studies in Jamia. They live in Zakir Nagar. Khalid works in a reputed IT firm, and Asma is teaching in a neighbourhood primary school.

Khalid Zafar and Zafar Iqbal Khalid is a 23-year-old chartered accountant. His father has a workshop manufacturing handicrafts catering to export markets. Khalid's father Zafar sahab stayed back in Delhi during Partition, while his entire extended family left. They are residents of Chitli Qabar, Jama Masjid. My conversations with them took place at their home. Khalid's mother was also present and participated in the conversations; her parental family had also left for Pakistan. Khalid also accompanied me in walking through Chitli Qabar, Bazaar Sita Ram, and Bawarchi Khana, among others.

Mohd Mohsin Mohd Mohsin is a 21-year-old resident of J-Block New Seelampur, pursuing a Masters degree. His father buys insulated wire and subcontracts the work of wire stripping to middle men, who distribute it to home-based labour stripping copper wire of its plastic/rubber insulation. Apart from his studies, his major engagement is helping his father in this work. Mohsin is preparing for the UGC-NET (University Grants Commission-National Eligibility Test) and aspires to become an academician. The conversation with him took place in a group discussion with youth from J and K blocks, New Seelampur. Most of these young men are involved in the scrap business.

Mohd Sultan Small manufacturer of electronic goods, originally from Amroha, as a young bachelor, Mohd Sultan worked in a workshop in Old Delhi, where he learnt the trade. He shifted to Chauhan Bangar in Seelampur, where he brought his family and now owns a small manufacturing workshop himself. My conversation with him took place at his home. His children and wife also contributed to the discussion occasionally.

Monis Siddiqui Monis Siddiqui is a manufacturer of metal sheet cabinets from Chauhan Bangar. My conversation with him took place in his workshop office. Mr Sultan and two other manufacturers from the garment industry also participated in this discussion.

Moin Ahmed and Ranam Ahmed Moin is a software engineer originally from Ranchi, Jharkhand. His education and training is from Aligarh Muslim University. After coming to Delhi for work, he lived briefly in Malviya Nagar. He shifted to Zakir Nagar to a rented flat upon his marriage with Ranam. Ranam is from Patna, and was a graduate when she came to Delhi. She enrolled in Jamia for her master's degree. They now live in their own flat in Shaheen Bagh in Jamia Nagar. The interview with them took place at their home.

Mr Jaffry Eighty-year-old Mr Jaffry is a senior member of the Taj Enclave society. At present he is the president of the society, and actively looks after all its affairs. The conversation with him took place in the flat of another resident.

Mr Merajuddin Qureshi and family A worker on lathe machine in Bara Hindu Rao, Merajuddin has a very small workshop with a single lathe that he owns and operates himself fashioning metal parts for various machines. My conversation with him took place at his workshop. Later, I was invited to his home, where I met his wife, daughters, daughter-in-law, and grandchildren.

Naghma Begum Thirty-year-old Naghma is a housewife and mother of two. She is originally from a village in Bulandshahr. The interactions took place at her home.

Sumaiya Sumaiya is an Urdu teacher at Rabia Girls' School, Daryaganj. She lives in Basti Hazrat Nizamuddin since her marriage. She has researched Urdu programming on All India Radio for her doctoral degree. The conversation with her took place at her home in Basti Hazrat Nizamuddin. Her mother-in-law is a Punjabi Muslim from Malerkotla. She was also present for part of the interaction.

Mohd Naim Thirty-five-year-old Naim is a resident of Taj Enclave, having shifted there from Sarai Khalil. He has been living there with his family for the last 10 years. The conversation took place at his flat. Naim's wife Nisha was also present and participated in the conversation.

Qamar Akhtar Sixty-seven-year-old Qamar sahab owns a bridal garments shop in Chandni Chowk. His father moved to Delhi after Partition. Qamar sahab's family moved to Zakir Nagar only a few years ago. He is deeply familiar with the dynamics in Old Delhi, Nizamuddin, as well as Jamia Nagar. He was used as the first 'excellent' participant[1] of the study from the point of view of theoretical

---

[1] I have borrowed sampling method for the ethnographic fieldwork in this study from grounded theory. The technique is termed 'theoretical sampling' in which the process of data collection is determined by the development of theory as it emerges. Decision related to thus recruitment for participants are crucial. Study essentially starts by recruiting a few 'excellent participants', who not only have an experience of the subject matter of the enquiry but are able to comment articulately and reflexively. Excellent participants must be willing to spend considerable amount of time on the research.

exploration. Qamar sahab also helped me meet his brother who has written extensively on Old Delhi.

Ovais Sultan Khan A 22-year-old resident of Chauhan Bangar, Ovais Sultan Khan was placed as a social work student trainee for fieldwork in Seelampur K-Block. A student activist, Ovais is intimately familiar with many community-based organizations and activists, as well as organizations that engage with issues related to communalism. Conversations with him took place at his home and while walking in Seelampur and the walled city.

Rizwan Alam (name changed) Rizwan is a 45-year-old researcher and content writer in a PR firm in Gurgaon. Trained as a journalist, Rizwan is originally from Aurangabad, Maharashtra. He lived in Hauz Rani before moving to Zakir Nagar right before his marriage. Conversations with him took place at my house.

Sabiha Ahmed (name changed) A 40-year-old software engineer originally from Moradabad, Sabiha came to Delhi as a single woman with a master's degree in chemistry, but got further training in computers and software. She works with a small consultancy firm located near Jamia Nagar. She is now married and has two children.

Shaheena Begum Shaheena is a 62-year-old housewife. Shaheena is a widow and shifted from Moradabad only after all her children settled in Delhi after studying in Jamia and having gotten jobs and/ or being married in Delhi. Conversations with her took place at her son's house with her other children and grandchildren being present.

Shakeel Malik Thirty-seven years Shakeel and his family originally came from a village in Aligarh district and invested in land. He has dabbled in several businesses in Jamia Nagar—a garments workshop, dealing in scrap, and mobile phones, among others. Presently he is engaged as a builder and developer in real estate. He is my neighbour in Jamia Nagar. Conversations with him took place at my house.

Sibghat Ullah Siddiqui Principal of Shafiq Memorial School, Sibghat Ullah was valuable in helping me frame my enquiries into educational and professional aspirations in Delhi's Muslim localities.

FOCUS GROUP DISCUSSIONS

Youth from J Block and K Block of New Seelampur, mostly working in the scrap recycling business (only men).

Community elders and local political activists in Seelampur (only men).

Employees of Call Centres and other IT professionals in Jamia (Both men and women).

Class IX school children (boys and girls) in Jaffarabad at Dr Kamran's coaching centre.

REFERENCES

Adarsh, T. 2008. 'A Wednesday (Review of the Film *A Wednesday*), *Bollywood Hungama*, 2 September, available at http://www.bollywoodhungama.com/movie/a-wednesday/critic-review/.

Agamben, G. (trans. D. Heller-Roazen). 1998. *Homo Sacer: Sovereign Power and Bare Life*. Palo Alto: Stanford University Press.

Althusser, L. 1969[1965]. *For Marx*. London: Verso Books.

Anand, U. (2012, June 12). 'Jamia More Volatile after Batla House Encounter: Police to HC'. *Indian Express*.

Anderson, B. 1991. *Imagined Communities: Reflections on the Origin and Spread of Nationalism*. London: Verso.

Appadurai, A. 1996. *Modernity at Large: Cultural Dimensions of Globalization*. Minneapolis: University of Minnesota Press.

———. 2006. *Fear of Small Numbers: An Essay on the Geography of Anger*. Durham: Duke University Press.

Arad, Y. 1980. *Ghetto in Flames: The Struggle and Destruction of the Jews in Vilna in the Holocaust*. Jerusalem: Ktav Publications.

Arendt, H. 1951. *The Origins of Totalitarianism*. Prague: Schocken Books.

Ashok, S. and M. Ali. 2012. 'Housing Apartheid Flourishes in Delhi', *The Hindu*, 8 July, available at http://www.thehindu.com/news/national/housing-apartheid-flourishes-in-delhi/article3613994.ece.

Balshaw, M. and L. Kennedy. 2000. *Urban Space and Representation*. London: Pluto Press.

Banerjee-Guha, S. (ed.). 2010. *Accumulation by Dispossession: Transformative Cities in the New Global Order.* New Delhi: Sage.

Barthes, R. 1993. *Mythologies.* London: Vintage.

Basu, A. 2010. 'Encounters in the City: Cops, Criminals, and Human Rights in Hindi Film', *Journal of Human Rights* 9(2): 175–90.

Basu, S. (2016, November 6). 'The Women of Nizamuddin Basti: Aga Khan Trust for Culture Brings a New Light into Their Lives'. *Firstpost.com,* available at http://www.firstpost.com/living/the-women-of-nizamuddin-basti-aga-khan-trust-for-culture-brings-a-new-light-into-their-lives-3090938.html.

Baudrillard, J. 1995. *The Gulf War Did Not Take Place.* Bloomington: Indiana University Press.

Bauman, Z. 2004. *Identity: Conversations with Benedetto Vecci.* Cambridge: Polity Press.

Baviskar, A. 2004. 'Between Violence and Desire: Space, Power, and Identity in the Making of Metropolitan Delhi', *International Social Science Journal,* 55(175): 89–98.

———. 2006. 'Demolishing Delhi: World Class City in the Making', *Mute Magazine,* 5 September.

Bayly, C. 1986. 'Delhi and Other Cities of North India during the "Twilight"', in R.E. Frykenberg (ed.), *Delhi through the Ages: Selected Essays in Urban History, Culture, and Society,* pp. 224–32. New Delhi: Oxford University Press.

Benegal, S. 2007. 'Secularism and Popular Indian Cinema', in A.D. Needham and R.S. Rajan (eds), *The Crisis of Secularism in India,* pp. 225–38. Duke University Press.

Benjamin, S. 2010. 'Manufacturing Neoliberalism: Lifestyling Indian Urbanity', in Swapna Banerjee-Guha (ed.), *Accumulation by Dispossession: Transformative Cities in the New Global Order,* pp. 92–124. New Delhi: Sage.

Benjamin, W. 2009. 'The Work of Art in the Age of Mechanical Reproduction', in M.G. Durham and D.M. Kellner (eds), *Media and Cultural Studies: Keyworks,* pp. 18–40. John Wiley & Sons.

Bennett, T. 1995. *The Birth of a Museum: History, Theory, Politics.* London: Routledge.

Berry, C. 2001. 'Land Use Regulation and Residential Segregation: Does Zoning Matter?', *American Law and Economics Review,* 3(2): 251–74.

Bharucha, R. 2003. 'Muslims and Others: Anecdotes, Fragments and Uncertainties of Evidence', *Economic and Political Weekly* 38(40): 4238–50.

Bhaskar, I. and R. Allen. 2009. *Islamicate Cultures of Bombay Cinema.* New Delhi: Tulika Books.

Bök C. 2001. *Pataphysics: The Poetics of an Imaginary Science.* Evanston, Illinois: Northwestern University Press.

Burgess, E.W. 1925. 'The Growth of the City: An Introduction to a Research Project', *Publications of the American Sociological Society*, XVIII: 85–97.

Butler, J. 2004. *Precarious Life: The Powers of Mourning and Violence.* London: Verso Books.

Castells, M. 1976. 'Is There an Urban Sociology?', in C.G. Pickvance (ed.), *Urban Sociology*, pp. 60–86. London: Methuen & Co. Ltd.

———. 1989. *The Informational City: Information Technology, Economic Restructuring, and the Urban–Regional Process.* Oxford: Blackwell.

———. 1996–8. *The Information Age: Economy, Society and Culture*, Vols I–III. Cambridge: Blackwell.

Census of India. 1941. Vol 1. Government of India Press: Shimla.

Census of India. 1951[1953]. Vol. 1, Part 1-A. Government of India Press: Delhi.

Centre for Equity Studies: New Delhi, available at http://www.unesco-gym.org/wp-content/uploads/2015/06/MANDER_SAHGAL_Internal-Migration_Distress-Opportunities.pdf.

Chakravarty, S.S. 2011. *National Identity in Indian Popular Cinema, 1947–1987.* University of Texas Press.

Chandler, D. 2002. *Semiotics: The Basics.* London: Routledge.

Chandra, B. 1979. *Nationalism and Colonialism in Modern India.* New Delhi: Orient Longman.

Chatterjee, I. 2009. 'Social Conflict and the Neoliberal City: A Case of Hindu–Muslim Violence in India', *Transactions of the Institute of British Geographers*, 34(2): 143–60.

Chatterjee, P. 1993. *The Nation and Its Fragments: Colonial and Postcolonial Histories.* Princeton: Princeton University Press.

———. 2012. 'The Movement against Politics', *Cultural Critique*, 81(1): 117–22.

Chishti, S. 2011. 'Khursheed Says Sachar Report Not Quran, Sparks Off War of Words', *The Indian Express*, 28 June, available at http://archive.indian-express.com/news/khursheed-says-sachar-report-not-quran-sparks-off-war-of-words/809657/.

Chopra, A. (Director). 1995. *Dilwale Dulhania Le Jayenge* (Film). Mumbai: Yashraj Films.

Christopher, A. 1990. 'Apartheid and Urban Segregation Levels in South Africa', *Urban Studies*, 27(3): 421–40.

Clark, W.A. 1986. 'Residential Segregation in American Cities: A Review and Interpretation', *Population Research and Policy Review*, 5(2): 95–127.

Correa, C. 2010. *A Place in the Shade: The New Landscape and Other Essays*. New Delhi: Penguin India Books.

Coser, L.A. 1977. *Masters of Sociological Thought: Ideas in Historical and Social Context*. New York: Harcourt.

Cosgrove, Denis. 1998[1984]. *Symbolic Formation and Symbolic Landscape*. Madison: University of Wisconsin Press.

Dalrymple, W. 2003. *City of Djinns: A Year in Delhi*. New Delhi: Penguin.

Daly, G. 2006. 'Marxism', in S. Malpas and P. Wake (eds), *The Routledge Companion to Critical Theory*, pp. 28–42. Oxon: Routledge.

DDA (Delhi Development Authority) 2007. *Master Plan for Delhi 2021*. New Delhi: Delhi Development Authority.

Debord, G. 1983. *Society of the Spectacle*. Detroit: Black & Red.

Debray, R. 1967. *Revolution in Revolution? Armed Struggle and Political Struggle in Latin America*. New York: Monthly Review Press.

De Kock, L. 1992. 'New Nation Writers Conference in South Africa', *Ariel: A Review of International English Literature*, 23(3): 29–47.

Derrida, J. 1994. *Spectres of Marx: The State of the Debt, the Work of Mourning, and the New International*. New York: Routledge.

Dodds, K. 2007. *Geopolitics: A Very Short Introduction*. New York: Oxford University Press.

Douglas, Mary. 1966. *Purity and Danger: An Analysis of the Concepts of Pollution and Taboo*. London and New York: Routledge.

D'Silva, R. (Director). 2009. *Kurbaan* (Film). Mumbai: Dharma Productions.

Dupont, V. 2004. Socio-Spatial Differentiation and Residential Segregation in Delhi: A Question of Scale?', *Geoforum*, 35(2): 157–75. doi:10.1016/j.geoforum.2003.08.003.

———. 2008. 'Slum Demolitions in Delhi since the 1990s: An Appraisal', *Economic and Political Weekly*, 43(28): 79–87.

Dupont, V., E. Tarlo, and D. Vidal (eds). 2000. *Delhi: Urban Space and Human Destinies*. New Delhi: Manohar.

Eagleton, T. 1989. *Marxism and Literary Criticism*. London: Routledge.

Engineer, A. A. 1991. 'Socio-Economic Backwardness of Muslims in India'. Occasional Paper, No. 5, Vol. 7, May, *Institute of Islamic Studies*, Bombay.

———. 2002. *Gujarat: Laboratory of Hindutva*, available at http://www.dawoodi-bohras.com/spotlight/riots.htm.

Fainstein, S.S. 1999. 'Can We Make the Cities We Want?', in R.A. Beauregard, S. Body-Gendrot, and L. Beauregard (eds), *The Urban Moment*, pp. 249–71. Thousand Oaks: Sage.

Fainstein, S.S. and N.I. Fainstein. 1978. 'National Policy and Urban Development', *Social Problems*, 26(2): 125–46.

Falah, G. 1996. 'Living Together Apart: Residential Segregation in Mixed Arab–Jewish Cities in Israel', *Urban Studies*, 33(6): 823–57.

Faridi, F.R. and M.M. Siddiqi (eds.) 1992. *The Social Structure of Indian Muslims*. Institute of Objective Studies, New Delhi.

Fazal, T. 2013. *Millennium Development Goals and Muslims in India*. Oxfam India working papers series, OIWPS – XIII.

Field, E., M. Levinson, R. Pande, and S. Visaria. 2012. 'Segregation, Rent Control, and Riots: The Economics of Religious Conflict in an Indian City', *The American Economic Review*, 98(2): 505–10.

Flyvbjerg, B. 1998. 'Habermas and Foucault: Thinkers for Civil Society?', *British Journal of Sociology*, 49(2): 208–33.

Foucault, M. (trans. Richard Howard). 1973. *Madness and Civilization: A History of Insanity in the Age of Reason*. New York: Vintage.

———. (trans. Robert Hurley). 1979. *Discipline and Punish: The Birth of a Prison*. New York: Vintage.

———. 1982. 'The Subject and Power', in H. Dreyfus and P. Rabinow (eds), *Michel Foucault: Beyond Structuralism and Hermeneutics*, pp. 208–28. Chicago: Chicago University Press.

———. 1988. 'The Ethics of Care for the Self as a Practise of Freedom', in J. Bernauer and D. Rasmussen (eds), *The Final Foucault*. MIT Press: Cambridge, Massachusetts.

———. (trans. Robert Hurley). 1990 [1976]. *The History of Sexuality*, Vol. 1: *An Introduction*. New York: Vintage.

Fraser, N. 1997. *Justice Interruptus: Critical Reflections on the 'Postsocialist' Condition*. New York: Routledge.

Friedmann, J. and G. Wolff. 1982. 'World City Formation: An Agenda for Research and Action', *International Journal of Urban and Regional Research*, 6(3): 309–44.

Frykenberg, R.E. (ed.). 1986. *Delhi Through the Ages: Selected Essays in Urban History, Culture, and Society*. New Delhi: Oxford University Press.

Galster, G. 1988. 'Residential Segregation in American Cities: A Contrary Review', *Population Research and Policy Review*, 7(2): 93–112.

Gans, H.J. 1982. *Urban Villagers: Group and Class in the Life of Italian-Americans*. New York: Free Press.

Gayer, L. and C. Jaffrelot (eds). 2012. *Muslims in Indian Cities: Trajectories of Marginalisation*. New York: Columbia University Press.

Gerbner G., L. Gross, M. Morgan, and N. Signorelli. 1994. 'Growing Up with Television: The Cultivation Perspective', in J. Bryant and D. Zillman (eds), *Media Effects: Advances in Theory and Research*, pp. 17–41. Hillsdale: Erlbaum Associates.

Ghertner, D.A. 2011. 'Gentrifying the State, Gentrifying Participation: Elite Governance Programs in Delhi', *International Journal of Urban and Regional Research*, 35(3): 504–32.

Giddens, A. 1991. *Modernity and Self-Identity: Self and Society in the Late Modern Age.* California: Stanford University Press.

Glaeser, E. 1997. 'Ghettos: The Changing Consequences of Ethnic Isolation', *Regional Review*, 7: 18–24.

Goffman, E. 2010 [1971]. *Relations in Public: Microstudies of the Public Order.* New Jersey: Transaction Publishers.

Government of India. 2001. *Census of India 2001.* New Delhi: Office of the Registrar General and Census Commissioner, India, Ministry of Home Affairs.

Gramsci, A. 1971. *Selections from the Prison Notebooks of Antonio Gramsci.* New York: International Publishers.

Grewal, R. (Director). 2009. *Aaloo Chaat* (Film). Mumbai: Mirchi Movies Ltd.

Gupta, N. 1981. *Delhi between Two Empires.* Delhi: Oxford University Press.

Gupta, R. (Director). 2008. *Amir* (Film). Mumbai: UTV Spotboy Productions.

Habermas, J. 1984. *The Theory of Communicative Action*, Vol. I. Boston: Beacon.

———. 1994. 'Burdens of the Double Past'. *Dissent*, 41(4): 513–17.

Halbwachs, M. 1992. *On Collective Memory.* Chicago: University of Chicago Press.

Harriss-White, B. 2005. *India's Market Society: Three Essays in Political Economy.* Gurgaon: Three Essays Collective.

Harvey, D. 1972. 'Revolutionary and Counter Revolutionary Theory in Geography and the Problem of Ghetto Formation', *Antipode*, 4(2): 1–13.

———. 1976. 'Labor, Capital, and Class Struggle around the Built Environment in Advanced Capitalist Societies', *Politics & Society*, 6(3): 265–95.

———. 1978. The Urban Process under Capitalism: A Framework for Analysis. *International Journal of Urban and Regional Research*, 2(1–4): 101–31.

———. 1985. *The Urbanization of Capital.* Oxford: Basil Blackwell.

———. 1987. 'Flexible Accumulation through Urbanization: Reflections on "Postmodernism" in the American City', *Antipode*, 19(3): 260–86.

———. 1996. *Justice, Nature and Geography of Difference.* Oxford: Blackwell.

———. 2000. *Spaces of Hope.* Berkeley: University of California Press.

———. 2003. 'The Right to the City', *International Journal of Urban and Regional Research*, 27(4): 939–41.

———. 2009. 'The Urban Process under Capitalism: A Framework for Analysis', *International Journal of Urban and Regional Research*, 2(1–4): 101–31.

Hasan, M. 1990. 'Adjustment and Accommodation: Indian Muslims after Partition', *Social Scientist*, 18(8–9): 48–65.

———. 1997. *Legacy of a Divided Nation: India's Muslims since Independence.* New Delhi: Oxford University Press.

———. 2008. *Moderate or Militant: Images of India's Muslims.* New Delhi: Oxford University Press.

Hetherington, K. 2006. *Capitalism's Eye: Cultural Spaces of the Commodity.* London: Routledge.

Hindustan Times. 21 September 2008. "Neighbours Know Them as Helpful Chaps'.

———. 22 September 2008. 'Graduates with a Killer Degree'.

———. 22 September 2008. 'They Fooled Police, Media, Parents'.

———. September 2008.' Got Them?'.

Hillier, B. and J. Hanson. 1984. *The Social Logic of Space*, Vol. 1. Cambridge: Cambridge University Press.

Hillier, B. and K. Tzortzi. 2006. 'Space Syntax: The Language of Museum Space', in Sh. Macdonald (ed.), *A Companion to Museum Studies*, pp. 282–301. London: Blackwell Publishing.

Hirani, R. (Director). 2009. *3 Idiots* (Film). Mumbai: Vidhu Vinod Chopra Productions.

Hobsbawm, E. 1983. 'Introduction: Inventing Traditions', in E. Hobsbawm and T. Ranger (eds), *The Invention of Tradition*, pp. 1–14. Cambridge: Cambridge University Press.

Hodgson, M.G. 1974. *The Venture of Islam: Conscience and History in a World Civilization*, vol. 1. *The Classical Age of Islam*, Chicago: University of Chicago Press.

Horkheimer, M. 1982[1968]. *Critical Theory: Selected Essays.* New York: Continuum.

———. (trans. G. Hunter, M. Kramer, and J. Torpey). 1993 [1931]. 'The Present Situation of Social Philosophy and the Tasks of an Institute for Social Research', in *Between Philosophy and Social Science: Selected Early Writings*, pp. 1–14. Cambridge: MIT Press.

Horkheimer, M. and T. Adorno. 2007 [1972]. 'The Culture Industry: Enlightenment as Mass Deception', in *Dialectic of Enlightenment: Philosophical Fragments*, pp. 94–136. Palo Alto: Stanford University Press.

HRW (Human Rights Watch). 2011. *The 'Anti-nationals': Arbitrary Detention and Torture of Terrorism Suspects in India.* New York, available at https://

www.hrw.org/report/2011/02/01/anti-nationals/arbitrary-detention-and-torture-terrorism-suspects-india.

Humayun's Tomb—Nizamuddin Urban Renewal Initiative (2016, March 9). Mother and Child Park in Hazrat Nizamuddin Basti, available at https://www.facebook.com/NizamuddinRenewal/photos/a.341896242527742.95440.180959275288107/1253089021408455/?type=3.

Ihlanfeldt, K.R. and B. Scafidi. 2002. 'Black Self-segregation as a Cause of Housing Segregation: Evidence from the Multi-City Study of Urban Inequality', *Journal of Urban Economics,* 51(2): 366–90.

Jackson, K. 1985. *Crab Grass Frontier: The Suburbanization of the United States.* New York: Oxford University Press.

Jacobs, J.M. 1993. 'The City Unbound: Qualitative Approaches to the City', *Urban Studies,* 30(4–5): 827–48.

Jameson, F. 1979. 'Reification and Utopia in Mass Culture', *Social Text,* 1: 130–48.

———. 1981. *The Political Unconscious: Narrative as a Socially Symbolic Act.* Ithaca: Cornell University Press.

———. 1991. *Postmodernism, or, the Cultural Logic of Late Capitalism.* Durham: Duke University Press.

———. 1992. *Signatures of the Visible.* New York: Routledge.

———. 1998. *The Cultural Turn: Selected Writings on the Postmodern, 1983–1998.* London: Verso Books.

———. 2000. 'Globalization and Political Strategy', *New Left Review,* 4: 49–68.

Jasani, R. 2008. 'Violence, Reconstruction and Islamic Reform—Stories from the Muslim 'Ghetto', *Modern Asian Studies,* 42(2–3): 431–56.

Jayal, N.G. 2013. *Citizenship and Its Discontents: An Indian History.* Ranikhet: Permanent Black.

JTSG (Jamia Teachers' Solidarity Group). 2009. 'Encounter' at Batla House: Unanswered Questions, available at https://archive.org/stream/encounterAtBatlaHouseUnansweredQuestions/Batla_House_encounter_report_djvu.txt.

Jessop, B. 1998. 'The Rise of Governance and the Risks of Failure: The Case of Economic Development', *International Social Science Journal,* 50(155): 29–45.

Jha, M. K. 2011. 'The Un-Gandhian from Ralegan Siddhi', *Hardnews,* www.hardnewsmedia.com.

Johar, K. (Director). 2010. *My Name Is Khan* (Film). Mumbai: Dharma Productions.

JTSA (Jamia Teachers' Solidarity Association). 2009. *'Encounter' at Batla House: Some Unanswered Questions.* New Delhi: JTSA, available at https://archive.

org/stream/FramedDamnedAndAcquittedDossiersOfAVerySpecialCell/
JTSA-Report-Framed-Damned-and-Acquitted-Dossiers-of-a-Very-
Special-Cell_djvu.txt.

———. 2012. *Framed, Damned, Acquitted: Dossiers of a Very Special Cell.*
New Delhi: JTSA, http://www.kafila.org/.

Kamat, N. (Director). 2008. *Mumbai Meri Jaan* (Film). Mumbai: UTV
Spotboy Productions.

Katz, M.B. 1990. *The Undeserving Poor: From the War on Poverty to the War
on Welfare.* New York: Pantheon Books.

———. 1997. *Improving Poor People: The Welfare State, the 'Underclass', and
Urban Schools as History.* Princeton: Princeton University Press.

———. 2001. *The Price of Citizenship: Redefining the American Welfare State.*
New York: Metropolitan Books.

Kesavan, M. 1994. 'Urdu, Awadh and the Tawaif: The Islamicate Roots of
Hindi Cinema', in Z. Hasan (ed.), *Forging Identities: Gender, Communities,
and the State*, pp. 244–57. New Delhi: Kali for Women.

Khaitan, A. 2007. 'Dance of Hate: Safehouse of Horrors', *Tehelka Magazine,*
3 November, http://www.tehelka.com.

Khalidi, O. 1995. *Indian Muslims since Independence.* Chicago: South Asia
Books.

———. 2006. *Muslims in Indian Economy.* New Delhi: Three Essays Collective.

Khan, K. (Director). 2009. *New York* (Film). Mumbai: Yashraj Films.

Khan A. (25 September 2008). 'Uneasy Calm in Azamgarh village'. *The Hindu.*

Krips, H. 2010. 'The Politics of the Gaze: Foucault, Lacan and Žižek', *Culture
Unbound: Journal of Current Cultural Research*, 2: 91–102.

Kumar, R. (13 June 2012). For Muslim Women in Delhi, a Breath of Fresh Air.
New York Times, available at https://india.blogs.nytimes.com/2012/06/13/
for-muslim-women-in-delhi-a-breath-of-fresh-air/?_r=0.

Lacan, J. 1991. *The Seminar of Jacques Lacan: Book II: The Ego in Freud's Theory
and in the Technique of Psychoanalysis.* New York: WW Norton & Company.

Lefebvre, H. 1991. *The Production of Space.* Oxford: Blackwell.

Lévi-Strauss, C. 1955. 'The Structural Study of Myth', *The Journal of American
Folklore*, 68(270): 428–44.

———. 1963. 'The Effectiveness of Symbols', in *Structural Anthropology*,
pp. 186–205. London: Penguin Books.

Low, S.M. (ed.). 1999. *Theorizing the City: The New Urban Anthropology
Reader.* New Brunswick: Rutgers University Press.

Maher, F.A. and M.K. Tetreault. 1993. 'Frames of Positionality: Constructing
Meaningful Dialogues about Gender and Race', *Anthropological Quarterly*,
66(3): 118–26.

Mamdani, M. 2005. *Good Muslim, Bad Muslim: Islam, the USA, and the Global War against Terror.* Delhi: Permanent Black.

Mander, H. and G. Sehgal. 2012. *Internal Migration in India: Distress and Opportunities. A Study of Internal Migrants to Vulnerable Occupations in Delhi.*

Marshall, T.H. 1992 [1950]. 'Citizenship and Social Class', in T.H. Marshall and T. Bottomore, *Citizenship and Social Class*, pp. 1–85. London: Pluto Press.

Marx, K. 1978 [1856]. 'Speech at the Anniversary of the People's Paper', in R.C. Tucker (ed.), *The Marx–Engels Reader*, 2nd edn, pp. 577–8. London: Norton.

Masand, R. 2008. 'Any Day Watch A Wednesday' (Review of the film *A Wednesday*), available at http://www.rajeevmasand.com/uncategorized/masands-verdict-any-day-watch-a-wednesday/.

Massey, D.S. 1992. 'Politics and Space/Time', *New Left Review,* 196: 65–84.

———. 1994. *Space, Place and Gender.* Cambridge: Polity Press.

Massey, D.S. and N.A. Denton. 1988. 'The Dimensions of Residential Segregation', *Social Forces,* 67(2): 281–315.

———. 1993. *American Apartheid: Segregation and the Making of the Underclass.* Cambridge: Harvard University Press.

Mathur, S and Ray, D. 2014. Nizamuddin urban renewal initiative. Seminar. No: 657 (May), available at http://www.india-seminar.com/2014/657/657_shveta_&_deeti.htm#top.

McCombs, M. and D. Shaw. 1972. 'The Agenda-setting Function of Mass Media', *Public Opinion Quarterly,* 36(2): 176–87.

Mehra, D. 2012. 'Protesting Publics in Indian Cities', *Economic and Political Weekly,* 47(30): 79–88.

Mehra, R.O. (Director and Producer). 2009. *Delhi-6* (Film). Mumbai: UTV Motion Pictures.

Menon, A. 2012. 'Spicejet in Dock after Communal Slur on Naseeruddin Shah's Nephew Major Muhammad Shah', *Mail Today,* 20 July, www.indiatoday.intoday.in, available at http://indiatoday.intoday.in/story/spicejet-communal-slur-ex-major-mohammed-ali-shah/1/209245.html

Menon, N. 2004. *Recovering Subversion: Feminist Politics beyond the Law.* Ranikhet: Permanent Black.

———. (7 June 2009). 'And Aren't OBC women "women"? Loud Thinking on the Women's Reservation Bill' [blog post], available at https://kafila.online/2009/06/07/and-arent-obc-women-women-loud-thinking-on-the-womens-reservation-bill/.

Menon, S. 2012. 'Which Way to Ramgarh?', *Outlook Magazine*, 4 June, available at https://www.outlookindia.com/magazine/story/which-way-to-ramgarh/281004.

Merrifield, A. 2002. *Metromarxism: A Marxist Tale of the City*. New York: Routledge.

Mid-day 2006. 'Shock, Anger at Sabharwal's Mall a Mall'. *Mid-day*, http://judicialreforms.org/wp-content/uploads/2013/01/Shock%20anger%20midday.pdf.

Miller, D. 1987. *Material Culture and Mass Consumption*. Oxford: Basil Blackwell.

Mills, C.W. 1970. *The Sociological Imagination*. Harmondsworth: Penguin.

Mishra, M. 2008. 'Azamgarh: A Breeding Ground for Terror', *The Times of India* (Ahmedabad edn), 17 August, available at http://timesofindia.indiatimes.com/city/ahmedabad/Azamgarh-A-breeding-ground-for-terror/articleshow/3372589.cms.

Mistry, M.B. 2005. 'Muslims in India: A Demographic and Socio-Economic Profile'. *Journal of Muslim Minority Affairs*, 25(3), 399–422.

Mondal, S.R. 1992. 'Muslims in India: An Enquiry into their Minority Status, Backwardness, Special Rights and Development Problems', *Journal of the Indian Anthropological Society*, 7(2): 149–60.

Mulvey, L. 1975. 'Visual Pleasure and Narrative Cinema', *Screen*, 16(3): 6–18.

Nagar, R. and S. Geiger. 2007. 'Reflexivity and Positionality in Feminist Fieldwork Revisited', in Tickell, A., Sheppard, E., Peck, J., & Barnes, T. J., (eds), *Politics and Practice in Economic Geography*, pp. 267–78. London: SAGE.

NATO Summit. 2012. 'Obama's Speech at McCormick Place', *Huffington Post*, 21 May, available at http://www.huffingtonpost.com/2012/05/21/nato-summit-obama-speech_n_1533353.html.

Nattoji, I. (Director). 2009. *Aagey se Right* (Film). Mumbai: UTV Motion Pictures & Spring Films.

NCEUS. 2006. *Report on Social Security for Unorganised Workers*, National Commission for Enterprises in the Unorganised Sector. New Delhi: Government of India, available at http://nceuis.nic.in/Social%20Security%20-%20Cover%20and%20index.htm.

———. 2007. *Report on Conditions of Work and Promotion of Livelihoods in the Unorganised Sector*, National Commission for Enterprises in the Unorganised Sector. New Delhi: Government of India, available at http://nceuis.nic.in/Condition_of_workers_sep_2007.pdf.

NCRB (National Crime Records Bureau). 2016. *Prison Statistics India — 2015*. Government of India.

Nichols, B. 1976. *Movies and Methods*, Vol. I. Kolkata: Seagull Books.

Nomani, A.Q. 2008. 'Muslims: India's New "Untouchables"', *Los Angeles Times*, http://www.latimes.com, available at http://www.latimes.com/la-oe-nomani1-2008dec01-story.html.

Noorani, A.G. 2003. *The Muslims of India: A Documentary Record*. New Delhi: Oxford University Press.

Noordegraaf, J. 2004. *Strategies of Display: Museum Presentation in Nineteenth- and Twentieth-Century Visual Culture*. Rotterdam: Museum Boijmans Van Beuningen: NAi Publishers.

Oakes, J.P., S.A. Haslam, and J.C. Turner. 1994. *Stereotyping and Social Reality*. Wiley-Blackwell.

Oliveira, N.D.S. 1996. 'Favelas and Ghettos: Race and Class in Rio de Janeiro and New York City', *Latin American Perspectives*, 23(4): 71–89.

Outlook India. 2012. 'Mumbai Police Commissioner Transferred: Home Min', 23 August, available at https://www.outlookindia.com/newswire/story/mumbai-police-commissioner-transferred-home-min/772888.

Paddison, R. 1993. 'City Marketing, Image Reconstruction and Urban Regeneration', *Urban Studies*, 30(2): 339–49.

Pandey, G. 2001. *Remembering Partition: Violence, Nationalism, and History in India*. Cambridge: Cambridge University Press.

Pandey, N. (Director). 2008. *A Wednesday* (Film). Mumbai: UTV Motion Pictures.

Park, R. 2005. [1936]. 'Human Ecology', in Jan Lin and Christopher Mele (eds), *The Urban Sociology Reader*. London: Routledge.

Park, R.E. 1915. 'The City: Suggestions for the Investigation of Human Behavior in the Urban Environment', *American Journal of Sociology*, 20(5): 577–612.

———. 1926. *The Urban Community*. Chicago: University of Chicago Press.

Park, R.E. and E. Burgess. 1921. Introduction to the Science of Sociology. Chicago: University of Chicago Press.

Patel, S. 2009. 'Introduction: Urban Studies—An Exploration in Theories and Practice', in Sujata Patel and Kushal Deb (eds), *Urban Studies Reader*. New Delhi: Oxford University Press.

Patel, S. and K. Deb. 2009. *Urban Studies Reader*. New Delhi: Oxford University Press.

Perappadan, B.S. and R.S. Zaman. 2012. 'In Delhi's Nursery Classes, Muslim Children are a Rarity', *The Hindu*, 18 March, available at http://www.the-hindu.com/news/national/in-delhis-nursery-classes-muslim-children-are-a-rarity/article3009826.ece.

Perlman, J. 2009. *Favela: Four Decades of Living on the Edge of Rio de Janeiro*. New York: Oxford University Press.

Perlman, J.E. 2007. 'Globalization and the Urban Poor'. Helsinki: United Nations University-WIDER.

PMHLC (Prime Minister's High Level Committee). 2006. *Social, Economic and Educational Status of the Muslim Community of India: A Report.* New Delhi: Cabinet Secretariat, Government of India, available at http://www.minorityaffairs.gov.in/sites/default/files/sachar_comm.pdf.

Prasad, M.M. 1998. *Ideology of the Hindi Film: A Historical Construction.* New Delhi: Oxford University Press.

Punwani, J. 2008. 'Rendezvous with SIMI', *The Times of India,* 10 August, available at http://www.newageislam.com/radical-islamism-and-jihad/india-rendezvous-with-simi/d/512.

———. 2012, August 15. 'So What's New about Mumbai Burning'. *The Hindu* http://www.thehindu.com/todays-paper/tp-opinion/so-whats-new-about-mumbai-burning-our-response/article3773557.ece.

Rajadhyaksha, A. (ed.). 1987. *Indian Cinema.* New Delhi: Directorate of Film Festivals.

Ramachandran, R. 1989. *Urbanization and Urban Systems in India.* New Delhi: Oxford University Press.

Ramachandran, S.K. (2012, April 12). 'Zenana Bagh Gives Women a Space of Their Own', *The Hindu,* available at http://www.thehindu.com/news/cities/Delhi/zenana-bagh-gives-women-a-space-of-their-own/article3306719.ece.

Raman, B. 2012. 'A Second Look at Police Handling of Rampaging Muslim Mob in Mumbai', *Eurasia Review,* 23 August, available at http://www.eurasiareview.com/23082012-a-second-look-at-police-handling-of-rampaging-muslim-mob-in-mumbai-oped/.

Rauch, L. and D. Sherman. 1999. *Hegel's Phenomenology of Self-Consciousness: Text and Commentary.* New York: State University of New York Press.

Ritzer, G. and D.J. Goodman. 2004. *Classical Sociological Theory.* New York: McGraw-Hill.

Roberts, B. 2006. *Micro Social Theory.* Hampshire: Palgrave Macmillian.

Roy, A. 1 October 2007. 'Scandal in the Palace'. Outlook Magazine, available at http://www.outlookindia.com/magazine/story/scandal-in-the-palace/235689.

———. 2009. 'Why India Cannot Plan Its Cities: Informality, Insurgence and the Idiom of Urbanization', *Planning Theory,* 8(1): 76–87.

Roy, B. (Director and Producer). 1953. *Do Bigha Zamin* (Film). Bombay: Bimal Roy Productions.

Said, E.W. 1998 [1981]. *Covering Islam: How the Media and the Experts Determine How We See the Rest of the World.* New York: Vintage Books.

Sassen, S. 1991. *The Global City: New York, London, Tokyo*. Princeton: Princeton University Press.

———. 1998. *Globalization and Its Discontents: Essays on the New Mobility of People and Money*. New York: New Press.

———. 2002. 'Towards a Sociology of Information Technology', *Current Sociology*, 50(3): 365–88.

———. 2010. 'The Global Inside the National: A Research Agenda for Sociology', *sociopedia.isa*: 1–10.

Sauer, C.O. 1963 [1925]. 'The Morphology of Landscape', in J. Leighly (ed.), *Land and Life: A Selection from the Writings of Carl Ortwin Sauer*, pp. 315–50. Berkeley: University of California Press.

Saunders, P. 1981. *Social Theory and the Urban Question*. London: Hutchinson.

Saussure, F. [2017(1913)]. 'Course in General Linguistics: Nature of the Linguistic Sign', in J. Rivkin and M. Ryan (eds), *Literary Theory: An Anthology*, pp. 137–77. John Wiley & Sons.

Scott, J. 1990. *Domination and the Arts of Resistance: Hidden Transcripts*. New Haven: Yale University Press.

Sengupta, A., K.P. Kannan, and G. Raveendran. 2008. 'India's Common People: Who Are They, How Many Are They and How Do They Live?', *Economic and Political Weekly*, pp. 49–63.

Severin W.J. and J.W. Tankard. 2000. *Communication Theories: Origins, Methods, and Uses in the Mass Media*, 5th edn. New York: Longman.

Shah, N. 2012. 'Resisting Revolutions: Questioning the Radical Potential of Citizen Action', *Development*, 55(2): 173–80.

Sharma, J. 2011. 'Anna Hazare Is the Icon of Banal Hindutva', *Mail Today*, 17 October, available at http://indiatoday.intoday.in/story/anna-hazare-hindutva-rss-vhp-bjp/1/155206.html.

Sharpe, M. and G. Boucher. 2010. *Žižek and Politics: A Critical Introduction*. Edinburgh: Edinburgh University Press.

Sheikh, Z. 2016. 'Every 4th Person Categorised as "Beggar" in India is Muslim', *Indian Express*, available at http://indianexpress.com/article/explained/muslims-polpulation-in-india-muslims-beggar-unemployment-census-data-muslim-economic-survey-2941228/.

Sheppard, E. 2000. 'The Spaces and Times of Globalization: Place, Scale, Networks, and Positionality', *Economic Geography*, 78(3): 307–30.

Sheth, D. L. 2003. 'Growth of Communal Polarization in Gujarat: The Making of a Hindutva Laboratory?' *Lessons from Gujarat*. Mumbai: Vikas Adhyayan Kendra.

Singh, U. 1999. *Ancient Delhi*. New Delhi: Oxford University Press.

Singh, R. 2008, September 20. 'Braveheart Inspector's Death a Huge Loss.' NDTV. com, available at https://web.archive.org/web/20080921002031/http://www.ndtv.com/convergence/ndtv/story.aspx?id=NEWEN20080066025.

Smith, D.E. 1988. *The Chicago School: A Liberal Critique of Capitalism.* Basingstoke: Macmillian.

Spear, T.G.P. 1937. *Delhi: A Historical Sketch.* Bombay; Chicago: H. Milford; Oxford University Press.

Spodek, H. 2010. 'In the Hindutva laboratory: Pogroms and Politics in Gujarat, 2002'. *Modern Asian Studies*, 44(02): 349–99.

Statistical Abstract of Delhi. 2014. Government of NCT Delhi, available at http://www.delhi.gov.in/wps/wcm/connect/f508bc8046667b0e9cf6bc-f5a4ed47e7/Stattistical+Abstract+of+Delhi+2014.pdf?MOD=AJPERES& lmod=66436406&CACHEID=f508bc8046667b0e9cf6bcf5a4ed47e7.

Stiglitz, J. 2002. *Globalization and Its Discontents.* London: Penguin.

Susewind, R. 2017. 'Muslims in Indian Cities: Degrees of Segregation and the Elusive Ghetto'. *Environment and Planning Asia*, 0308518X17696071.

Tagma, H.M. 2009. 'Homo Sacer vs. Homo Soccer Mom: Reading Agamben and Foucault in the War on Terror', *Alternatives: Global, Local, Political*, 34(4): 407–35.

Tarlo, E. 2003. *Unsettling Memories: Narratives of the Emergency in Delhi.* New Delhi: Permanent Black.

Taylor, L. 1973. *Deviance and Society.* London: Nelson.

Thomas, W.I. and F. Znaniecki. 1958 [1918–20]. *The Polish Peasant in Europe and America,* 2 vols. New York: Dover Press.

Times of India. 24 September 2008. 'The terror map from Pakistan to the Indian Heartland'.

———. 25 September 2008. '5 IM Suspects Held in Mumbai'.

Tripathy, R. 22 September 2008. '3 Atiq Aides Held, Say He Had Planned 20 More Bombings', *Times of India.*

Tudor, A. 1976[1974]. 'Genre and Critical Methodology', in Bill Nichols (ed.), *Movies and Methods. Volume 1*, pp. 118–25. Seagull Books: Calcutta.

Turner, J.C. 1999. 'Some Current Issues in Research on Social Identity and Self-Categorization Theories', in N. Ellemers, R. Spears, and B. Doosje (eds), *Social Identity: Context, Commitment, Content*, pp. 6–34. Oxford: Blackwell.

U.N. Habitat. 2008. *State of the World's Cities 2008/2009: Harmonious Cities.* London: Earthscan.

———. 2016. *Urbanisation and Development: Emerging Futures. World Cities Report 2016.* United Nations.

Van Dijk, T. 1985. *Discourse and Communication.* Berlin: Walter De Gruyter.

———. 1991. *Racism and the Press.* London: Sage.

———. 1993. 'Principles of Critical Discourse Analysis', *Discourse & Society*, 4(2): 249–83.

Varshney, A. 2002. *Ethnic Conflict and Civic Life: Hindus and Muslims in India*. New Haven: Yale University Press.

Vithayathil, T. and G. Singh. 2012. 'Spaces of Discrimination: Residential Segregation in Indian Cities', *Economic and Political Weekly*, 47(37): 60–6.

Wacquant, L. 2008. *Urban Outcasts: A Comparative Sociology of Advanced Marginality*. Cambridge: Polity Press.

———. 2009. *Punishing the Poor: The Neoliberal Government of Social Insecurity*. Durham: Duke University Press.

———. 2011. 'A Janus-faced Institution of Ethnoracial Closure: A Sociological Specification of the Ghetto', in R. Hutchison and B.D. Haynes (eds), *The Ghetto: Contemporary Global Issues and Controversies*, pp. 1–32. Boulder: Westview Press.

Wajihuddin, M. 2008. 'Terror's "Secular" Roots', *The Times of India*, 7 September, available at http://timesofindia.indiatimes.com/home/sunday-times/Terrors-secular-roots/articleshow/3453605.cms.

Weber, M. 1918 (2009). 'Class, Status, and Party', in *Max Weber: Essays in Sociology*, pp. 180–195. London: Routledge.

West, R.L. and L.H. Turner. 2007. *Introducing Communication Theory: Analysis and Application*. McGraw-Hill.

Whyte, W.F. 1943. *Street Corner Society: The Social Structure of an Italian Slum*. Chicago: University of Chicago Press.

Wirth, L. 1928. *The Ghetto*. Chicago: University of Chicago Press.

———. 1938. 'Urbanism as a Way of Life', *American Journal of Sociology*, 44(1): 1–24.

World Bank. 2001. *Cities in Transition: World Bank Urban and Local Government Strategy*. World Bank: Washington, DC.

Wollen, P. 1976[1972]. 'The Auteur Theory', in Bill Nichols (ed.), *Movies and Methods. Volume 1*, pp. 529–41. Seagull Books: Calcutta.

Zieleniec, A.J. 2007. *Space and Social Theory*. London: SAGE.

Žižek, S. 1989. *The Sublime Object of Ideology*. London: Verso.

———. 1997. *The Plague of Fantasies*. London: Verso.

———. 2002. *Welcome to the Desert of the Real*. London: Verso.

———. 2009. *First as Tragedy, Then as Farce*. London: Verso.

INDEX

· ·

governmentality, technologies
impact on 113
government institutions 10, 10n5
government service 10, 10n6
Gramsci, Antonio 16, 30, 97,
172, 199
GRCs of Mission Convergence 111
Greater Kailash 66
gross domestic product (GDP),
Muslim population contribution
towards 10
Gujarat pogrom (2002) 8, 73, 90n6,
108, 164
Gupta, Narayani 4–5

Haji Ali *dargah* 147
Hali 3
Hamdard Educational Society 177
Hamdard Public School 177
Hamdard Waqf 177, 177n1
Harijan (people of God) 198n2
*harijan basti*s 198, 198n2
Harijan colonies 36
Harvey, David 16–17, 24–5, 28,
39, 69, 81–2, 172, 195, 199
Hasan, Mushirul 149
Hazrat Nizamuddin (Sufi Saint) 84
heritage conservation 86
Heritage Conservation Committee
(HCC) 52n2
heritage walks 52
high modernity 23
hijab 188
Hindu Gujjars 71, 82
Hinduism 99
Hindu Jat 87
Hindu–Muslim marriage 155
Hindu nationalism 145
Hindu refugees 44
Hindu, The 116
Hindutva rhetoric 119

historicism (archaeology) 112
History of Sexuality (M. Foucault)
110
Hollywood cinema/films 134–5,
138, 144
homogenous slums 34
Horkheimer, Max 136, 157, 172,
190, 192–3
emphasis on emancipatory aim
of research 23
human society, emphasis on 22
speech at Frankfurt school
inauguration in 1931 22
human ecology, notion of 14
human happiness 193
human reality 192
human society 22
Humayun Tomb 85
Humayun Tomb- Sunder Nursery—
Nizamuddin Basti Urban
Renewal Initiative 85–6
Hyderabad 4

Ibn-e-Batuta 3
ideal city 30, 193, 195, 198, 202
ideal Delhi 195
building of good life and
happiness 193
highlighting and amplifying
tensions 192
provision of space for
happiness 193
identity formation 127–31
identity markers 140
identity of Muslim 124
negative aspersed characteristics
186–7
as a political position 182
ideological state, Althusserian 128–9
ideology
Marxist notion of 138

sepoy mutiny of 1857 (*ghadar*)
4, 40, 54
Muslims' role in 98
Shafiq Memorial School 176
Shaheen Bagh 184
Shahjahanabad 51
Sharma, Mohan Chandra 160
shehr (the city) 5
Sheila cinema theatre in Paharganj
40n1
Sheppard, Eric 24
Shergill, Jimmy 150
Shibli College 163
Shivdasani, Aftab 153
Shiv Sena 116
Sikh cities 37
Sikh refugees 44
SIMI 115, 163
Sindhi refugees 87
situational approach 15
slum(s) 13, 58–9, 68, 90n6,
106, 184, 199
colonies 36
dwellers 12, 105
homogenous 34
Mumbai 146
urban 37
Small, Albion 14
soccer hooligans 122
social control 2
social distance 18
social interaction 19
social organism 14
social philosophy 192
social relationships 128
social reproduction 2
social shift 135
social situatedness of
researcher 24
sociological absurdity 22
socio-political agency 129

socio-religious communities (SRCs)
10n9
socio-spatial inequalities 36
solidarity(ies) 173–81
burden of building 108
politics of 107–9
sovereign power 112–13
sovereignty 96, 111–12, 122
absolute 114
sovereign violence, on physical
bodies 122
Soviet Bolsheviks 16
space(s) 28
commodification 47–57
cultural records 53
form material spatial axis 57
instrumental view of 25
organization of 24
production of 24–6
representational 26
representation of 26, 57, 127–31
Spain 184
spatial decoding 25
spatialization of inequality in
Delhi, in slum and resettlement
colonies 36
spatial practices, definition of 26
spectacle 48, 186
Sriniwaspuri 44
state sovereignty (Nazi) 111
Station House Officer (SHO) 165
stock
characters 141, 141n3
situations 141, 141n3
Street Corner Society (W. Whyte)
15
structural adjustment programme
7, 13, 17
structural analysis 132
subaltern classes, definition
of 97

About the Author

· ·

Ghazala Jamil is Assistant Professor at the Centre for the Study of Law and Governance, Jawaharlal Nehru University, New Delhi. Her core research interests are urbanization, social movements, minority rights, and materiality and spatiality of culture.

She has earlier taught at the Department of Social Work, University of Delhi, as an adjunct faculty, and at the School of Planning and Architecture (SPA), New Delhi, as a visiting faculty. Jamil has a master's degree in social work from Jamia Millia Islamia, New Delhi, and PhD from University of Delhi.

She is associated with several grassroots collectives working in the areas of social justice and communal amity. Jamil is interested in poetry of protest and has translated works from Hindi/Urdu and Punjabi to English. She has co-translated an Urdu book on popular history of Delhi by Intizar Hussain, titled *Once There Was a City Named Dilli* (Yoda Press, 2017).